To Venus –

I hope you enjoy reading about these great women of Pakistan.

Best Regards.

Moneeza

Sept. 2014

© All rights reserved. No part of this publication may be reproduced, stored in a retrieval system, or transmitted, in any form or by any means, digital, electronic, mechanical, or otherwise, without the prior permission of the Publisher/Author.

ISBN-10: 969-35-2697-X
ISBN-13: 978-969-35-2697-4

923.5	Hashmi, Moneeza Who am I?/ Moneeza Hashmi.- Lahore: Sang-e-Meel Publications, 2014. 224pp. 1. Biography. I. Title.

2014
Published by:
Niaz Ahmad
Sang-e-Meel Publications,
Lahore.

Designed by Grafix.
Printing by Print Professional.

www.sangemeel.com

Sang-e-Meel Publications
25 Shahrah-e-Pakistan (Lower Mall), Lahore-54000 PAKISTAN
Phones: +92-423-722-0100 / +92-423-722-8143 Fax: +92-423-724-5101
http://www.sangemeel.com e-mail: smp@sangemeel.com

This book is dedicated to my two grand daughters
Zainab Mehtab Hashmi and Alina Ali Hashmi
with the hope (and prayer) that as they pursue their own paths in life
they too may find a place somewhere beside these great women of Pakistan.

WHO AM I ?

Moneeza Hashmi
Foreword Bapsi Sidhwa

SANG-E-MEEL PUBLICATIONS

ACKNOWLEDGEMENT

This book is a result of the efforts of so many people that I find myself at a loss to start listing them all but I must name a few without whose support this would never have "come to pass".

There are three broad areas of gratitude which need to be mentioned here.

The first is the recording of the interviews by PTV. I am most grateful to the PTV management of 1999 who agreed to let me conduct these interviews and later telecast them continuously over the course of several years. PTV policy at the time did not permit employees to appear on camera. Special permissions had to be sought, arguments in favour had to be strong and someone somewhere had to be willing to support the case and take it to a positive conclusion. I was fortunate enough to have friends in decision making positions in PTV at the time who supported my passion for promoting the cause of Pakistani women in the electronic media. I must also mention the technical staff of all PTV centres who devoted extra time and made extra effort to accommodate these recordings. The one person who deserves special mention by name is Shaukat Zain ul Abedin who was the producer and director of this series. He must be credited for his enormous contribution to the project. No more with us, Shaukat was not only my friend and a professional colleague but in many ways my mentor and my guide.

The second part of the acknowledgement is reserved for the actual book itself.

Six young dynamic women teamed up with me in this labour of love.
Aisha Sarwari, who translated the interviews and edited the book draft several times.
Khuzaima Fatima Haque and Maryam Abbasi who are responsible for devoting many, many hours of their time researching and gathering the background material of all the personalities mentioned.
Amina Ali, MahvashHaider Ali and Farha Noor who formatted, edited and arranged the original draft and the many that followed. I am deeply grateful to them all for their efforts and support over the past two years in egging me on to complete this book.

And lastly I must thank all these wonderful women who shared their lives, their dreams, their struggles, their achievements and their frustrations with me. They are all pioneers in their fields and are our role models. They are beacons we must follow and emulate. I am privileged to have met them and will cherish the time spent in their company.

Moneeza Hashmi
October, 2012

LIST OF CONTENTS

- Foreword — 6
- Abida Parveen {Music} — 9
- Babra Sharif {Film} — 15
- Bahar Begum {Film} — 25
- Bano Qudsia {Urdu Literature} — 35
- Bapsi Sidhwa {English Literature} — 45
- Benazir Bhutto {Politics} — 57
- Fatima Bilquis Edhi {Social Work} — 69
- Dr. Fatima Shah {Social work/Visually Impaired} — 79
- Ruth Pfau {Social work/Leprosy} — 89
- Fareeda Khanum {Music} — 101
- Malika Pukhrag {Music} — 111
- Nasim Wali Khan {Politics} — 117
- Sabiha Khanum {Film} — 127
- Salima Hashmi {Fine Arts} — 135
- Shamim Ara {Film} — 145
- Swaran Lata {Film} — 155
- Tahira Mazhar Ali {Political/Social Activist} — 163
- Viqar-un-nisa Noon {Social Work} — 173
- Zari Sarfaraz {Political/Social Activist} — 183
- Zehra Nigah {Poetry} — 195
- Biographies — 206

FOREWORD

It is an honor to be asked to write the foreward for this book by Moneeza Hashmi, creator and anchor of her TV series "*Tum Jo Chaho Tu Suno*". In this book, Moneeza has transcribed the interviews of twenty prominent women hosted on her series. She has also included her own impressions and memories of each personality she interviewed and vignettes of what went on behind the scenes during the recordings.
"*Tum Jo Chaho Tu Suno*", was inspired by a series titled "*Face to Face*", which was shown on PBS in the 1960's. It ran on Pakistan Television from 1997 to 2002 and derived its title from the following verse by Faiz Ahmed Faiz: "*Tum Jo Chaho Tu Suno, Aur Jo Na Chaho Na Suno*"

More than 100 top achievers, both men and women in the fields of Politics, Law, Arts, Poetry, Music, Science, Sport, Performance, Literature, Theatre (to name a few), were interviewed on this series. As well as being hugely popular, the series is considered amongst the best professional productions of PTV. "*Tum Jo Chaho Tu Suno*" meant to give these exceptional people an opportunity to share their lives candidly with the viewers, and at the same time allow the viewers to "walk" into the lives of celebrities they had only seen from a distance or read about in magazines and newspapers. It facilitated a unique meeting between the two.

Creator Moneeza Hashmi set an innovative trend of anchor-guest relationship on the mini-screen. In a departure from the normal trend of interviews, "*Tum Jo Chaho Tu Suno*" never showed the interviewer on camera. Instead, all questions overlapped with the guest's facial expression. Moneeza Hashmi explained, "*I wanted all eyes to be on the guest and the audience's focus to be on what the guest was saying or feeling. I wanted them to empathise with the guest. I wanted to elevate the guest to a position of importance and respect*".

I was one of the fortunate women she interviewed in this way. Once she posed a question, she did not ever interrupt. Her guest spoke her (or his) piece until it was time to move on. Ms. Hashmi said, "*I would get awfully irritated while watching a host interrupt the guest to ask long-winded questions in order to show off their own knowledge of the person they were being asked to interview; they might also try to 'trip' the guests and embarrass them in front of millions of people. It was rude and overbearing. My objective during the entire show was to give the invited guest due respect and listen to what they had to say.*"

True to her vision, she interposed no questions when she interviewed me.

Moneeza Hashmi exuded a warmth and openness that put me at ease right away. She established a sense of friendship and even of intimacy so naturally that I felt I could trust her not to embarrass me or try to trip me up. Not that she shied away from asking difficult questions; she asked them. But the questions were pertinent and would be of interest to the viewer. Over all, I felt she brought out the best in me.

This collection of Interviews could be appropriately described as the first step towards documenting the lives and works of leading Pakistani feminists in their own respective fields. Ms. Hashmi also intends to bring out this book in Urdu, as well as a sequel featuring prominent men.

Bapsi Sidhwa

Place of Birth
Larkana
Marital Status
Married
Number of Children
Two daughters and one son
Area of Expertise
Singing
Area of Interest
Gardening, Photography and Music
Moment of Pride
Finding Allah-Sain
Moment of disappointment
There is no disappointment
A trait I am embarrassed about
There are lots of weaknesses in a person
A trait I am proud of
My listeners keep me in their prayers
The first question I would ask myself
Who am I?

ABIDA PARVEEN

October 1997. The first thing that struck me as I entered the rather simplistic sitting room of Abida Parveen's house was a large photograph of my father in the center of the room. It was a very cheerful looking Faiz Ahmad Faiz who smiled benevolently down at me. I remember being both curious and moved on seeing that photograph. Abida's living room at that time was a *farshi* style set up. This was before she became a household name, famous and somewhat of a Sufi Dervish. I sank down onto a floor cushion, guided my camera crew to set up the lights as I waited for her to make an appearance. She "flowed" into the room. There is no other way to describe her movements. One would think her massive frame and the volume of mass that surrounds her all around should make it awkward for her to move. Quite the contrary, on the several occasions I have been with her she moved gracefully and with ease, in a sort of flowing rhythmic musical movement as gentle as her voice, as soft as her personality.

She came into the room saying "*Bismillah, Bismillah*" half a dozen times before she descended onto the cushion opposite me. "*Zahaynaseeb. Hamaray peer murshid ki beti hamaray ghareeb khanay par tashreef laeen hain*" (We are fortunate that the daughter of our mentor has graced our home). I was taken aback and touched by her genuine affection and respect for my father. This was perhaps only my second or third actual meeting with her. Truth is I knew who she was and was very much aware that she was a rising star in the field of Sufi music but her style of performance was entirely unique. I felt somewhat at a loss of where to begin with my questions. The childhood approach usually gets the ball rolling, so I tried it again and sure enough, Abida began to share her memories with me.

My experience with talking to singers has never been easy. I have found wonderful performers on stage struggling to find words to answer simple questions. Speaking in monosyllables they have mumbled most of the time and preferred to even just nod on some occasions. I was prepared for another encounter of the same but Abida surprised me with her vocabulary and her desire to speak. Not much is known about this great and versatile performer from Sindh. Not much has been written about her either. I found her an extremely humble and low profile personality. At the time when this interview was taking place Sheikh Sahib, her husband was present. It was quite obvious that he doted on her and she looked up to him no end. He was her moon and stars and quite obviously her manager and administrator. She certainly did not appear to have either the desire of making her performance bookings, schedules, negotiating payments or even selecting her wardrobe. Indeed she did confide in me that Sheikh Sahib did all of that and more. He hovered around as we set up the tech equipment and then disappeared into the kitchen. We started recording without any interruptions from household staff or her kids who were somewhere around in the beginning but melted away later. I found our conversation just "happening". One question flowed into another, naturally, in sequence, almost musically. She was a person without airs, without pretences, without any false facade. She was simple, open hearted; completely at home in front of half a dozen strange men moving across her line of vision. She focused on the task at hand.

We finished talking and lo and behold! Sheikh Sahib appeared followed by a trolley bearing cookies, cakes and hot tea. He served each one of us himself. He gently persuaded all of us to pile up our plates despite our refusals. Abida smiled and sat silently watching this charade of hospitality. She did not move a finger. She was quite obviously the "queen" of the house and used to being treated as such. But there was no arrogance in her attitude and demeanor. We wrapped up and got ready to depart. That's when she unfolded out of her sitting stance, held both my hands and bowed low as we left, never raising her eyes or her head until we were in the car. Abida Parveen has since risen in fame and stature. She is a performer par excellence. When on stage she transforms from being just a singer to a medium that can communicate with the souls of her audience. She herself says there are times when she feels she is touching a "higher plane".

I am fortunate to have had those private moments with her one-on-one all those years ago and still more privileged that even today when we meet, she bends down to meet me and places my hands on her eyes as a token of respect for my father. Truly a great artist and an even greater human being.

Moneeza Hashmi: Who do you sing for?
Abida Parveen: I sing for my inner self. One must satisfy that self before entertaining others.

Moneeza Hashmi: When did you discover you could sing?
Abida Parveen: I grew up in a musical environment. My father was a singer. My mother also sang beautifully. I think of singing as an extremely natural process, almost like the way birds learn to sing. I would often compose my own music on the harmonium, and that was how I was trained. My father was a very soft hearted musician, but he was an even better teacher. He taught me all there was to know about this beautiful art. My husband too is very gifted.
I was surrounded with music by the grace of God. But I am still searching for beautiful melodies.

Moneeza Hashmi: You belong to a place where women are rarely seen in fields such as music?
Abida Parveen: I was brought up in the Sufi tradition by my parents. I believed what they believed. That was my destiny. This tradition wasn't attacked by conservatism at all.

Moneeza Hashmi: How would your father teach you?
Abida Parveen: He never put me in a situation where I found the lesson

difficult. It all came very easily to me. People came to learn music from my father and in a few days he would manage to teach the person to sing well and play the harmonium. He asked Ustad Salamat Ali Khan to be my Ustad. These are the kind of oceans that flow towards a thirsty soul.

Moneeza Hashmi: They say girls are very close to their fathers?
Abida Parveen: I was "in love" with my father.

Moneeza Hashmi: Your mother never sung with you?
Abida Parveen: She passed away too soon. But she had a beautiful voice and great control over her voice.

Moneeza Hashmi: This profession demands a lot of time, effort and passion. How do you get so much time to devote to your music?
Abida Parveen: All my time is for music. I 'am' my music. It is not separate from my identity. At home I am with my music and outside I am with my music.

Moneeza Hashmi: What do you feel when you sing?
Abida Parveen: I feel I am there but actually am somewhere else. When you speak with your Maker you are bound to feel lost. I am fortunate to have felt this.

Moneeza Hashmi: How do you select the 'kalam' (text) for your performances?
Abida Parveen: Good music is a bridge to good 'kalam'. *Hazrat Amir Khusroo Rehmatullah Alaih* (God's blessings on him) said that music is a way of getting your message into another person's soul. It is like reading the Quran with a certain tone and voice. The beauty of the human voice cannot be underestimated. The story of *Hazrat Dauood* illustrates that.
The beauty of voice transports the beauty of the words onwards. Music is a strong bond of communication with yourself and your Maker. Both are bound to each other and cannot be separated. Every person possesses this feeling of being alive through music. All other forms of art are only a shadow of music. Music opens doors to other arts.

Moneeza Hashmi: Do you remember your first public performance?
Abida Parveen: It was at the *Urs* (yearly celebration) of *Hazrat Shah Abdul*

Latif Bhitai Rematullah Alaih (God's blessings on him). There was a gathering of approximately 30,000 people. I was only 15 years old at the time. My father was with me. I was of course very nervous and prayed that I should perform well. Even today I stand with my hands folded in prayer at that *dargah* (shrine). Singing before people is the best feeling for a performer. People are a reflection of God; it is through their souls that you connect to the Almighty. The smell of the flowers tells you where God is.

Moneeza Hashmi: Was your husband supportive in your 'calling'?
Abida Parveen: My fame is because of his contribution. I met him at Radio Pakistan. He knew the importance of words. He would help select my kalam *(text)* and ghazals *(poems)*. He would always be present when we were working on a melody. He was not just a critic but effectively corrected the course of something that wasn't moving in the right direction. He may have his own opinions but would also seek advice of others. That is how he made a performer out of me.
He is not separate from me. He is always with me. He has taught me like a pigeon feeds it's young. My connection with my listeners is just the same. God has been kind and I haven't felt his (my husband's) absence in my work.

Moneeza Hashmi: Do you get sad?
Abida Parveen: People who live by love always live in sadness.

Moneeza Hashmi: What are you most passionate about?
Abida Parveen: Good poetry and good *kalam (text)*. The *faqeers* (devotees) in the *darbars* (shrines) have the most beautiful *kalam* (text). I would listen to their singing for hours. I always went to Faqeer Abdul Ghafur for inspiration. A good *kalam (text)* is for everyone to sing, it is everyone's copyright.

Moneeza Hashmi: When you are just about to perform before a live audience, what is it that you think about?
Abida Parveen: Every event seems like it is my first and maybe my last.

Moneeza Hashmi: Your daughters are grown up. Are you friends?
Abida Parveen: I am like their servant. I enjoy talking to them about life. They remind me of the grace of God and everything about them brings so much joy and enjoyment to my life.

Place of Birth
Lahore
Marital Status
Unmarried
Area of expertise
Acting
Area of Personal Interest
Jewelry designing
Moment of Pride
When my first film became popular
Moment of disappointment
When any of my films would turn out to be a flop
A trait I am embarrassed about
Sometimes I am so engrossed in my work that I forget to respond to people
A trait I am proud of
Not really
The first question I would ask myself
Why is an actor's life so short-lived?

BABRA SHARIF

September 1999. Her perfectly flawless skin, wrinkle-free even in her late 50s would make any one envious. Her hazel brown shining eyes brimming with mischief are fascinating to watch as they dart around the room. Her soft honey voice even when she is screaming out a frustrated film dialogue is not irksome. If anything, Babra Sharif suffers from a lack of torso. She is short by any standards but somehow even that gets over looked when she is prancing around as a carefree college girl or as a younger poor cousin of the chocolate hero who has turned up after many years in search of his roots or some other such unbelievable film plot twist. She goads and teases the hero into submission and a declaration of love. His mother, her aunt, threatens suicide or an equally ridiculous plan. The story plods on and on melodramatically until love conquers all. Throughout, Babra is the saving grace. Her soft facial expressions, her underplaying of the hysterics required, her tear jerking dialogues, her singing on mountain tops are all gimmicks to make any film carrying her name a huge commercial success at the box office. She contracted a disastrously short marriage with Shahid, her leading man and since her divorce, has lead the life of a semi recluse surrounded by friends and family. She is still top biller if she ever agrees to grace an event or fashion show. She is still a top model face for any corporate client that can afford her charges; she is still as fresh and bouncy as ever if one is lucky enough to meet her. She is strangely elusive, media shy and a very private person.

I had met her here and there but never actually struck up a relationship or even an acquaintance.The trouble with most tinsel town dwellers is that they appear extremely genuine at that particular moment when they shake your hand but a follow up is virtually impossible. It takes string pulling and personal contacts to get through which is usually both exhausting and frustrating. Hence Babra, although a dear friend of a dear friend, was simply out of my visual field until I wanted her in the studio sitting opposite to me. So several phone calls were made, untill they were answered and positively so! She turned up for the interview and I was genuinely surprised and delighted.

I recall that as we were being 'lit up' and 'wired' she looked quite at ease facing a total stranger. She knew of me, and I obviously knew of her, but there were no ruffles. Her cherubic face was simply charming minus any cakey make up. Eye lashes beautifully 'mascarraed', each lash separately curled. Hand and toe nails manicured, painted and polished. Legs folded over one another gracefully. Eyes focused on me clear and enquiring. She did not sink too low into the sofa as I would have thought due to her height. Maybe my assistant had gotten her a cushion before I came in. She did have the tech crew in a buzz as they walked around briskly setting up the show. I didn't blame them.This could be their first and last glimpse up close with the first lady of the screen at the time. She didn't ask what the interview was about or any others details. Could it be she felt comfortable with a female interviewer or had the mutual friend who set up this appointment told her to 'be cool' and not worry. I would never know.

We started off with the usual investigative questions about her back ground and how she came into films. Slowly I felt her unwind and relax.It is quite an accomplishment for me as an interviewer to be able to make my guests feel at ease surrounded by bright lights and whirring machines. Being in a TV studio can prove to be an intimidating experience. Being asked personal questions even more so. Being asked to expose your life and thoughts in front of millions of strangers is worse. It takes courage and confidence to grit your teeth and sit through a dialogue with a total stranger unaware of where the next blow might be coming from.

Babra did all of that with grace. She gave me all the answers I was looking for. She shared personal anecdotes with ease. She was all present and willing to go on if we had the time. She was performing and did it exceedingly well. Goodbyes were said and I heard her heels clicking as she walked out of the studio.
I have not seen her since.

Moneeza Hashmi: What was your first experience of the film world?

Babra Sharif: The first day I went on the set I cried a lot. Mr. Munawer Zareef was there and started to make fun of me. I was wearing yellow clothes. He called me a plate of *"Zarda"* (sweet rice). I guess I was very young at the time.
I started crying. He then explained to me that as a comedian that was what he did for a living and I shouldn't take it personally.

Moneeza Hashmi: People think being an actress is all about glamour and glitz, fame and glory. New clothes, new people, new places. Is this an easy field to get into?

Babra Sharif: Not at all.
I did not join it for fame and glory. That was not my ambition at all. This is a very tough profession. People think it's about traveling and fun, comfort and socializing. But that's not the way it is. People do not witness what happens off screen. They don't know what happens backstage and what we have to go through. Sometimes we have to change 5 costumes for one shoot. It's not fun. It's cumbersome. Sometimes you're acting as a princess. Other times a pauper. You are flipping characters like a coin.
One is so engrossed in the role that nothing must distract you. You have to really focus on the delicate and intricate

nuances.

Moneeza Hashmi: When you are playing a character do you also put an emphasis on all details?

Babra Sharif: Yes I do. But often I would be thinking ahead of the shootings that still had to be scheduled and not really focus on the story I was supposed to be listening to. I knew it would be months before the actual planning of the film would begin. Then I would have to study all aspects including the costumes again, and that is when I would really focus on that particular role. At present I have to empty my head and only think about the work at hand.

Moneeza Hashmi: There was a time when you were an extremely busy actress. How would your day start and end?

Babra Sharif: Don't ask! My father was not alive then, but my mother was, and I wouldn't even see her for many days. I would come home late and she'd be asleep. When I would leave in the morning she would be out somewhere. I would hardly meet my nieces and nephews for several days on end.
This all seemed very strange to everyone including myself! Friends and relatives would accuse me of becoming very proud and arrogant. The reality was that there was very little time to do anything else.

Moneeza Hashmi: Sometimes you must have woken up in the morning and found out that shooting for that day had been cancelled. On that particular day what would you do?

Babra Sharif: I would meet family and friends, and play with my nieces and nephews.

Moneeza Hashmi: We hear that actors don't get enough time to read the scripts. We also hear that sometimes the story changes during shooting. What kind of relationship did you have with the writers?

Babra Sharif: I've never really had any direct contact with the writer. I would always deal with the director. There would be changes in the script, but those would mostly not come from me but from the directors themselves. We would do our preparation based onthe script given to us. But sometimes when the director would insist on a complete change of script I would resist. Because I had taken on that film for its original idea as it had been narrated to me. Unless the change was something I agreed with, I refused to accept it.

Moneeza Hashmi: I know you are a very conscientious actress who takes her work very seriously. You do not make compromises other people might. In the event that you might be asked to play a role that you wouldnít or could not agree with, a role that you perhaps thought was not realistic enough who would win that argument, you or the director?

Babra Sharif: Most of the time the directors I have worked with were wonderful people. They were the kind of people that you never really had the courage to disagree with. For example professionals like Shahbab Kiranvi, Pervaiz Malik or Nazar-ul-Islam would know how to convince us. When they cast us in a certain film, they would be making a conscious choice. We understood their reasons for selecting us and so we were on the same page as them.
A new director would perhaps sometimes try to create a song that they feel would be a hit, and this would become the cause of a conflict with me as I would feel the original story was being compromised.

Moneeza Hashmi: You are an extremely talented performer. How much of this talent is God-gifted and how much is your own effort?

Babra Sharif: This is a profession where luck plays an equally important factor. I didn't really want to take this field on as a profession while I was in the middle of my education. Yet I also am grateful to God that ever since my first film, I have always been cast in a leading role.
When I watch some of my old films I cannot believe I acted like that. Believe me I am not claiming here to have performed exceptionally well but there were scenes back then which I did rather well and that still surprise

me. Although at the time I did not have the seriousness towards my work which I have now, I still managed to do pretty well.

I did a film with Hassan Tariq called *'Maazi Haal Mustaqbil' (past, present, future)* in which I worked with Nayyer Bhabhi for the first time. She was a very experienced and seasoned actor and I was friendly and candid with her on set. I think it is very important to maintain a positive atmosphere around one's workplace. Tariq Sahib got irked about my constant bantering and he actually had to ask the camera man to tell me to stay in character. I am answering your question in detail to explain that most of the time I was not aware of how or what I was supposed to do.

In a dramatic scene from the same film I became conscious of the criticism he had levied about my non-serious attitude. When the scene was shot and completed in one single take and I got his instructions right the very first time he commented in Punjabi and said, *"Aye kee cheez ai, aye kee kuri ai!"* (What is she? What kind of a girl is she?)

After that day he didn't mind if I joked around a bit or got carried away. He understood that if he restricted me I wouldn't be able to deliver.

Moneeza Hashmi:	Obviously you had a gift. This brings me to my next question. You've done really good comedy and you've also performed well in melodramatic roles. Which do you prefer most?
Babra Sharif:	Definitely comedy.

Comedy is an extremely difficult genre. The timing has to be spot on. Crying is something I can do just sitting here. All you have to do is put glycerin in the eyes, make your voice grainy put on a somber expression and that's it. But getting someone to laugh is next to impossible. Getting a reaction in a comic scene is the world's toughest task. I love doing it because it's a challenge every time.

Moneeza Hashmi:	Is Babra a funny person?
Babra Sharif:	Yes. I play a lot of practical jokes. My close friends would vouch for this.

Moneeza Hashmi:	You've made a lot of sacrifices on becoming a public figure. Would you much rather prefer being a private person?
Babra Sharif:	I am thankful to God for placing me in this position of fame and recognition. What more could I ask for? Regarding the drawbacks I'd say I really don't sweat the small stuff. These are little irritants that I choose not to make an issue about. I've done so much work, and have been so busy doing more work that I never got the time to worry about what people would say. And whatever has been said about me doesn't really have an effect on me because I felt strongly about continuing in the direction that I have set for myself. I have discontinued acting the past few years by choice. I often meet so many people who demand that I come back to films. They also ask why I am not acting on TV, and that's a good feeling. But the women I don't like are the ones who ask: "Why do you look the same (so good) even now?" I get to hear this at least 20 times in a day! (laughs)
Moneeza Hashmi:	What does that question mean?
Babra Sharif:	I am not exactly sure myself. In fact I've asked that of a few people, and they say "You've got great skin". I respond "You've got great skin too!" Then they say they want to know how I've kept up with this 'beauty'. I tell them it's important to maintain yourself. It's not necessary to eat so much that you can't even get up from the chair you are sitting in! So this one statement: "Gosh you look so young" makes me want to ask them if they are referring to my height or my age!
Moneeza Hashmi:	What would irritate you the most on a set during a shoot?
Babra Sharif:	Many things. For instance they would want me or my co-star to come walking towards the camera from a distance, and I'd know instantly that to be a bad idea. It just would not gel with the mood of that particular

scene or the dialogue.
Then our costumes were so elaborate, and so completely unrealistic. We were portraying a world of fantasy. We would sing and dance which doesn't exactly happen in real life.
You have to put up with it because the public demands it.
People would comment on my costume and say that it was way too simple for the audience. I would get irritated with these kind of comments.

Moneeza Hashmi: A creative artist is never satisfied. Correct?
Babra Sharif: I would come back home after a long day at the studio and review the work I had done that day. I would mull over the good and the bad shots. I would consult with my co-stars the next day and ask them if they had been up last night obsessing as much as me. I only asked those who I knew really worked hard and took pride in their performances. They would all tell me how they had spent the night critiquing themselves.
One can never feel complete.
Those who weren't so committed said they had slept deeply and well!

Moneeza Hashmi: An honest answer please. Do you miss your film life now?
Babra Sharif: No. It is not necessary to be involved in a single profession for one's entire life. When people say I look young and I should continue to act, I tell them I've worked very long and very hard in films. I do not need to 'belong' to it forever. I never said I had retired. I simply said after I got married I would not work in films. The people who are used to working cannot sit idle.

Moneeza Hashmi: And when will you get married?
Babra Sharif: One can try to make the effort but circumstances also have to be in sync. Sometimes it doesn't work out. It could be because of me. It could be because of other people. If God has designed it in my destiny it will happen someday.

Place of Birth
Lahore
Marital Status
Married
Number of Children
Two sons
Area of Interest
Acting
Activities of Interest
Keeping house
Moment of Pride
When my professional work is appreciated
Moment of disappointment
When I got divorced and returned to Lahore
A trait I am proud of
I am proud of my professional position
A moment of embarrassment
When people behave improperly at social gatherings
The first question I would ask myself
Why did I decide to opt for character roles and not ask to be cast as the heroine?

BAHAR BEGUM
(KISHWAR)

April 2000. I cannot claim to know Bahar Begum very well. For a long time my only introduction to her was from her films. She had a commanding presence on the screen: tall, upright and broad. Every inch the *'Chaudry's wife'* or

'Thakurani' which were her frequently assigned characters. Her eyes blazed fire as she looked at her adversary, male or female. Her body shook with tension, every muscle taut, every sinew tight, and every nerve ready to brace itself for the onslaught of a degrading dialogue or insult which was sure to be flung her way from the actor opposite her in the scene (usually Sultan Rahi, the great).

What did fascinate me about Bahar Begum was the little-known fact that she was the only 'English' speaking actress of her time. This always intrigued me. She had a convent education and had passed her Senior Cambridge level examination when she entered this field. She fluently expressed herself in English which endeared her to me as a teenager. Why would an attractive young educated woman choose films as a career when (at first glance) it appeared she could have become a doctor or a teacher?

I was an avid film-goer at the time and not the only one I may add. Going to the Sunday Matinee in those days was an activity anticipated by all teenagers of our 'era'. We would dress up in our 'Sunday best', reach Plaza or Regal early to 'check out the scene'. We all had our eyes focused on someone or the other each week. Somehow we had managed to get in contact through mutual friends and dropped hints about being at the movie that Sunday afternoon. Young handsome boys, hair combed back in a slick style which was all the rageback then, wearing hip hugger jeans, pretending to be casual while 'eyeing'

their 'dates' from afar. Heart a flutter, tickets in hand we would shuffle into the cinema hall. Would 'he' be in the same row? Close by? Avoiding eye contact under the strict gaze of elder cousins or sisters we always managed to exchange indirect glances, shy smiles, all for a lucky piece of paper with a scribbled message that might find its way into our hand somehow and make the whole effort worthwhile.

English movies were the rage back then. My favorite heroes were Gregory Peck, Dirk Bogard, David Niven, Cary Grant, Paul Newman even Burt Lancaster with his broad mouth baring all his teeth when he wanted to emphasize a dialogue! Lana Turner, Audrey Hepburn, Ava Gardner, Rita Hayworth, Jean Simmons were show stoppers and then Grace Kelly came along! She had a royal presence and sure enough became the fairy tale princess by marrying Prince Ranier. Her tragic death in a car accident saddened me to no end, I recall.

I went to see Pakistani movies with equal fervor. The magical musical melodies of Khursheed Anwar, accompanied by soulful voice of Madame NoorJahan were a sheer delight to listen to and watch. Bahar Begum at the time was a young actress breaking into the film industry which had the likes of Sabiha Khanum, Nayar Sultana, Shamim Ara, Neelo, Panna to name a few. She faced tough competition for sure. She did not possess the childlike innocence of Sabiha Khanum, nor the angelic beauty of NayarSultana but her towering presence on screen certainly kept her up there decades after the others bade the screen farewell. Another factor which went in her favour was the fact that she made a comeback in character roles and she was an instant hit. The tall commanding presence of an imposing *Chaudharani* appeared to be just her cup of tea. She was a natural in that setting. Her partnership with Sultan Rahi brought her laurels which resulted in more films and Bahar Begum was back on top after an absence of many years. Not many actresses have been able to pull that off successfully and maintain such a position unchallenged for over a decade.

There has never been a scandal or adverse gossip shadowing her throughout her acting career spanning more than three decades. That must most certainly be a record of sorts.

Yes. Bahar Begum would be an interesting person to talk to, I thought. She should indeed have some thoughts to share on how to survive in the film industry of Pakistan, keeping your reputation and dignity intact and safe from being torn to shreds by rivals. Over to you Kishwar!

Moneeza Hashmi:	If you told me you had always wanted to be an actress, I would find that hard to believe.
Bahar Begum:	No, I never really wanted to become an actress. Coming into films for me was purely accidental. I never even dreamt of it. I remember when I was a student my younger sister loved getting autographs of players during cricket matches. Back then we had separate enclosures for film stars to watch the matches. I would have arguments with her about this. I would find it upsetting that she would go into the enclosure of the film stars asking for autographs. As fate would have it, years later I too would be giving autographs to young students standing outside those very enclosures.
Moneeza Hashmi:	So how did you enter the film world?
Bahar Begum:	I was a Senior Cambridge student when I met Mr. Anwar Kamal Pasha. I had gone to visit my uncle in Karachi. Pasha Sahab was a family friend. After meeting me, he insisted I join films. He was not in favour of my continuing my education. He said I would only end up doing some small office job. He made a really good case for my joining the film world at the time.

I have thought about this many times over the years and agree he was right. In those days films provided a very positive environment for girls like me.
I was quite perplexed back then about how to commence my career in a professional field I knew nothing about and for which I really had no aspirations but destiny had carved out another role for me.
In my very first film, Pasha Sahab cast me as a heroine. He made a bet with me saying if the film was a hit then he would cast me in his next film as well and that too as a heroine. That is exactly what happened. I got a second film and my career was launched.

Moneeza Hashmi: Tell me what you were like in school?
Bahar Begum: I was a tomboy! I loved playing outdoors. I loved sports. Even today if I have an option I would rather be playing some competitive sport. In school I was popular because I did so well in sports. I did go back to participate in several sport competitions even though I had decided not to continue my education. I won a trophy for my class in that tournament. Those are some of my most cherished memories from back then.
I was an average student, not too clever. At home I loved playing putkunni.

Moneeza Hashmi: What was that?
Bahar Begum: Little girls get together and pretend to cook food in tiny little saucepans and cooking pots. I thought it great fun. We also arranged wedding ceremonies of our dolls.
In a strange way, I had two personalities. I was a tomboy and a domesticated girl. I was my maternal grandmother's pet. She adored and spoilt me rotten. Everyone in the neighborhood knew not to mess with me or there would be hell to pay.
Once I remember I was cycling home and got hurt on my forehead. I still have a scar to show for it. The boy who got me down was in big trouble because I came home crying. My grandmother actually went and injured his head in retaliation. You can now imagine the scale of how spoilt I was!

Moneeza Hashmi:	Do you ever regret not continuing your education?
Bahar Begum:	At times I do. Being the eldest of my family, I had to work. Even if I had continued my education and got a job, I was going to be the bread winner. It was not desperate in the sense that I absolutely had to, but my siblings needed an education and a future. I needed to make a contribution towards domestic expenditure very early on in my life.
Moneeza Hashmi:	What was it like for you when you became an established actress?
Bahar Begum:	For the longest time my heart was not in it. I did it out of a sense of duty. The thought of facing a work day of acting was not my cup of tea. On the days I would have to shoot a musical number, I would barely be able to drag myself out of bed.
Moneeza Hashmi:	Was it because of the dancing?
Bahar Begum:	Yes. I found that part terribly difficult. I have still not figured out why. I tried to learn but to no avail. It just wasn't in me. Things are done well when they are connected within the heart. When I had to shoot a sad tragic song I was more willing, but dance numbers were hell!
Moneeza Hashmi:	Who taught you to act?
Bahar Begum:	I was taught by Anwar Kamal Pasha, Sheikh Iqbal who was his writer and the story writer Baba Alam Siahposh. These people would sit me down and make me practice my dialogues. They would give me practical tips on how to enunciate words correctly. They would ask me to speak loud enough so I could hear my own voice in my own ears. When I started working in Punjabi films I didn't speak Punjabi although it was my mother tongue. I had studied in a convent school where we were only allowed to speak in English. At home we spoke Urdu so Punjabi was not a language I was comfortable with.
Moneeza Hashmi:	Any problems when trying to remember dialogues of a scene?
Bahar Begum:	I don't recall trying to cram my lines; a lot of that would come very naturally to me. Especially the second time round

I came back to films. The second time I really had to act. As a heroine you have to sing a few songs, act a few romantic scenes with a hero, and that's the extent of your work. After I started taking on character roles, I realized how much more effort was required. Understanding your craft was essential; the weight of the entire story sometimes rests on your shoulders.

If I really like a role it becomes a part of me. I take it very seriously. Until a crucial scene is over I don't even want to talk to anyone. If there is any disturbance on set I ask people to leave and insist on my peace while playing the scene the way I think it ought to be done.

Moneeza Hashmi: Why have you acted in more Punjabi films?

Bahar Begum: Our film industry has gone through different phases. There was a time when more Urdu films were being produced. Then it changed to more Punjabi films.

When I quit the film industry (the first time), I had done some Urdu films and some Punjabi films; but when I rejoined the situation had completely turned around. It was the era of mostly loud Punjabi films. I was not comfortable with speaking so loudly and wondered whether I would actually fit into that scenario. I am a bit stubborn. When I make up my mind about something, I usually end up doing it.

Moneeza Hashmi: Why did you leave acting?

Bahar Begum: It was by choice. I believed that film and married life could not co-exist. The film industry had no timings. You need to devote time to your family and in building up your home. Men also think a wife should dedicate herself to her home. They take this for granted.

The choice however was mine because I no longer wanted to work at the time. There is a distinct possibility that if I had been asked to leave (by my husband or in laws) I would have refused because I do have a strong mind of my own.

Moneeza Hashmi: Did you feel alienated from the creative side of your personality?

Bahar Begum: I immediately conceived my first child and that kept me very involved. Like other girls I too dreamed of having my own home, children and a domestic life. That dream

happened very quickly for me, so I felt no void.
It was when I was planning to return to the film world I contemplated long and hard. That was a difficult decision.

Moneeza Hashmi: What compelled you to come back?
Bahar Begum: I tried not to return. Because I am stubborn and for me it was strange to go back to something I had left by choice. I worried what people would say. I tried to look for a job instead. Friends supported and networked for me to work in one place or the other. I also got a few offers. I thought about going to work and saying 'yes-sir' for 30 days and getting a paycheck which I would have to extend my hand to receive. It just didn't feel good.
You tend to get pampered in the film industry; you are like a spoilt brat with people running around you.
That being said, my vanity was hurt thinking I would have to go to people asking for work. That was a tough period for me. When I returned to Lahore, I was offered work immediately. I got an offer for a title role. I accepted this new turn of fate and I was back.

Moneeza Hashmi: Fame disrupts private life, how did you take it?
Bahar Begum: There are definitely some irritants. They become even more problematic when people misbehave at parties or when someone stalks you. However most of the time it feels great. It is also very difficult to digest fame, most people can't handle it.
In public places, I tend to not bother about the fact that I am well known. If someone cuts me off on the street, I shout at them. With time your perspective changes. As I have gotten older I realize I shouldn't do that. After all it is the same public that has given me this prestige and fame.

Moneeza Hashmi: You have spent some time being a single parent...
Bahar Begum: It has been a long time. It has been almost 24 years. I was divorced in 1975.

Moneeza Hashmi: Divorce is a very difficult decision for both parties, especially for a woman with two sons. How did you make that decision and how did you continue with your life?

Bahar Begum: Yes. It took me a very long time to take this decision. I tried to fix things. I tried very hard. It took me a year and a half to finally decide. I wouldn't like to discuss it since my ex-husband has passed on and it would not be appropriate. Essentially both our parents, his and mine, told us that we should separate amicably if issues continued to remain unresolved. Their support helped me a lot. One party cannot alone change things. The issue persisted and I eventually had to decide. I never really considered myself so unimportant as to give up my life for one man, and turn into a psycho case. I had two sons at the time. Rather than give up on life, I decided that it was better if I got divorced. Life is very precious. You only get one shot at it.
I told my husband we should separate. At the time it seemed very unimportant. Later when the realization hit him he tried to win me back. I had told him there would be no turning back for me once the decision was made.

Moneeza Hashmi: What difference do you see between the Bahar of "Chanmahi" (name of her film) and the Bahar of today?

Bahar Begum: Frankly I don't remember that time because I didn't do that much work back then. Agreed that it was a 9 year initial stint but I made much fewer films. There would be one shift in the day and one shift at night. When I returned to films the second time I realized what real acting entailed. I became a student again. There were several days I had 8 shoots in a day and did not get tired. I felt my real calling was now being realized.

Place of Birth
Ferozepur, Punjab
Marital Status
Married
Number of Children
Three sons
Area of Personal Interest
Reading, Writing, Cooking and Traveling
Moment of Pride
When I see my grandchildren looking at me with love
Moment of disappointment
When I ignore my husband or sons because I am busy
A trait I am proud of
Pride is the flip side of arrogance so I never considered being proud
A trait I could do without
My afternoon nap
The first question I would ask myself
Have I fulfilled my responsibilities?

BANO QUDSIA

April 1997. It was the fall of 1969 when I moved to Model Town from Mozang in Lahore. The house was bought by my parents from my mother-in-law and her siblings. It had been her ancestral house so there was a nice ring to the entire transaction. My parents had been looking to invest some money in property and this seemed an obvious choice. Of course it needed huge repairs and much face lifting (which still continues I may add, 4 decades later) but at the time it was a godsend. We moved into what appeared at the time a different town. It was miles from Mozang. It still obviously is but somehow either the roads have shrunk or we have become immune to travelling longer distances playing with our mobile phones oblivious to the dust and garbage alongside as our air-conditioned car speeds towards its destination. There were no lights on the roads back then. There were stretches of dark and desolate emptiness before taking the turn into Model Town.

All grocery shopping had to be done before we undertook the tedious journey home. Transportation was another problem. I recall often jogging along in the back of a tonga from Icchra where I would go to visit a paternal aunt or pick up essential supplies like freshly slaughtered chicken brought home still dripping blood in its plastic cover. It was isolated and lonely in the beginning. The only saving grace was the noticeable drop in temperature as one entered Model Town. It's still there but less noticeable now - too many buildings and cars all around.

My introduction to Bano Qudsia who I still refer to as *"Bhabi ji"* is connected closely to my move to Model Town. She and Khan Sahib as we affectionately called Ashfaq Ahmed lived just around the corner from us. My elder son Ali who was just a few months old started getting used to his surroundings outside the new house at the time. So he became a frequent visitor to Bhabi ji's home every morning when he went for his morning stroll in the pram with his maid. He would be most fondly spoilt by both husband and wife while he toddled around their garden . chasing butterflies or playing with mud Bhabi ji looked forward to his visits and usually had a snack ready for him upon arrival. Ali was a big boy (and still is I may add!) so any extra food was always welcome. Sometimes I walked him there. Those were good days I recall when I spent time sitting and talking to these two learned people who willingly shared so much of their experiences and affection with both myself and my son. Khan Sahib continued to call Ali by his full name Ali Madeeh which very few people ever knew!

Later I acted in a few PTV dramas upon the insistence and encouragement of Mohammad Nisar Hussain, a senior producer in PTV of much repute. All of them were written either by Bano Qudsia or Khan Sahib. In those days the actor would have long sittings with the writer and discuss the role. On several occasions I remember listening to both these writers explain the intricacies of each dialogue to the drama team highlighting the back ground of each sentence, even the reactions that were needed.

My friendship and admiration for Bhabi Ji continued to grow in the years that followed. Our paths would cross off and on socially or at PTV events. She would always be dressed simply; head covered with her dupatta, an earthy perfume probably khasor sandal trailing behind her as she moved. She abhorred make up and had an argument each time with the makeup person prior to a PTV recording about too much powder being patted on her face. She refused to put on lipstick ever. She was humility personified, oblivious of her talent and extremely shy to acknowledge it. She wanted to and continued to remain in the shadow of her husband whom she admired and served. Her days began and ended with his desires and commands. She negated her own creative genius constantly and no one could change that opinion. She is a deeply religious person, devout is perhaps a more accurate definition but she had an amazingly dry sense of humour which cut through the most serious of discussions.

She once gave me a very important lesson in feminism which I still remember. I asked her to participate in another talk show to be shown in the transmission specifically meant for women audiences. She regretted saying *"Main zananay dabay main nahin baithoon gi"* (I will not sit in the compartment meant only for females).

She hated being interviewed or given any public projection. She would have none of it but I was adamant. I badgered her, bullied her, blackmailed her, reminded her of her affection for me and Ali, evenbegged her. I promise to agreed to her strict timing, her selection of venue, day, whatever-just to get her on camera. I knew it would be a scoop because she has not to date given an interview of such length to the media. I played my final trump card one day by bringing up the one name I had been holding back. She looked at me with such affection and said in her soft lyrical voice *"Your father was someone I admired and respected profoundly. He gave me the same affection back. You are his daughter. I love you like my own and therefore I cannot say no to you"*.

We agreed on the time and date. I landed at her house since she refused to come to PTV for reasons best known to her. I respected her wish for privacy and there on the floor of her *baithak* recorded one of the best interviews I have ever done. It was from the heart, one on one. She was very candid indeed and I am grateful for that. She will always remain one of my most favourite people and one of the best ones I have had the good fortune to know.

Moneeza Hashmi:	My first question quite obviously is when and how did you decide to become a writer?
Bano Qudsia:	All creative people have to suffer a loneliness of the self. In this loneliness the person discovers that he or she is different, from their siblings, their mother, father and friends.
	This realization takes them into a cave, where they sit and contemplate what to do. For the longest time this realization does not come easily- will they be an Einstein, Faiz or Mir Dard are questions that can begin to haunt

them. This isolation is like a shell of loneliness until the loneliness transforms into its final form and becomes a pearl.

Sometimes people get opportunities and they can immediately sense their calling. They soon realize what is to be their destiny.

There are however some people who do not come upon that realization until quite late. I am one such person. To date I do not understand what really is the purpose of my life. I still wonder what is it that I was destined to do: Raise kids, stay captive in my husband's life or am I to write?

I have spent these past ten years searching for the real me so I could understand the meaning of my own life. But to answer your question, I knew in fifth grade that perhaps I am to become a writer. If however, I had not been awarded the 'gift of loneliness' I would have ventured in another direction. I would have been social with many things to be done and achieve.

Recently someone told me their dream. Mr. Mumtaz Mufti met this person in his dream and asked him to tell Bano (me) that an apple tree only produces apples. I interpreted this as: leave all else and get down to writing. Writing has been the least of my priorities. For example I am busy giving advice to people which they don't appreciate. I involve myself in other people's lives too much, which is also wrong, but I can't stop myself. I also cook experimental foods that no one really likes to eat but I have to do this only to keep busy. I keep attempting to clean my house which is impossible to clean anyway. You will find 20 books here and 20 books there which makes it difficult to keep the house tidy and clean. Plus there are too many small items all around. I also keep trying to fulfill my duties as a family member which again is next to impossible. I pay my brother a visit once a year, and then my sister-in-law the next year. I have always placed so much value on keeping contact with my relatives but have been unable to live up to that commitment. I think the problem begins when you try to be a jack-of-all-trades and eventually turn out to be a master of none. That is a fundamental problem with me. If someone wants to be perfect at everything they usually end up being good at nothing. I have tried to realize that if I cannot do things right, I might as well leave some things well alone. Following that thought, the first thing I gave up was appearing on and writing for television.

Moneeza Hashmi: You have gotten recognition for your writing. Who would you give credit to for that achievement?

Bano Qudsia: Not myself certainly.

It is my considered opinion that wherever there is a support system in place there will be a potential to do good quality work.

The first credit for my success goes to my husband. He felt that I may not be that competent but that I could get the work done. In the early days of our marriage we brought out a magazine. We were dirt poor. To run that magazine he assigned me the task that if any author did not submit a story, I would fill that space under a pseudonym.

Whenever he would come home he never asked me what was for dinner or anything about the children. It was always regarding how many pages had I written or how many hours had I spent writing that day.

The second person I credit for my success would be my mother. I am enjoying the fruits of the lessons my mother gave me as a child. She told me to be wary of creating domestic disputes over non-issues. She encouraged me to speak but only with love. She always told me to understand the other person's point of view. Most importantly she taught me never to waste time. I was only twelve years old at the time. She insisted that my sleep, meals, gossip should all be tabulated and prioritized. She brought me a *charka* (spinning wheel) which I would work on when all my other chores were done. Everything was about putting a value on time.

I am very grateful to her. Even now when I am just sitting by myself and thinking I can hear her asking me, 'Why are you wasting your time?'

The third person to whom I owe any credit is my maid who is also my cook. She does not understand my work because she is completely illiterate and she has been with me for 30 years. In the beginning she would ask me why I spent long hours at my desk writing. Why would I not rather lie down? I told her that I wanted to write. I remember she asked me if this made me happy. When I said it did, she said "This is what you should be doing" and freed me from the drudgery of cooking. After that incident she would not let me go into the kitchen. I am so fortunate to have her. My mornings are now free to dedicate to my writing.

Moneeza Hashmi: What are you like when you are in a creative mood and then what are you like after you have expressed yourself or are done with writing?

Bano Qudsia: I once met a poet from Oslo who wrote beautiful poems but none of them were ever published. He sent me a couple of poems after translating them. He said that creativity is like living the Day of Judgment in your head. You can neither sleep nor rest.

Think of it another way, you put a kettle to boil, and then seal the passage where the steam comes out from. Whatever happens to the water inside is what happens to a creative person during the time of his or her creation. It is such a strange phenomenon, that people around you are incapable of understanding what you are undergoing.

Creative people appear to have a horrid expression or their eyes are terrifying and they look disturbed, whereas in reality that person could be close to achieving a breakthrough. They search for solitude and silence at that time. People may brand him or her a snob, because they do not respond, and other people around him or her seem to have ceased to exist. People don't understand that this person is in another dimension, in another world.

All creative artists live in a world full of internal activity and chaos. So much is jumbled and needs constant sorting. Imagine having to go on a long flight with only a few minutes available to pack. An artist is in that constant state of mind.

When it is expressed, it is such a relief. Not because of

the final product but because you get out of such immense pressure. Most creative people have these compulsions.

Moneeza Hashmi: Can writing be improved with practice?

Bano Qudsia: You've touched on a very important and sensitive topic. Take the example of a watermelon. If the seed is good and sown in sandy soil conducive to its growth, it will turn out red and succulent from inside. If you sow it in wet soil and the seed is neither good , it will turn out pale and tasteless. Likewise if someone has the DNA to develop into a star, and gets the right environment, chances are he or she will flourish. If someone gets the right partner, the right environment, the right teacher then the work produced will be of a certain standard. Now think of a person who does not have a good voice but practices for years, he will never make it to be first class performer. So what I am saying is that it is the inner talent which counts more than the routine daily labour.

Moneeza Hashmi: You are a wife, a daughter, a mother-in-law, a grandmother and a writer. Which of these roles comes first?

Bano Qudsia: With much guilt I have to admit that my performance as a mother-in-law has been the worst. I have not been able to give enough time to my grand children or my daughters-in-law as I got split into so many roles. I played the mother's role badly as well. I wasn't good at it. I couldn't give the kind of time my kids required from me.
I don't believe in the myth of quality time. Kids just need time. They are like sunflowers that follow the sun. A child follows the mother until they mature.

Moneeza Hashmi: So you're not a good mother-in-law, you're not a good grandmother by that standard. I will ask your husband if you are a good wife. That leaves us with the writer's role. Are you a good writer?

Bano Qudsia: This is for other people to judge. You tell me: am I a good writer?

Moneeza Hashmi: Are there any regrets about being a writer?
Bano Qudsia: Insecure people, such as me, keep thinking that we haven't worked much at all and now that it's time to go, what will happen no? No work of grandeur was done. Whatever little work was done, none of it was brilliant.

Moneeza Hashmi: What inspires you to write?
Bano Qudsia: When I write a drama there is much conflict in it. It follows the life of some or any human being. It could be that a particular person is being oppressed. At times there is no visible injustice, nothing is wrong but someone has silenced himself in his environment, and does not say anything. There begins to formulate a question in my mind about his demeanor: why did he behave in that way? Why didn't this person clean up for seven days? These are the types of questions that force me to examine that person's world. Sometimes a person near your house leaning against your wall will catch your eye as you pass by. You make eye contact and it sets you thinking about who he is and why is he here outside your house leaning on your wall? In the middle of the night in a quiet moment you recall his eyes. Are they the eyes of someone who has lost the ability to comprehend and is confused about the affairs of the world? We have all seen those. They have a sense of panic, sometimes sadness.
So many eyes and faces come before me as I sit to write. Now as I talk to you I have seen your eyes.
These eyes will visit me another time and entice me to meet you again, if not in real life then on paper, so I can find out what is in your heart. When you enter a room you can get to know a lot through the body language of the people present. Their eyes tell you a lot. So do their clothes. You see someone standing in a window looking outside. You try to guess what is wrong. You come up with scenarios about where she has lost her husband or her job or is her child sick or is she married for the third time, or has she been left by her lover? Innumerable questions. And it is these questions that lead you to a story as you find the answers. You slowly see a path, and that path is paved by those characters whose eyes you have seen.

There are other times when a phrase strikes you, a phrase that is not there written on the piece that you are reading in the paper at the time. I may come up with a phrase and it is "The anger and bitterness that he filled himself with was not developed in a day". Then that phrase joins itself with another phrase and the process begins. Till today I have not written about a real person or a real event. I cannot write such journalistic pieces. I cannot take something from my environment and write about that. I cannot write biographies or obituaries. I write in the shadows of whiffs of perfumes. I hear about things and conflicts and as I delve deeper I find my stories. Sometimes I don't find them, other times I do. An artist would be tongue tied but not be able to tell you how he or she creates their art. Because a flower does not know how it creates its perfume. There is no self awareness in the process itself. No flower can express it. Similarly, no artist can tell you about the demon that haunts him/her.

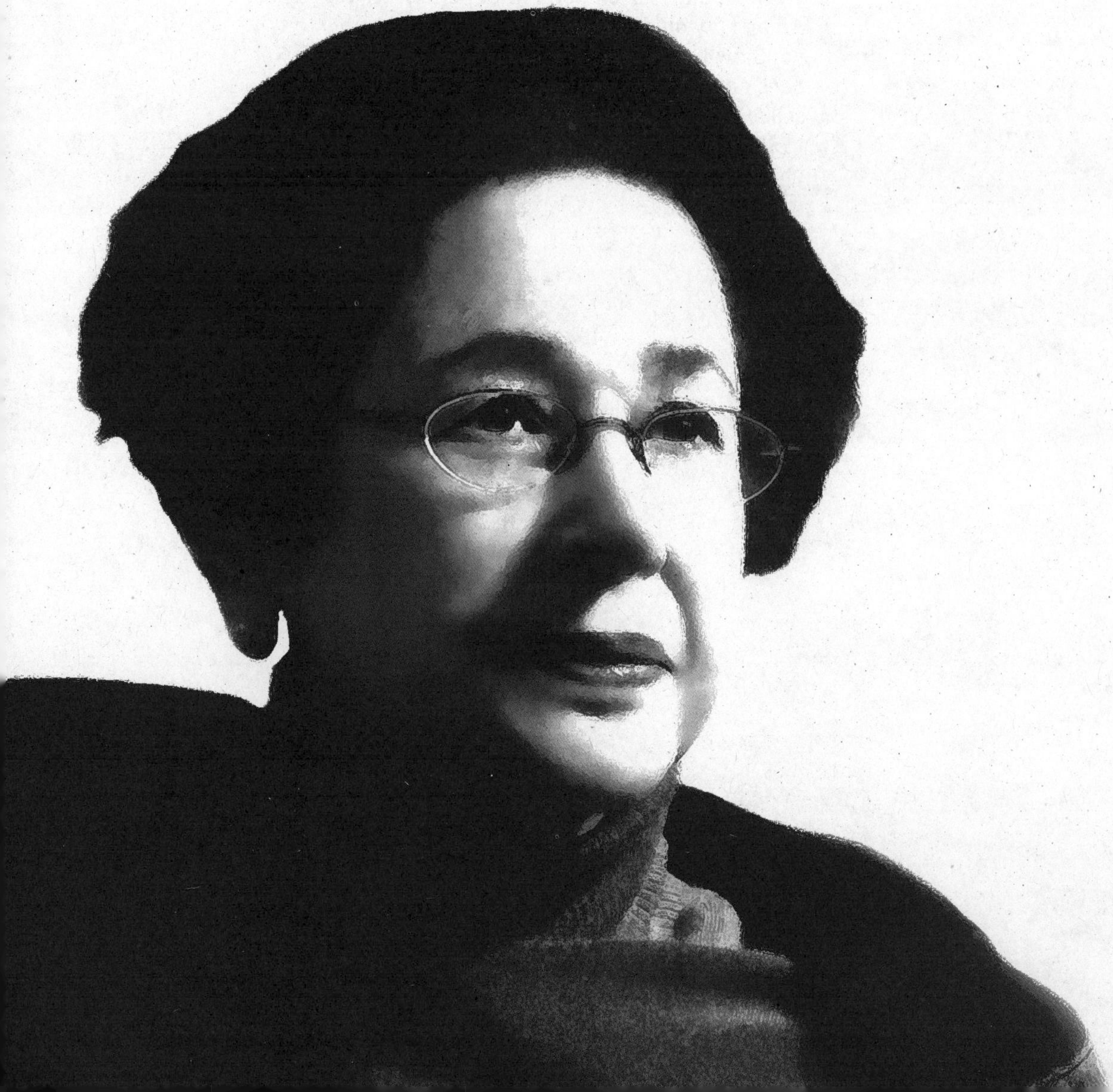

Place of Birth
Karachi
Marital Status
Married
Number of Children
Two daughters and one son.
Area of Expertise
Writing, Reading and Teaching
Area of Personal Interest
Film, theater, writing and music
Moment of Pride
When I got a Sitara-e-Imtiaz in 1991
Moment of disappointment
There are too many to state
A trait I am embarrassed about
Over-eating, lack of discipline
A trait I am proud of
Being able to write
The first question I would ask myself
I always wonder what is going to happen after I die.

BAPSI SIDHWA

December 1999. I had heard and read about Bapsi Sidhwa frequently before actually meeting up with her. What I did not know was how my father had been instruemental in getting her book published or how high he held her in his esteem. All of this was revealed as we got talking.

I arrived at her lovely home in Lahore Cantt on a lunch invitation several years ago. I remember being quite in awe of meeting up with the author of "The Bride" which had struck several inner cords with me. Was it the young girl's passionate liaison with her lover so beautifully described? Was it the loneliness of the young bride? Was it just 'connecting' with a young starry eyed female 'in love with the notion of being in love'? I had read that book in one sitting and was thinking of dramatizing it for PTV when I received her lunch invitation. Bapsi's daughter Parizad had been a student of mine at the Lahore American School. I had discussed her mother's literary pursuits with her on and off while maintaining the distance of a teacher with her student. She was a shy and withdrawn teenager not at all easy to draw out. So I never got closer to knowing more about Bapsi, her writing habits or creative flows.

"Please come in" said a soft tinkling voice. Before me stood a petite, pretty person in a peach colored trouser outfit. Short auburn curly hair. Petal curved mouth exuding a gentle smile. Bright sharp eyes, twinkling behind spectacles. She led the way inside a tastefully decorated home, into a bright and open living room. That was my first introduction to Bapsi Sidhwa whom over the years, I grew to vastly admire for her soft spoken gentleness, her inner strength that shone through the mild exterior and most of all her choice and selection of words as we discussed a variety of subjects. Oh yes - and her sense of humour! She would pass the funniest of comments with a completely straight face or just laugh that tinkling laugh to show she was really not that serious.

Over the years I have continued to meet her in Lahore, in Houston where she now lives permenantly, in seminars, at lunches and dinners, in hotel lobbies accidentally and at airport lounges. Each time she has greeted me with much affection, much grace. Each time I moved ahead with a sense of pride of having shared a few moments with a legend of her time. I have read an Urdu methaphor when someone's diction or voice has been described as "bells tinkling or rose petals falling" *(ghantian bajti hain, phool jhartay hain)*. Bapsi has that music in her voice and beyond doubt, in her words.

My interest was to find out how and when she wrote. Creativity for me has always been a passion to explore. I have spent time with several creative geniuses (in my opinion) and queried them about their creative "muse". Each time I heard different words basically describing the same process. Some compared it to the painful process of 'child bearing' but the result being just as exhilarating, just as satisfying. A few said they paced like restless tigers in a cage until the 'beast' within came out. Some talked about wanting to curl up in a dark room to sort out their thoughts. Others wanted to be alone, in an unknown place amongst strangers to design their creativity into a tangible shape. There were still some who sat down every day in a regimented routine to 'create' and then walked away to resume their normal day as if nothing exceptional had occurred. I found all these explanations fascinating. I found each one unique. I found every one different, individual but similar. The similarity was that inner voice, that inner idea, that inner feeling which had to find expression. Be it colour or words or musical notes. Be it to soothe eyes or ears or nose. The overall objective remained the same - to transport and elevate the mind to another level; to enhance the sensitivity of fellow human beings; to connect with other minds on some mystical level. Yes, creativity holds enormous power which when passed on can soften a stony heart and mellow a stern exterior.

I wanted to know Bapsi's secret.

When I sat down to talk to her that afternoon in the PTV studio she looked her normal calm self as the crew went about their business. She was that kind of person. Always at ease. Comfortable in her surroundings. She gave me a feeling of being at peace with herself and the world around her. I have seen her in her home in Houston laying the table, bringing out the food, setting up the table ware, making the fruit punch, greeting her guests with the same aura of ease and peace. No fuss, no ruffles.

And here was a world renowned writer who had never been to school, was a recovered 'polio' victim, who had missed out on much in her childhood.

I had to know more.

"Madam we are ready" said Shaukat Sahib's voice on the intercom from the control room above.
I turned to Bapsi. She smiled that gentle smile which lit up her face as always.

We began to talk.

Moneeza Hashmi:	What was your childhood like?
Bapsi Sidhwa:	As a child I had polio. The doctors convinced my parents not to send me to school because I wouldn't be able to handle the pressure. I had to have several operations so I couldn't attend school regularly. I started to take private tuition and more or less studied at home. You can say I am completely self taught.
Moneeza Hashmi:	Do you remember those days?
Bapsi Sidhwa:	Very vividly.
Moneeza Hashmi:	Were they happy or sad?
Bapsi Sidhwa:	My childhood was pretty lonely because I didn't go to school. But now I feel it worked out to my advantage. The loneliness made me read a lot and that is what made

me into a writer. It was a happy time nonetheless, not a bad time.

Moneeza Hashmi: When did Bapsi Sidhwa discover she wanted to become a writer?

Bapsi Sidhwa: After I was married and had had two children. I went on the Karakorum Highway where I heard a story about a girl from Punjab who lived in the Kohistan Mountains having run away from home. She had been married into the Kohistani tribal clan. They live by an extremely strict code of honor, are extremely poor and totally locked in by the mountains. The story was told to me by the people who were building the KKH.

Within a month of her marriage, the bride had run away with some one else which was an intolerable insult to those people and to their code of honor. They hunted out and killed the couple. When I came back from the mountains, I wanted to tell the story of this girl. I wanted to describe the hill tribesmen, the beautiful Indus, the gorgeous Karakorum Mountains. At the time I thought I would write a short story. Without my conscious effort, it became a long tale as I started to describe where this girl came from, her family, how she met the tribals. By the time I moved along to the point where I wanted to actually tell the story a whole novel had developed. I called it *The Bride*.

Moneeza Hashmi: How does one become a writer?

Bapsi Sidhwa: It is an innate gift definitely to begin with. That is the most important thing. Imagination plays a very vivid role but it is only your own imagination. What I did however later learn was how a novel is structured. Whatever entertained me or appeared interesting to me I wrote about that. Not consciously, just naturally because I had absorbed all of it through my subconscious. When I started to write it flowed very easily and very naturally.

Moneeza Hashmi: You are one of the very few people from Pakistan who writes in English. When you began you were the only one.

Bapsi Sidhwa: Not many people read English in Pakistan. Not many people have an English-Medium education either. Our literacy rate is very low, for women in particular. Out of a million people maybe one would be really inclined to write or have the gift of writing. And of course the biggest reason for not having many writers is also the fact of not having enough publishers.

When I wrote my first book, 'The Crow Eaters', there were no publishers, so I self-published that one. That was quite a humiliating experience. Not only did I pay for publishing the book; I had to go from shop to shop trying to market it as well. It was quite exilierating when the book was finally published by Jonathan Cape from Britain.

Moneeza Hashmi: Did you have any regrets at the time?

Bapsi Sidhwa: I had written two novels by then, and though I had a very good agent in America and in Britain, I found it took a lot of effort and energy to find an agent; it is also very hard to find the right one. Since they invest a lot of time and money in an author they are selective in their choices. Once I had an agent, I now had to get a publisher. I still got a lot of rejection slips. The usual reason was that Pakistan was too remote in time and space at the time. It was not a commercially viable project for them.

Moneeza Hashmi: What year was this?

Bapsi Sidhwa: Around 1975 / 1976. I self published in 1978. Then a British publisher picked up the book. After that a demand for my books seemed to develop.

Moneeza Hashmi: Do you remember the feeling when you actually held your book in your hand?

Bapsi Sidhwa: Yes. At every stage there were some remarkable incidences. One of them had to do with Mr. Faiz Ahmed Faiz. Mr. Javed Iqbal had loved *The Crow Eaters* and insisted I self-publish. He had liked the front and back covers and passed it to a few friends including Mr. Faiz Ahmed Faiz. He happened to be traveling on the same flight as my brother. He said to my brother, "This book is written by a Parsee woman, would you know who it is?" My brother leafed through it and he said, "Yes. This is my sister."

Faiz Sahab came straight home and made some very encouraging remarks about the book. It gave me a feeling of tremendous self-confidence and wonderment I remember.

Moneeza Hashmi: Now how many books do you have to your name?
Bapsi Sidhwa: I have four novels starting with *The Bride*, *The Crow Eaters*, *Ice Candy Man* which is known as *Cracking India* in America and lastly *An American Brat*.

Moneeza Hashmi: What makes a writer?
Bapsi Sidhwa: There may be a hundred reasons or more. In my case it was the loneliness of my childhood, the habit I developed of fantasizing, of being entertained by books for years and years. I did enormous amounts of reading in those years. There were also long silences in my life. When I didn't get a chance to communicate with anyone; writing became a way of filling that silence. It became a means of communication, my means of self-expression.

Moneeza Hashmi: You teach creative writing in the United States. Can one teach writing?
Bapsi Sidhwa: You can polish the gift somebody already has. You cannot teach the gift of storytelling. That has to be innate. Of course you can help with editing, advising them what needs more dialogue, more dramatization. There are certain crafts associated with writing which I didn't know about myself either. After I started to teach I learnt "how" to write.

Moneeza Hashmi: So you are self-taught there as well?
Bapsi Sidhwa: Yes, I did self educate there too. But I learned to teach.

Moneeza Hashmi: How about creativity. Can you teach that?
Bapsi Sidhwa: Everybody has their own form or manner of creativity. Some people are wonderful cooks, some are novelists. I think we are all born with some creativity. Creativity is innate. But the direction it takes depends on your own particular set of genes, your circumstances, the interests you have and what you are exposed to.

Moneeza Hashmi: Can one practice writing?

Bapsi Sidhwa: No. You just plunge into writing. They say fools rush in where angels fear to tread. You just rush into it and see what happens. That is a form of practice in itself. I became a writer when I wrote my first novel. Gujrati was my mother tongue but I knew Urdu perhaps better at that stage than English. While I was writing I studied the thesaurus a lot because I wanted to be very careful about each word I was putting in my book. It used to give me a great thrill to find the exact word. English is a rich language which offers different nuances and each one opens a new world. By the time I had written *The Bride* I had become a writer.

Moneeza Hashmi: I am interested to know what really inspires you to write.

Bapsi Sidhwa: Sometimes it's images I see; sometimes it's the memory of something very vivid in my mind. In the case of *The Bride* I had heard the story and I wanted to tell it. I wanted to describe the gorgeous black mountains, the scintillating air, the width of the Indus, the color of the river. These were images I was compelled to describe. Then the story of the girl was compelling too because it is shared by so many girls in Pakistan. It doesn't matter what class or society they belong to. Women have very little control over their livesin Pakistan. Often there is a need to make a statement and say what you feel very strongly about. Writing is also about telling stories.
In the case of *The Crow Eaters* I wanted to talk about the Parsee way of life. I feel we are a diminishing community - almost an endangered species. I wanted to convey the humor and the charm of our community. That was my main reason for writing *The Crow* Eaters. I felt very little had been written about partition although it was a historically defining moment at that time in the world at that point. So I wrote *Cracking India /Ice Candy Man*. I wanted to talk about people who were displaced. The roar of the mobs is a permanent image etched in my childhood memory. I had seen the fires. I had seen the scene where a bunch of goons raided our house to loot it. My mother came out with her hands on my

brother's head and mine. The cook came out of the kitchen. They asked if Hindus lived in the house. Our cook told them that the house belonged to Parsees and they went away on hearing that. That is still a vivid memory in my head.

When I began to write, all these stories, all these images came back to me. There were also women who were kidnapped. I knew of some of them.

I wanted to write about those days, although at the time I had no clear idea of where I was going with the story. Some instinct in my subconscious just steered me throughout. I eventually got the whole essence of what I wanted to say.

Moneeza Hashmi: How does Bapsi write?

Bapsi Sidhwa: Very spasmodically. No discipline. Sometimes I write for 18 hours a day and sometimes for 10 days a month at most. When I am traveling I have months of not writing. Everything else at one stage in my life took priority over my writing. Everything suddenly becomes more important - you are a mother, a wife, a hostess, a sister and whatever roles demand from you. Writing was not considered very worthy of my time.

So that meant that I would write whenever I could and that could mean gaps of six months at a time, but the book would remain always in me. Whenever I got down to it, it was always there.

Also you need a period of gestation between heavy writing. You need time to wallow. You need time to fill your mind; your subconscious fills it in so that when you put pen to paper again, out it flows.

Moneeza Hashmi: I have heard that creative people become moody, irritable, restless and some even nasty when they are passing through a creative phase. How does Bapsi Sidhwa behave?

Bapsi Sidhwa: I am quite the opposite of all that. When I'm writing I am very calm. I also become a little spaced out. I am not very alert at that time and someone else has to take control of my life. It's when I am not writing that I am irritable. I lose my temper more often and that is when

I am not happy. I am happiest most when I am writing. If a sentence comes to mind which is framed well, I write it down on any handy scrap of paper, the back of a cigarette packet, anything that I can lay my hands on. I can write anywhere so I keep pieces of paper handy. Sometimes I write in notebooks to use the sentences later. Each novel of mine takes roughly four years because I give it huge gaps.

The Crow Eaters I wrote in one summer. It just rolled out and wrote itself. It was an internal book about the Parsee and Punjabi communities. It was me. It was also a funny book which amused me as I was writing it. Then of course I took a lot of time revising it, editing in bits and pieces. That took about 2 years. *The Bride* took about 4 years. *The Crow Eaters* also took that long. *An American Brat* took 3 to 4 years as well.

Moneeza Hashmi: Who is your best critic?

Bapsi Sidhwa: In a way my husband. I used him as a sounding board since I had no community of writers to give me any feedback. If he felt bored or yawned I knew it wasn't going very well. He was a responsive person and a good critic. Then later my brother was always a source of encouragement.

One does need encouragement because it gives you the confidence to write. Positive feedback helps a lot. Criticism can often break you.

Moneeza Hashmi: Writing requires a very supportive environment. It requires solitude, peace and harmony. How did you tell your "environment" to leave you alone?

Bapsi Sidhwa: In the milieu I was I had a lot of time on my hands. There was also a sense of boredom at times. We were all addicted to coffee parties and tea parties, which can be a little numbing at times. I needed something a little more intellectually stimulating. The boredom actually helped to write.

Also the convenience of servants gave me space and time. Although the bedroom where I wrote resembled a railway station with servants coming in and out, it didn't exactly disturb me. I had a lot of time to dream. A writer needs that kind of time. When you are idle you dream. In my opinion idleness leads to writing.

Moneeza Hashmi: What was your family's reaction to your writing? Supportive, demanding, rejecting?

Bapsi Sidhwa: The family didn't know I was writing till the first two books were done except for my husband, who was happy and encouraging about it. My children at the time were a little resentful because it meant that I was spending too much time at my desk. Everybody is very supportive now.

Moneeza Hashmi: What are your strengths and your weaknesses as a person?

Bapsi Sidhwa: Too many to innumerate. I have no discipline and no self control in many matters. I am too "happy go lucky" in many ways. I allow people to take care of me in many ways, which is not fair. My strengths would be that I have an optimistic outlook. I have an ability to write. I am an affectionate person, very fond of my friends and my family with a certain sense of loyalty. I don't know if this is true of me or not but I would like to believe that!

Moneeza Hashmi: You obviously made a conscious decision to move out of Pakistan. What keeps drawing you back?

Bapsi Sidhwa: It wasn't a conscious decision on my part. My husband at that stage wanted to move so we all went. It was a difficult decision for me. I wasn't ever exposed to living abroad; however once I had moved I did enjoy my life there. I feel a sense of personal freedom. I developed more as a woman and as a person. I developed more confidence.
Of course I will always be drawn back to Pakistan because this is where my roots are. I need to come back every now and again to get a sense of self worth and a sense of my own individuality. This is where I get my definition from.

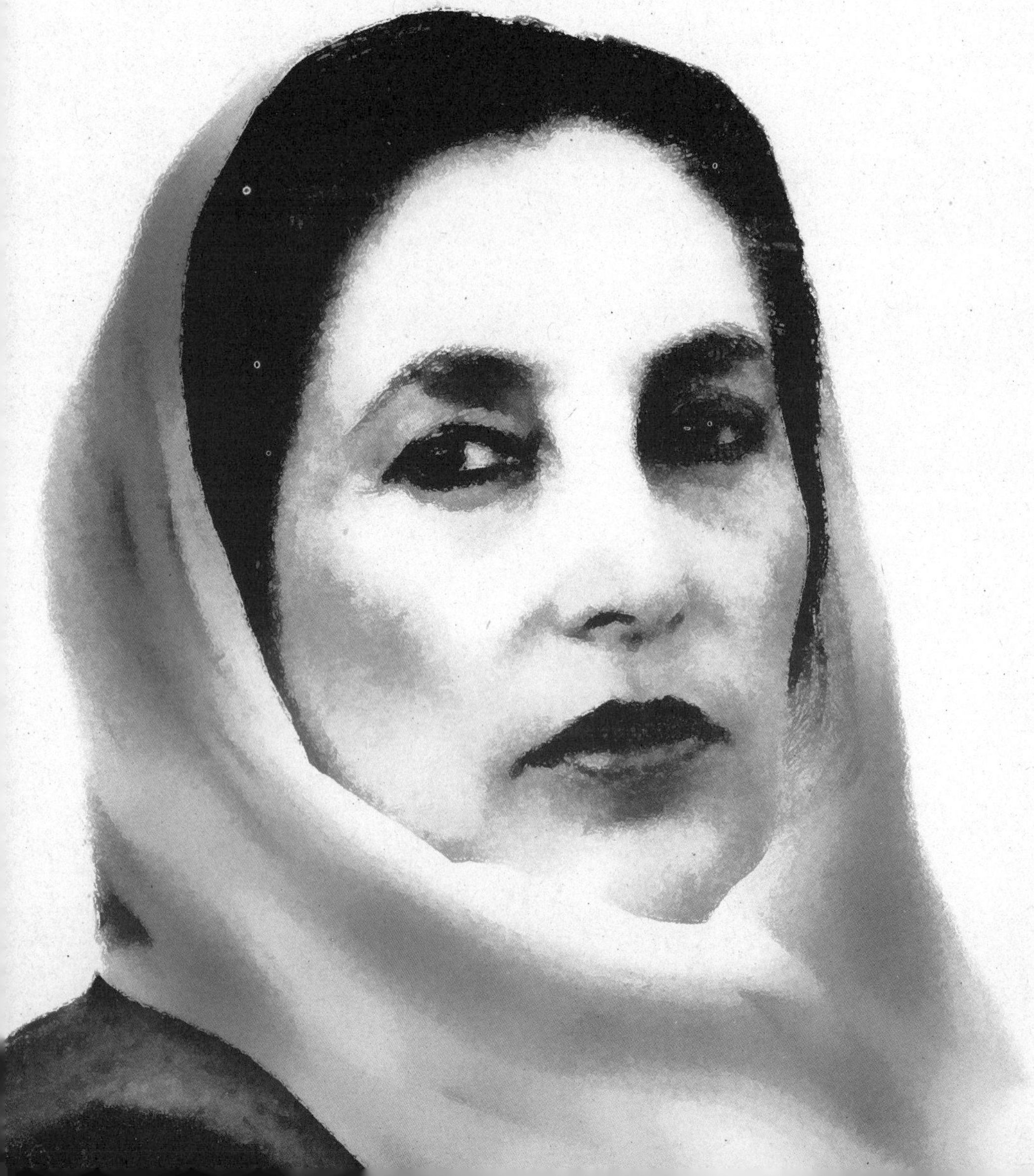

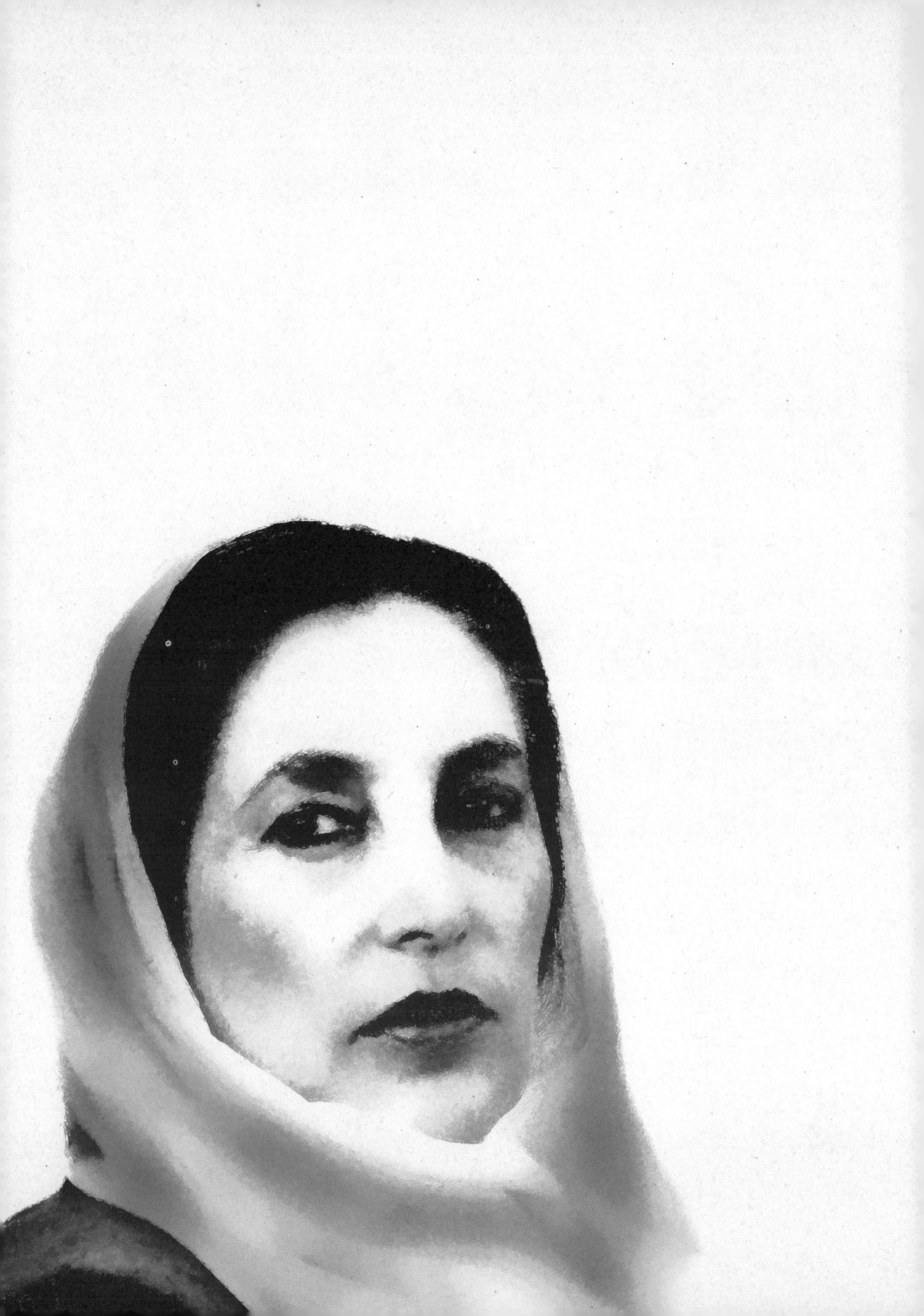

Place of Birth
Karachi.
Marital Status
Married
Number of Children
One son and two daughters
Activities of Interest
Politics
Moment of Pride
When I took oath as the first woman Muslim Prime Minister of Pakistan
Moment of disappointment
I do not think negatively
A trait I am proud of
My dedication to the people of Pakistan
The first question I would ask myself
Have I achieved what I wanted to for my people?

BENAZIR BHUTTO

February 1995. What does one ask a sitting Prime Minister? How do I address her? What am I doing here? And many more questions crowded my mind as my flight landed in Islamabad that crisp spring afternoon.

It had all happened too fast. A dream come true for any media journalist but a nightmare too if one was caught unaware or took it too casually. I am not sure exactly which of those two categories I would fall into but certainly I was nervous to the point of biting my nails. Totally unlike me for all of those who know me well. I can talk, argue, volley, discuss but to be at a loss for words was just not my style. I just had to discuss this with someone who knew "her" and me equally well.

"You address her as Madam Prime Minister. Don't worry, she is a very easy person to talk to and not someone who stands on ceremony" was how Shahnaz Wazir Ali described Benazir Bhutto. Shahnaz at the time was Minister of State for Education and counted as a member of BB's closer circle. Shahnaz was also and still is a dear friend of mine. I trusted her advice and felt somewhat relieved after that phone call.

The morning dawned bright and clear. Flowers were out in full bloom as I drove up to the PM house. My technical recording team was already in place when I entered the living room. Mics were in place waiting to be hooked on. The final lighting touches were being put in place. Just about everyone looked tense and that included me. I sat down in the assigned chair, my mic was hooked up. I laid my notes with the questions already sent ahead next to me and cleared my throat, looking around the elegantly decorated room.
It was now a question of waiting.

A few minutes later it appeared as if an electric charge had swept into the room. Bodies straightened up. My producer Sarfaraz Ahmad, who was going to record the programme, sent me an almost invisible eye signal. The service staff suddenly vanished. I heard a loud voice which sounded like hers coming closer. Then some more murmurings of male voices and she regally swept into the room. Farhat Ullah Babar followed. I immediately stood up and got pulled down by the wire of my microphone! Not a very graceful way to greet a Prime Minister in hindsight. I planked down as I greeted her and apologized for my rudeness. I don't think she noticed or at least did not mention it. "Where do I sit?" she asked addressing no one in particular. Farahat ullah stepped forward and pointed to the chair opposite to mine. I greeted her, to which she answered graciously as she sat down. I signaled the audio man to wire her. His hands were shaking visibly, I noticed as he fumbled slightly but finally got it right. That makes two of us, I thought! She was making small talk with Farhat Ullah as we did a voice test unobtrusively. Tech details over, she turned to me and smiled. "I hope I don't look like a fundo!" she said and then laughed. I had to go back later and ask someone what she meant by the phrase 'fundo'!

"Madam Prime Minister shall we begin?" I asked.
"Yes. Please do" she said.
While I waited for the recording signal from Safaraz I said "Ma'am, I am so nervous".
"Why should you be nervous? I am the one giving the interview" and she smiled again.

"Tape rolling" came the signal and we were on record.
What else do I remember of that historic morning in my entire career?

She was easy to talk to as Shahnaz said. I deviated from the laid out questions quite a bit. I prodded her a bit about her family life. She went through the whole interview without batting an eye lid. She was a 'pro' and that one could tell. My tension eased up a bit as we proceeded. Her eyes were clear and focused on my forehead. Her face was unlined and very fair. She had long fingers, nails perfectly manicured but unpainted. Throughout the interview her hands remained clasped in her lap. Her feet were tucked under the sofa. Her back was erect. Her duppata was probably pinned at the back because it did not move a centimeter as she talked. She wore a pinkish lipstick and eye kohl. There were some freckle marks on her cheeks other than that her skin was almost translucent. She was the epitome of regality and confidence. She was every inch the Prime Minister I had imagined.

Later I found out it was her very first interview for PTV and that made it all the more special.
We shared a cup of tea afterwards. She told me how her father had respected mine. She said how she was partial to putting women at the helm of affairs and wanted to see them take the lead. She swept out of the room for an official photograph session already scheduled. Every time I see that photo which adorned every government office for years to come it reminded me of that precious hour I had shared with Prime Minister Bhutto alone. How many people in Pakistan could be that fortunate?

Moneeza Hashmi: You had a lot of other professions to choose from, why did you decide on politics?

Benazir Bhutto: It was not my choice. I was 'thrust' into politics. I was just a child when my father Zulfiqar Ali Bhutto had a dispute with Ayub Khan over the Tashkent declaration after which they parted ways. After that there were attempts on his life. Every time my father would leave the house I would be fearful something might happen to him. I would pray for him return safely.
I would also say to myself I will never choose this way of life for myself. I will become a journalist, or join the foreign office, work on foreign policy and serve my country. I abhorred politics and didn't want anything to do with it. I associated it with fear and terror.
When I completed my higher education and returned, there was martial law in Pakistan and all democratic forces had been toppled. There was a false case registered against Mr. Bhutto, who was fighting for his life at the same time. This whole scenario was responsible for

politicizing not only myself but thousands of others who believed in democracy. Several ministers, MNAs and MPAs were distancing themselves from us because they were not willing to sacrifice their comforts and for being associated with the PPP at that time. A different wave of new people and political workers were taking their place. I would dream of the day when my father would return from jail and I would be standing outside the gate of Rawalpindi jail with garlands of flowers waiting to welcome him. There would be thousands of people alongside me.

But that day never came. I would assist my mother writing statements of protest on her behalf and meet many people. With time however, she started to distance herself from politics because she was becoming more and more unwell. So this responsibility was then thrust upon my shoulders without my wishing or wanting it. I remember once I was sitting with my father in our Rawalpindi house and reading an interview of Indira Gandhi in which she said for her father, politics was a romance but for her it remained a responsibility. My father tossed the paper aside and commented "Look at how little this lady understands politics". Now when I look back, it is the same scenario where it is a responsibility for me and was a romance for my father. It is a responsibility I had to take on for my father, for my people and for all those political workers who sacrificed precious years of their lives in jails.

Some people think you end up easily in the National Assembly but let me tell them that the path of politics is not an easy one. One needs to cultivate a lot of patience to be successful in this field. Unless you can compromise and learn to forgive, you cannot succeed. There is no room for ego in politics. Only causes unite people. Those who are striving for the same cause can walk the same path. When I first entered politics it was a very tough journey for me. I never understood how people could become friends overnight after being enemies for generations. It was strange that you'd fight with someone a day before but resolve that dispute the very next day. I think of it like a cricket match where there are too many players. So if you drop a certain number (of players) you simply replace them from the opposite team. Politics is very much like a mathematical game of numbers. You have to calculate precisely the number of players which will enable you to get a winning combination.

One of the most important things in politics is to keep your bond with the people, but it should not be a mere connection. It must be used to empower the people. You learn to make people aware of their own issues and to make the right choices with that awareness for themselves.

I had to learn all this on my own. I had only read politics at university level. Practical politics and theoretical politics are worlds apart.

Moneeza Hashmi: Madam Prime Minister, you are aware of the kind of politics we have today. It is the politics of force, it has very little dialogue and debate. It involves loss of life and property. How do we convert this negativity into a positive force?

Benazir Bhutto: Women have softer hearts than men. Women tend to forget grievances. Men nurture grudges. Women don't think as much of revenge and tend to leave things to be settled in God's court. They are by nature, gentler human beings.

Women can play a central role in creating this shift in politics (from negative to positive). It is my personal desire to see women play their proactive role in every profession and every field.

In two years time we are hoping to start Muslim Women's Olympics in Pakistan. The first Muslim country to host the Muslim Women's Olympics was Iran, and Pakistan will be the second country to host these games. When I first brought this up with the Ministry of Sports, I was informed we do not have too many such facilities for women. I am really saddened that we are lagging behind in the field of sports.

We have now started to train our sportswomen for these Olympics and I hope that at least one Olympic game will come Pakistan's way.

Politics becomes terror when there are restrictions

placed on it. When there are restrictions on newspapers, when there is injustice, when there are politically motivated cases filed or when the judiciary is not free or when you have military courts, then people become desperate. It is desperation that breeds force. The moment they choose to tread a path of violence they merge with other criminal forces. Robbing a bank for politics or for poverty are both wrong acts.

On the flip side when democratic forces return to a country, people don't automatically discard their previous methods. In the past, politicians have used terror to further their agendas. The line between politics and terror has become blurred. We are now trying to separate the two. We have to accept verbal criticism but we have to keep an eye out for actual protests also.

Moneeza Hashmi: What would be your answer if I asked you whether you learnt more sitting in the opposition or as head of government?

Benazir Bhutto: My early education was first when Mr. Bhutto was Foreign Minister, and then when he was in opposition. I used to distribute badges for his release when he was imprisoned in Mianwali Jail. Soon after, I appeared for my senior Cambridge exams. I would stand outside crowded cinema houses and hand out badges to people as they came out. So in a way for me politics began very early.

Then another kind was the politics in theory alone which I learned at University.

Yet a third kind of politics I learned when I myself was in jail where I had so much time on my hands. I was not allowed many visitors, that too only every 15 days. Also, it was restricted to three guests at a time and for just one hour. We were not allowed newspapers. All one could do was pray or think. I learned of patience while I was imprisoned.

When I came into the world of politics I used to think everyone was idealistic like me. I couldn't comprehend that people can be manipulative also. I would take every thing at face value.

When I became Prime Minister the first time, I realized people do not mean what they say. Those who I considered friends were not really my friends. Those who were advising me were actually using me for their own personal agendas. All this came as a shock to me. When I cam into the opposition, I learnt the lesson which I discussed earlier - that there are only so many players in the field, and I cannot fight on the fronts of both Prime Minister and President. If we wanted to have a playing team we would have to create a tactical alliance with either of them. We needed to mathematically add it up to a number where one or the other party was included. We tried this combination with first one and then the other, but both did not want to walk with us. We ended up joining other alliances.

We believe in meaningful alliances. We can only have an alliance on principles. Our principle was that we wanted free and fair elections, and we only wanted to have an alliance with those who were willing to hold a dialogue with us asking for fair elections.

Moneeza Hashmi: This is not a scripted question but I must ask it. Where did you have a better time, in opposition or in power?

Benazir Bhutto: None of them were any fun. There is certainly more satisfaction in power. It is only when you are in power than you can actually implement your dreams and ideals. There is more satisfaction now. When there was load shedding and power shutdowns and I was in opposition, our party could not do anything about those issues but now that we are in power we have a plan which we have put into action.

When I would go to a village and see children with polio, I would feel very helpless. Pakistan is on serial five in the world among countries which are polio affected. This means that one in five children has polio in Pakistan. We could not do anything then, but now we have a campaign to eradicate polio in five years from Pakistan. There are some villages that have children with goiter, because of iodine deficiency. Working on these issues is very important because this is where we can make a big difference. There is no bigger pain than to witness diseases in children.

We are working towards bringing in investment into Pakistan. We want to spur jobs and cut down on unemployment. The world is entering a new media era and Pakistan is lagging behind. We are launching computer literacy programs.

There is a huge problem of over population. We need to cut down on our population growth. In 1947, each family had two acres of land and now there is only half an acre left to feed that family. Imagine what will happen in the next few years if we cannot control the growth rates. At this rate we will not be able to sustain ourselves, much less feed our children.

It gives me tremendous satisfaction to know that something is being done regarding these issues by my government. There is no time for myself though. I cannot sit and read a book. If I do get even half an hour to myself I have to give that time to my children or my husband. I don't get time to relax or to meet my girlfriends. My children demand that time from me, or my husband demands that time. No time to rest.

When I travel all night and arrive home the morning, despite the jet lag there are events I must attend. I have to speak on politics, economics or investment. There are so many subjects that I must be well versed about.

The primary duty of a Chief Executive is to package and sell their country. A country has now become a marketable commodity. If you do not sell it well you will not be able to secure investment. Pakistan's voice needs to be heard for investments to be brought in. Investment and influence are interlinked. Bringing in investment will bring in influence.

Moneeza Hashmi: What image do you have of the Pakistani woman?
Benazir Bhutto: People think that the Pakistani woman is trapped indoors. People also think that the Pakistani woman is draped in a cloak from head to toe and does not step out. They think that she has no voice or opinion and that she is not empowered. This is a false concept.

If you travel to the rural areas of Pakistan you will see women out in the fields. They not only harvest but also manage the household. We are not like the women in

the UAE. We are not restricted.
However it is true that we do not possess independent means. Even the working women in Pakistan do not have complete control of their hard-earned money. It goes either to the brother, or the father or the husband. This is despite the fact that Islam allows women to inherit property. What is surprising is that although Islam gives women this right it is snatched away by their own family members. You can have the right but whether you can exercise that right is the real question. We are now undergoing a communication revolution. Sitting here we can see what is going on around the world. This new change will affect the way people think. When my father died, I realized he had left me with the training and tools with which I could launch my career in politics.
Today I believe that women have to stand up for their rights in all spheres.
Take domestic violence for instance. If a husband beats his wife, what can she do? She doesn't have another home to go to; she doesn't have the means to support her children. She is helpless. The only way to get out of this helplessness is to open the doors of economic empowerment for women, through jobs and through entrepreneurship.
It is with this aim in mind that I launched The First Women Bank, which is a bank which finances and also employs only women. We hope that more women will come forward to play their role in the financial world. We have also initiated women police stations and brought in women into the judiciary for the first time. This is part of the broader scheme to empower women and to give them the respect they duly deserve. A woman must also be given all those means which would make them independent. This would enable her to make decisions for them selves, regardless of whether she is a housewife and managing her home and her children which is a full time job - So is cooking and ironing your husband's shirts, and of course managing your husband.
When I went to Norway and met the Norwegian Prime Minister, I asked her: "How does your husband assist

you since you are kept so busy?" She said that her husband was so caring that he would iron her clothes as well as his own. When I came back and mentioned this to Asif his answer was that this could not happen in Pakistan!

Regardless of whether a woman is a housewife or a working woman, choices should be available to her. She must decide her own path.

If we want to put an end to victimization and give our citizens their due rights then we have to focus our energies on the issues facing our women. We need to focus on that fifty percent of our population. After all, a sea is made up of tiny droplets. Each one of us is similar to that one drop. If we combine our energies we can become a force of love and progress.

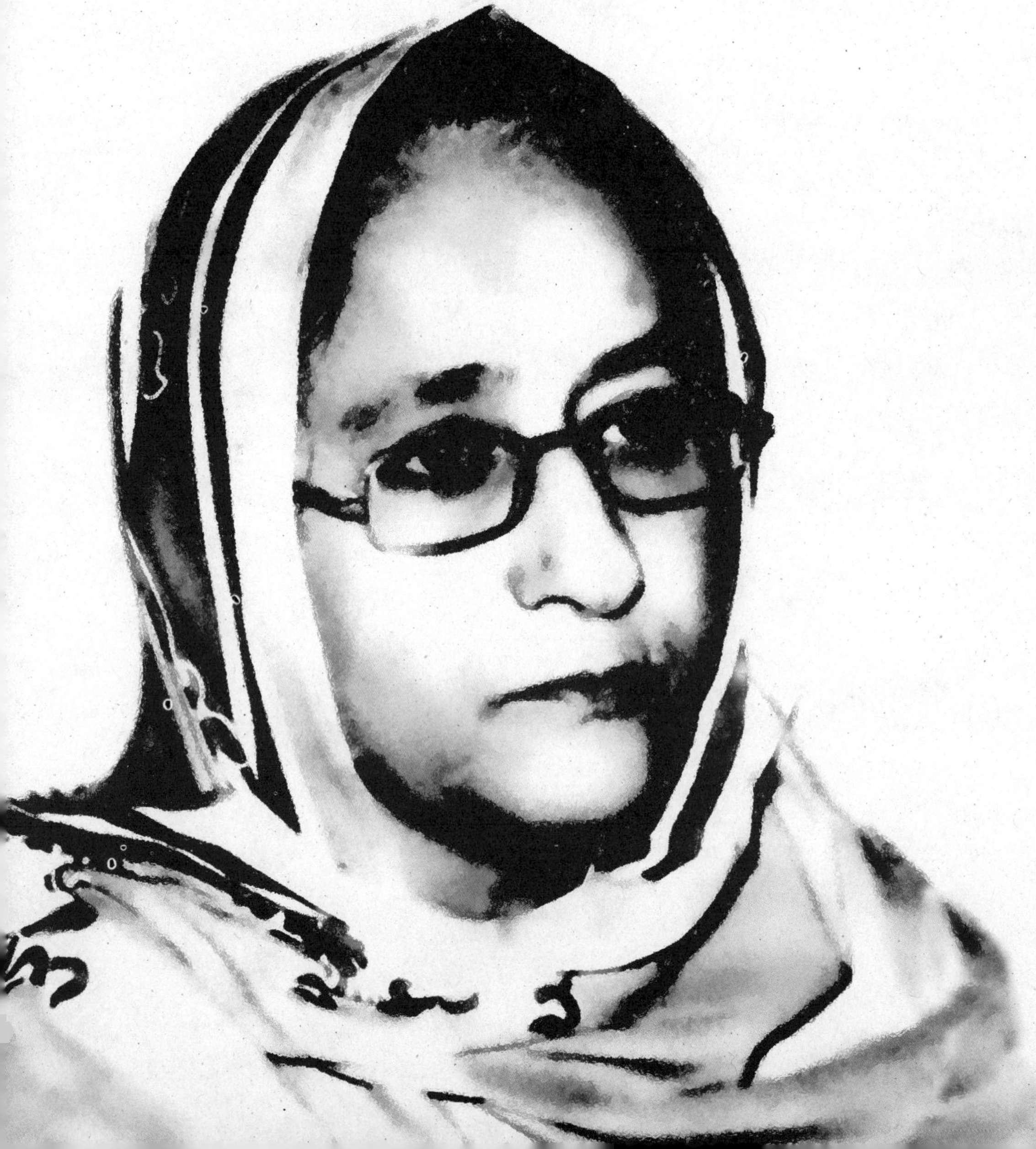

Place of Birth:
India
Marital Status
Married
Number of Children
Four
Activities of Interest
Social work
Moment of Pride
When I do something that I believe to be worthy
Moment of disappointment
When I see orphans
A trait I am proud of
I am grateful to God that he extracted humanity from me
A trait I am embarrassed about
My lack of formal education
The first question I would ask myself
I want no one to be harmed by my hands or my tongue

FATIMA BILQIS EDHI

May 1997. My impression of Abdul Sattar Edhi and his wife pretty much borders on "demi god" status. How anyone in Pakistan could be so filled with "milk of human kindness" syndrome has always been a question I could never wrap my head around. I once stopped my car to a skidding halt at Liberty Chowk when I saw that familiar figure in a grey crumpled *kurta-shalwar* standing in the hot sun with his j*holi* (shirt) extended. "Would you take a check?" I asked since I almost never carry cash on me. I didn't think he would be carrying an ATM machine on him! He answered "*Aap kuch bhi dain gi hum khushi say lain gay*" (whatever you give we will accept with pleasure). I remember writing out a cheque for 10,000/- and handing it over. He smiled over his long unkempt beard and saluted me. For him it was all in a day's work. For me the memory of having "met" a legend.

"What would his wife be like?", I remember thinking as I piled in the van with my crew. We were guided into a palatial house situated next to the Clifton shrine in Karachi. Marble floors; huge rooms; open spaces; long shining corridors; airy windows. I saw her walking towards me from the end of a long corridor. Simply dressed. Large spectacles. A smiling face. We greeted each other. The equipment started being set up.
"What should I call you?" I asked breaking the ice "Bilquis Apa". "But you are younger than me" I remarked. *"Bhaee. Humain sab yehi pukartay hain"* (everyone calls me that) she answered jovially and that set the tone for the interview. She was easy to talk to, giving more information than I asked for. Sitting opposite her, as our conversation progressed I felt totally comfortable even though she was a complete stranger. An inquisitive head would peer at us from a crack in a door and then disappear. A small kid would wander in and then out again. Voices could be heard somewhere nearby. It was a "*gharailu mahol*" (homely ambience). As we wrapped up recording I asked her where we were seated exactly and out came the most amazing story.

A rich man had built this huge palace like home for his only son who died tragically and suddenly. Since he could not bring himself to live in it himself after the boy's death, he came to the Maulana and handed the keys over to him and walked away, never to return. The Edhis set it up as a home for destitute women and abandoned girls. Bilquis Edhi took me for a walk around the place. I saw young teenage faces, mature women and small children roaming around enjoying the early evening sea breeze. Laundry was hanging out to dry. Music was playing somewhere. There were sounds of laughter here and there. It was a happy home. There was a curious look here and there. A stare now and then as we walked past. And then came the biggest surprise for me. We walked towards a huge godown. Bilquis Apa asked the guard on duty to open the massive door and there in front of my eyes I saw rows and rows of beddings. Shelves upon shelves of dry food rations. Stacked high up to the ceiling were shoes, bundles of clothes, blankets, and toiletteries. I was completely taken aback. I had never in my life seen a store so big and as well stocked. Bilquis smiled at my surprise. "It's the same almost every day. The gate bell rings. A guard goes to see who it is. There are trucks standing outside. No names are given. Some 'meharban' has sent a donation. We unload the trucks and send the provisions all over the country to needy people or refugee camps. The next day or the day after more trucks come. From the same people or others we never find out. *Yeh roz ka mamool hai.* (This is normal practice every day) As I drive away my thoughts are with these two 'angels' amongst us. Selfless, caring, dedicated and simple. How wonderfully content they appear to be! How fortunate we are to have them! But how much do we actually value them and their work?

Moneeza Hashmi: What were you like as a child?
Bilqis Edhi: I was very naughty and disobedient. I would be extremely destructive, and wouldn't adhere to the discipline required at school. My teacher would be very cross when the work she had assigned me wasn't completed. She would slap us and tell us to leave the class. That used to work out just fine for me because I would get to help sell chickpeas with the hawker near school. A bunch of my friends and I would spend the whole day selling chickpeas. It was great fun because we didn't get to do any class work. I was known in my neighborhood as someone who could beat up girls my age. I was a real bully. When my class fellows went to play on the swings, I would instead go play *guli danda (a boy's game).*
My parents had a cycle store. I had two younger brothers. I loved riding a bicycle. Unlike now, it was encouraged in those days. Times were much more simple back then.

Moneeza Hashmi: So you were a sort of tomboy?
Bilqis Edhi: Yes I was.

Moneeza Hashmi: How did you meet Maulana Edhi?
Bilqis Edhi: I was in class seven. I hated going to school, although, I was intelligent and got good grades when I applied myself. My mother was obviously very concerned about my future and really wanted me to get a good education. A few girls in my neighborhood decided to study nursing. Their white clothes fascinated me. I told them to take me along and enrolled in the evening courses. Then the '65 war happened. I started working as a nurse at the Edhi center. Edhi Saab and I worked closely during the war and after that we got married.

Moneeza Hashmi: What convinced you to spend the rest of your life doing this kind of work?

Bilqis Edhi: I didn't consciously choose this path. One thing led to another and I found myself following this destiny. I got a marriage proposal from Edhi Saab and said yes. Now this is my life.

Moneeza Hashmi: There is a considerable difference in age between both of you?

Bilqis Edhi: Yes there is a significant age difference.

Moneeza Hashmi: Why did you say yes to his proposal?

Bilqis Edhi: I didn't have that much awareness or insight about such things at the time. In fact there wasn't much thought given to it. Back then girls were getting married to men who already had four children from previous wives. There was also a lot of aversion to men with beards. I would say to myself, having a beard is better than him having children from a previous marriage. I respected him tremendously for the work he was involved in. So the age factor didn't really matter.
Neither did the fact that he had an extremely bad temper. Girls would caution me about marrying a *sadist*. They said he would torture and keep me locked indoors because he is a *maulvi* (bearded religious teacher).
I would say to them if he did then I am strong enough to escape, and not afraid.
Our marriage was a very simple affair. We did not host any guests for dinner. He did not ask for a dowry and neither did we offer him one.

Moneeza Hashmi: So first Edhi Saab was your boss, but then he became your husband. Did you change your attitude toward him after you got married?

Bilqis Edhi: No, I had no change of attitude. I have inherited this attitude of consistency from my mother. We never act to control anyone. We speak softly and with love.

Moneeza Hashmi: And do you get controlled?

Bilqis Edhi: Yes, I must say I let my husband get bossy with me, but he is the only person to whom I have given this privilege.

Moneeza Hashmi:	What do you like best about him?
Bilqis Edhi:	There is not a single personality trait which I can identify as non likeable. He has dedicated his entire life to the service of humanity. Women come to me because their men gamble, are violent, don't contribute financially, or seek other women. I counsel them not to leave the man or their children. I tell them the children are their responsibility and cannot be abandoned. Besides I ask them: how can they be sure the next person they marry would be different?
	I tell them to deal with their situations with compassion. Not every man has the same temperament. Men and women are fundamentally different. Women must try and adjust within the circumstances they find themselves in. Not immediately, but slowly, getting her way in one instance and then letting him get his way in another. This is the way the car of marriage can work and move ahead. That is how I have handled my marriage.
	By saying this I don't mean to say that the women who come to me are always at fault or that they do not comprehend the situation. They do, but they need to try and make things better for themselves even when the man is at fault. It is always for them to sacrifice that much more.
Moneeza Hashmi:	Did you ever think there would be a day when you would become so famous?
Bilqis Edhi:	Am I famous?
Moneeza Hashmi:	You do agree you have achieved a tremendous amount especially for women?
Bilqis Edhi:	Yes absolutely, I have done a lot of work. My work is now a part of me. But it is nothing compared to Maulana Saab's.
	Here you will have to separate me from him. Women who work with me do much more work than me, but they do it without the Edhi name, so they don't get the projection that I do. I am being absolutely honest here. The women who work with me are the real executers. I tell them what to do and it gets done.

Moneeza Hashmi: What's your typical day like?
Bilqis Edhi: I retire early in the evening so I am up by 5:00 or 6:00 am. I try and offer my *tahajud* (early morning) prayers. After my fajar prayers I read the Quran for a short while. Then I go to the hospital to prepare breakfast. We both have our breakfast at the hospital.

Moneeza Hashmi: Why don't you eat breakfast at home?
Bilqis Edhi: He hardly comes home. He actually has two wives, me and the hospital. He spends much more time with her! We have a light breakfast. We both begin our work after that. I have a room with a kitchen in the hospital where I go to later. I have a woman who assists me in the kitchen. The other staff has orders that if any one comes to see me, I am to be called immediately. No one is to be kept waiting. I cook my lunch, and sometimes go to the market nearby to buy chicken or vegetables. Actually after my mother died, much of this work has now become my responsibility. When she was around I hardly needed to take care of these things. She raised my children. Whatever charity work I have been able to do and whatever little assistance I have provided Edhi Saab, it was due to my mother's support. There were times I would have to stay back at the hospital and be extremely occupied with my work, but I had nothing to worry about vis-a-vis my domestic situation.
The house was a very short distance from the hospital. I was just a phone call away. Whenever my mother called I would be there in no time. I was extremely fortunate in that way.

Moneeza Hashmi: Didn't your mother complain and ask you to spend more time at home?
Bilqis Edhi: No. Most of the time my mother worried only about my well being, especially after I was diagnosed with Diabetes. Since I was her only daughter, she obsessed about me. But that would not stop me from tricking her. I would say that I would be back soon, and decide to stay back at the hospital until the next morning!

Moneeza Hashmi: Coming back to your day what do you do after

	you finish cooking?
Bilqis Edhi:	I usually call Edhi Saab for lunch. Sometimes he would eat if he was in a good mood, and if he was annoyed with someone he refuses to eat. He has always been the kind of person who takes things to heart, then frets over what someone has said for days, until the grievance fades from his memory. Only then will he let go. But in the meantime, he refuses to eat and disappears into his silent shell. I try and cook his favourite foods and reach through the shell.
Moneeza Hashmi:	Like a child?
Bilqis Edhi:	It is all I can do. In the evening, I then take a few of the senior girls who work with me in the *Women Edhi Center* and we go to the Vegetable Bazar to buy fruit and vegetables from the money Edhi Saab would give me. We feed everyone and then come home. It becomes a long day, and at times extremely tiring.
Moneeza Hashmi:	Tell me more about where we are right now. This is such a beautiful place.
Bilqis Edhi:	One day Maulana and I were having lunch and an Arab walked in. He wanted Edhi Saab to see two houses he wanted to donate to the center. Edhi Saab was not very happy about this proposition. Usually people donated houses, and then wanted a center to be opened right there and then. These would be small houses in residential areas. Opening up centers in such places create problems for the people in the surrounding areas. So we turn down such offers. We told him to come back the next day. Edhi Saab went on his own to survey the houses. He came back a little awed, and tried to tell me how huge the beautiful house was. He is such a simple man. Sometimes it's laughable to see how simple he is. Anyway I told him whatever he thinks to be beautiful is usually unattractive and under-resourced. He wanted to show me the house. I saw it and it was grand as you yourself have said. When we came here we had 14 gardeners and 20 guards.

The keys to this place were so heavy I couldn't lift the bag they were in. We told the owners we would not need all the staff and guards. There was nothing to steal. We wanted to keep only one gardener. They all started to wail! It took us some time to figure out how to use this facility. We decided that women would be on the first floor and handicapped children on the second.

Moneeza Hashmi: Does social work leave you any time for yourself?
Bilqis Edhi: I have lots of time. I go wherever I want. I attend whichever meetings I wish to. There is no wedding or funeral that I miss. I visit my children and my relatives. I don't want you to think that I am obsessed with social work. Work is delegated. This place is a well-oiled machine. Socially I am as connected as the next person. I had to be socially connected to get my children married.

Moneeza Hashmi: Where is Bilqis Edhi's own life in all of this?
Bilqis Edhi: Its right here, mingled with everything and everyone else.

Moneeza Hashmi: Tell me more about Edhi Sahib's two marriages?
Bilqis Edhi: This is an area of contention between us. I fight with him about the time we get to spend together, and then after I calm down I realize I am wrong and he is right. What he is doing has a purpose and is far more important. When I am upset Edhi Saab stays quiet. When he is upset, he also chooses to remain silent.

Moneeza Hashmi: How social is Edhi Saab?
Bilqis Edhi: He is not social at all. I complete all his social obligations on his behalf. I go on my own to all events.

Moneeza Hashmi: The Edhi Center is a large institution with so much responsibility. Do you ever wonder what will happen to it after you are gone?
Bilqis Edhi: I have full faith my children will take our mission forward.

Moneeza Hashmi: Whenever someone takes a few steps forward to good work people create obstacles in your way. Have

Bilqis Edhi:	you ever faced this?
	Yes we have faced these at all levels. But I believe there must be some sense of competition and resistance that allows you to work better. Opposition to good work is very essential.
Moneeza Hashmi:	This work must have its own kind of dangers associated with it?
Bilqis Edhi:	We have always played with danger. We started off with a donation of Rs. 5000 and one broken van. Now we have over 400 ambulances, helicopters, airplanes and we get donations in millions. As our donations increased so did our expenditures. Despite this we have constantly expanded our operations. This palace where we are is worth over Rs. 2 billion. We've been receiving and we've been spending. Despite the pace at which we have expanded we have not had to slow down. Isn't that something to be grateful for?
Moneeza Hashmi:	Why haven't you faced any slowdown?
Bilqis Edhi:	I'll tell you why. Because whenever anyone has criticized and attacked us, we have chosen not to respond. A person who attacks good work does so to weaken the other party and get them to waste their time obsessing over what was said. We simply chose never to do that. Our work and its results are our response to these insults and attacks.
Moneeza Hashmi:	What gives you the most satisfaction when you look back?
Bilqis Edhi:	I have led such a successful life. People have so much money and they are unable to find a way to spend it. They spend sleepless nights agonizing over that. God has made us work hard to put back wealth where it would be used best. I am very grateful to be a part of that entire process.
Moneeza Hashmi:	Where does the strength come from to do the same good work every day?
Bilqis Edhi:	God chooses his people and assigns them work accordingly. If he had not chosen me, it would have been someone else.

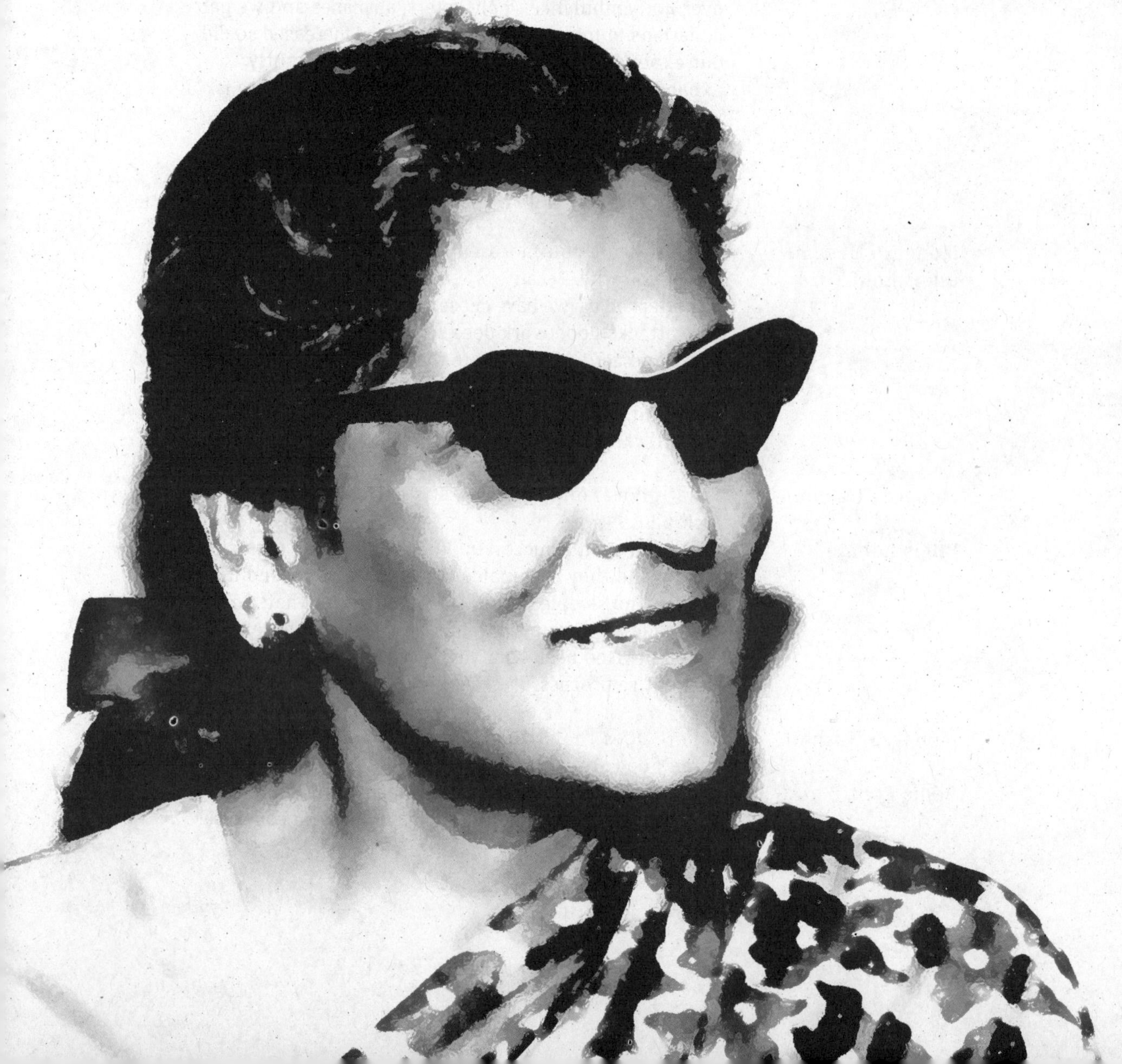

Place of Birth
Sargodha
Marital Status
Widowed
Number of Children
Two daughters
Area of Interest
Social work, Poetry and Science
Moment of Pride
When I saw my first child's face after her birth. I have never felt like that ever again.
Moment of disappointment
When my husband remarried and I lost my sight despite all efforts
A trait I am proud of
Determination and love for those who are deprived in one way or another
A moment of embarrassment
I get angry quickly, then get embarrassed about what I said.
The first question I would ask myself
Despite loving my husband, why couldn't I have had a happily married life?

DR. FATIMA SHAH

May 1997. I knew of Dr. Fatima Shah through her daughter Gala (Ghazala) who I used to meet socially although somewhat infrequently in Karachi. She was a class fellow of a friend's sister so whenever I would visit this friend sometimes Gala would also be there. I heard of her mother Dr. Fatima Shah in the course of those visits. I found out much later about Dr. Shah's handicap, again from Gala and how the family was extremely protective of this amazing person who never ever let her blindness impediment overshadow her life on the whole. So in the back of my mind was the impression of an empowered and confident professional woman but I certainly had no idea of how much until Dr. Shah walked into that room where I was waiting with my crew. The appointment to record the interview had been set up by the Karachi PTV management on my behalf. I usually only indicated the names of the people I wanted to meet. The rest was done by the PTV centre of that particular city.

I still clearly remember that morning as I waited outside on the porch of a beautiful house somewhere in one of the up market housing communities. The bougainvilleas were in full bloom waving in the gentle Karachi breeze. The crew started unloading the equipment as I waited to be admitted into the house. A servant invited us in. Gala greeted me from the kitchen where she was probably setting up a trolley tray for us. We were shown into a living room which I quickly surveyed. After a short consultation with the engineer in charge I selected a corner appropriate for an interview setting. The crew started preparations while I prowled around the room looking at photographs displayed here and there. I have done that in the past in some of the homes I would shoot in. Small knick knacks would give me clues at times which I would store in my mind and if or when needed draw into the conversation as the interview progressed. I never felt guilty about doing this. After all if the stuff was on public display it really could not be a family secret was my usual defense. It does hold solid even today. The lighting was being set up when I heard a voice asking "Is the TV team here?" and Dr. Shah walked in.

My first impression of her was the rather imposing height and the confidence with which she moved despite wearing dark glasses which quite obviously suggested her handicap. She was using her cane to guide her inside the room. She greeted us all and I guided her to the sofa chair where I wanted her to sit. Perhaps I had over looked informing the crew about her blindness. I caught a couple of them staring at her in a sympathetic sort of way. It was a blessing that she was oblivious to them although I am sure this would be normal practice every where she went.

We wired her up and I asked if she was comfortable. The perfectly *"mohazab"* (cultured) lady that she was, her answer was *"Bilkul"* (absolutely).

I always had a general idea why I was interviewing whoever was sitting opposite me but occasionally I did not have enough information about them. There were times when I had to cram more interviews into my out of town visits so that we had programmes in reserve. Sometimes also there were 'no shows' at recordings so we fell short of our list and had to fill in with others as standby and I would be caught un-aware and be less prepared. Sometimes there were misunderstandings at the logistical end and more people turned up then we had scheduled and I would be walking in and out of the studio completing one interview, making a quick change of attire and be back for the next recording before any one could say *Jack Robbins!*. However I had had time to prepare for my meeting with Dr. Shah but was certainly ill informed about her struggle to keep her sight, her husband and as a result her sanity.

This was my first and last (alas!) meeting with Dr.Shah. As we began to talk and her story unravelled from her own lips I recall so clearly even today my admiration for the journey this woman had undertaken alone. She was not at all emotional whilst describing her husband's desertion. She was not uncomfortable discussing her onsetting blindness and the consequential inner battle, not to let it drag her down. She was quite at ease talking to a total stranger and further sharing this with millions, about the challenges of facing a life time of dependency and vowing never to give up. I listened to this amazing lady describe her achievements as casually as if she was talking about some one else. My emotions of horror at her husband's rejection of her, my sympathy at her being stuck in a new country unable to go back to her previous life, my empathy with her trying to set up an association for the visually impaired in Pakistan where even the normal people do not get their due rights, my immediate bonding with this woman's strength of character and my sensing an inner steel within this exterior gentle demeanor are all vividly placed in my memory even today after all these years. Before me sat a fair, imposingly attractive, slightly heavy set, middle aged lady but the image etched in my mind is of a woman who was respected for her courage and determination and who championed the cause of the less fortunate and marginalized visually impaired women of Pakistan.

Moneeza Hashmi: What were some of your recollections of your childhood?

Dr. Fatima Shah: I was a very rebellious child. Always up to no good my mother would tell me. If a teacher would fall asleep in class I would sprinkle water on her. If a teacher was short in height I would pick on her by hitting her with a shuttlecock. I guess I was the same way at home. One thing is for sure: I was a social worker even as a child.

Moneeza Hashmi:	How so?
Dr. Fatima Shah:	I would collect all the broken shoes that were left discarded, fix them up and polish them. My mother would ask me what I was doing. A 'good thing', I would reply. That was a very formative part of my life and this action was very symbolic.

Another very interesting thing about my childhood was when the midwife called me a "*blind baby*". Because I was so plump my eyes appeared as slits. I guess that was somewhat prophetic at the time.

My maternal grandfather was very keen that I should study medicine. He wanted my mother to become a doctor but it was very difficult to educate women of that generation. She only managed to pass her 8th grade. He insisted that I should become a doctor. No one asked me what I myself wanted to study. I was 14 years old when I completed my matriculation. Since they admitted only 16 year olds in Hardinge College, I appeared for my intermediate examination from Aligarh and later joined Lady Harding College in Delhi. Soon after I got married and quit school. I now entered into an absolutely bogus phase of my life. There was nothing to do in that phase except relax in luxury.

Moneeza Hashmi:	Isn't that what most young girls want?
Dr. Fatima Shah:	I believe this creates a rot in people. Servants, helpers, money and wealth, going for summer vacations to the mountains- all this exhausted me. I could have opened a clinic for poor people up in the mountains. My husband had agreed upon this once. I could have done my husband's work too but the servants were much better at it. Our childhood was rather disturbed because my mother had been taken ill when we were little. We saw our parents laughing in each other's company. We however never got to see what a wife does for her husband because my mother was mostly ill. She did however say that if even there was a crowd of a million people around, she would have eyes for no one except our father. However my childhood did not give me a normal and nurturing environment to understand the real world. I feel now I would not have made all the

mistakes I did had I grown up in a normal household. My husband wanted me to do some of his work. The reason I didn't was because I was afraid of my incompetence being exposed publically. My life was continuing in this useless way, and the Pakistan movement started. My husband asked me to go to Pakistan and start work there which I did. Sometime later when I was planning to return to India a friend advised me to stay on and witness *Quaid-e-Azam Mohammad Ali Jinnah's* swearing in and oath taking ceremony. I stayed on. We saw the event and even met Quaid-e-Azam. However, soon after the riots erupted and I got stranded, I met Abdul Rab Nishtar and begged him to send me back to Aligarh. He said that it was not possible as the Sikhs were attacking all the trains. I had packed only a few sets of clothes and told the gardener in Aligarh I would be back in a week. I haven't gone back till today. I heard in 1952 that my husband had remarried. There were three instances in my life when it appeared as if the earth had swallowed me up whole. That was one such time. I got a letter through registered mail after I had returned home after a day's work at the clinic. I didn't believe it at first, and read it over and over again. I felt everything had suddenly come to an end. I had both my girls with me and I was thinking about them too. I wrote him a letter but never heard back. Then slowly I realized that I was having some difficulty with my sight. I discovered I had lost sight in one eye. It was during the time when I had gone to London for treatment where I learned the other eye had also been damaged. I eventually returned and went back to work but the problem only got worse. My doctor told me my other eye now had a cataract and I should stop working. I tried many different methods to cure myself, but to no avail. I remember the day clearly still when I woke up one morning and could see nothing. I prayed to God then if I am to lose my sight, at least He should let me keep my sanity. I felt at that magical moment as if my prayer had been heard.

I came across a soothsayer in Aligarh once who I didn't

want to meet but my sister-in-law insisted I should. He took his 15 rupee fee, looked at my hand, read my face and wrote something on his papers. After much ado, he said I would travel the world. This was a time when I was almost completely blind. I asked him if I would travel to get operated upon for my eye sight. He said I would travel to represent my country all across the world. He also said I would write a famous book that would be placed in libraries around the world. At the time I felt that he was mocking me. But in time it all came true and I realized how prophetic his statement was.

Moneeza Hashmi: How did you handle the loss of your sight?
Dr. Fatima Shah: After the initial few days of trauma, I remember sitting in my room alone. I liked to be alone because being by people felt like they were closing in on me. I was told there was a lady waiting to see me. I reluctantly agreed. This cheerful woman said, "Hi, I am Esabella Grant, I am 60 years old. I have traveld 24 African countries and many Asian countries and am here today to meet you." When she said she was completely blind and asked for a seat, I became alert. I asked her if she could see anything at all. She said no. I asked her if she had someone accompanying her on her travels and she said Oscar was always with her. Then she handed me a white cane and said, "Meet Oscar". Her voice sounded so happy, and that contentment stayed with me for quite a while. She had taken a rickshaw from her hotel to come to see me and here I was cooped up in a dark room alone, moping. Dr. Grant told me that she had visited many blind communities and told me they were surviving on the good will of many people. "There needs to be more of an organized effort for the blind" she said. She asked me to start an association where I should promote self-help for the blind". She said she was looking for such leaders through her travels. I was an ideal candidate to be that leader for Pakistan: I had just lost my sight, I was a medical doctor, I was a social worker and I was educated. I remembered then the child in me who wanted to make a difference in other people's life.

	I confided in her how I was not knowledgeable about working independently with a disability. She explained how I would have to learn on the job. I would have to help myself because no one would give me my rights. She inspired me to start the blind organization. After that it has been endless work.
Moneeza Hashmi:	What do you miss most about not being able to see?
Dr. Fatima Shah:	I loved looking at nature. When I went to Switzerland I remember standing for hours looking at the mountains. I used to soak in those images which are still very fresh in my mind. I love three things: perfumes, which I can still smell, a moonlit night, though I cannot see. I still try and stand outside on those nights and thirdly sites of nature which I now cannot see at all. I miss them very much. The time I really felt the pain of not being able to see was when my daughters got married. Another time was when they had their kids. But life goes on.
Moneeza Hashmi:	How did you convince the government to give blind people facilities?
Dr. Fatima Shah:	Blind people neither need sympathy nor pity. When you see a child who is blind, you should think whether this child has got the opportunity to get an education or not, and if not then why not. If it's because of economic issues, pay for that child's education. This is real practical help. Being sorry for the child or handing him a few currency notes is useless. In my book *Disability, Self Help and Social Change*, I outline what issues there are of the blind community and how they can be solved.
Moneeza Hashmi:	How did you manage to travel so much around the world, like the soothsayer predicted?
Dr. Fatima Shah:	I travel completely independently without help. The first time I traveled for my rehabilitation, there was a cyclone in the US and I had to change many aircrafts. When I got off a lady asked me if someone was meeting me. I replied "There had better be or else I will return on the same plane because I now know how to travel!"

Moneeza Hashmi: Do you ever feel that you are a burden?
Dr. Fatima Shah: Yes I do. I am not as busy as I used to be. I am mostly busy with the book I am writing and some correspondence. When I was busy, I didn't feel I was a burden. But now that I stay around at home and need things to be done for me, I feel I am a burden.
Most of my life I have been very independent and have worked for other people. Now that I need assistance, it's a strange feeling.

Moneeza Hashmi: What gave you strength to cope with your disability?
Dr. Fatima Shah: So many people became dependent on me - People who were poor and had a worse disability than mine. I had money and a house, and they had nothing. These people looked up to me. That gave me my strength.

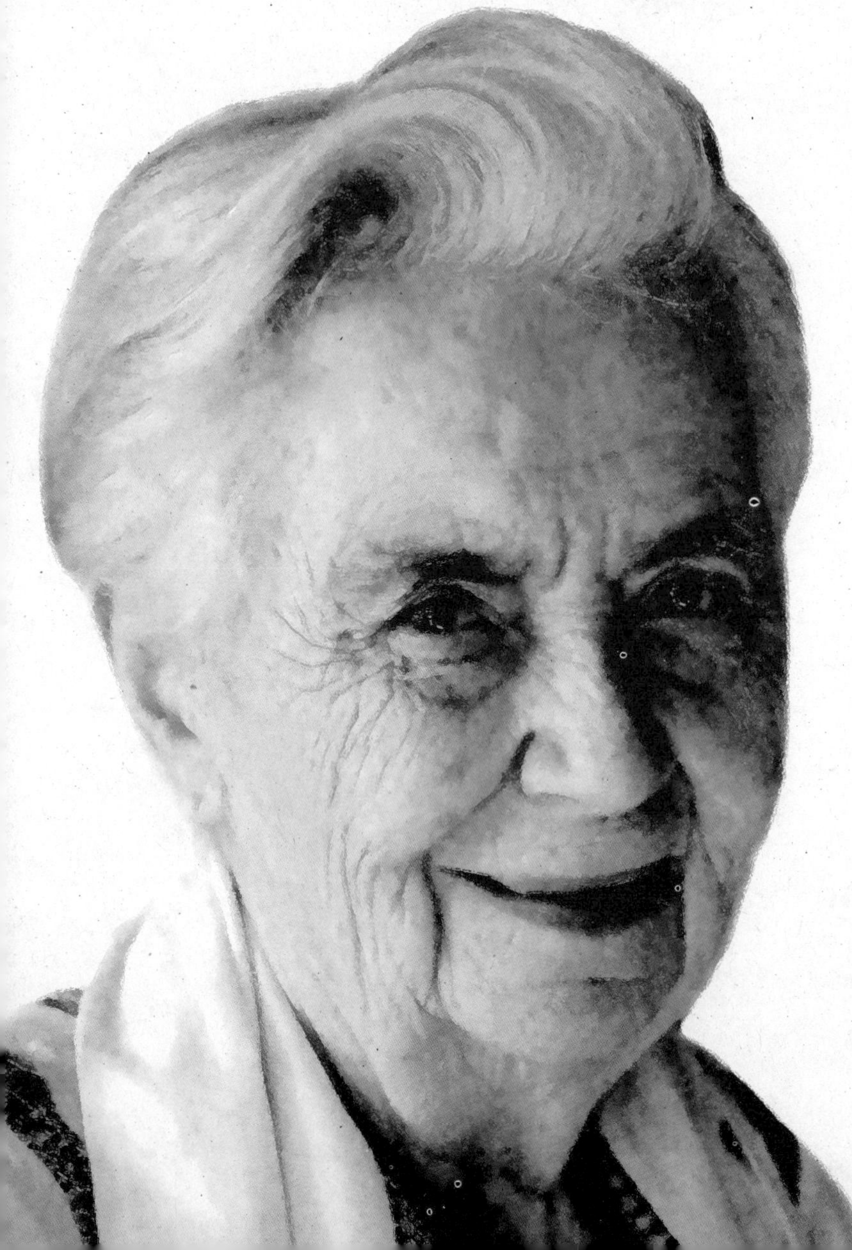

Place of Birth
Germany
Marital Status
Single
Area of Expertise
Eradication of leprosy
Moment of Pride
When I meet a patient cured of leprosy
Moment of Disappointment
When I see injustice in society
A positive character trait
Pakistan has controlled a disease like leprosy
A negative character trait
When a well-to-do person has no pity for the poor
The first question I ask myself
How will I face the Lord on the day of judgment?

RUTH PFAU

January 2004. I remember my mother mentioning her name with a great deal of respect and fondness. Coming from my mother, that was a good sign indeed. She was one difficult lady to please! To actually get her to praise you was quite an unsurmountable task, believe me! So Ruth Phau fascinated me for that reason as well the fact that this *"gori"* (foreigner) had forsaken the comforts of her homeland to serve the masses of Pakistan and that too lepers! Would I go and work with the lepers in Malir? I don't think so. I would probably dish out money and try to forget about their misery and needs to be rehabilitated into living normal lives as citizens of Pakistan. Like millions of Pakistanis such as myself I would prefer to look away and pretend this was not my responsibility. The Government's maybe? NGOs possibly? Charity organizations, could be? Anybody but me. Lepers? No, thank you.

My only exposure to Leprosy, I hate to admit, was from the movie *"Ben Hur"*. And all that I could recall of that too was how repelled the hero felt about his own mother and sister contracting Leprosy. Also that it took a miracle to make them well and heal their scars. So when I sat down in front to Dr. Pfau in the Karachi TV studio I felt grossly ignorant not only about the person but also her work. But the actress that I profess to be and with the superficial aura we TV *wallahs* (persons) ooze out, I was confident I would be able to swing it. I was surely in for a huge surprise!

Dr. Pfau is a petite, simple, gracious and gentle human being. This was my first meeting with her and still is to date. We were being wired up and I was thinking furiously of my opening question when she smiled and asked "How is your dear mother?" How she put two together I would never know but that touched a chord. We immediately connected. I had been accepted into her "fold" as it were. My antecedents had passed the litmus test and perhaps this interview was not going to be as difficult as I had imagined. Throughout the rest of the 40 minutes or so of our conversation I was taken into another world by this "Mother Teresa of Pakistan". Listening to her speak frankly and honestly about her hard and "contagious" work with poise and dignity has left an impression on me even after so many years. She was all praise for her team who are probably as simple and dedicated as herself.

We began our conversation by my mentioning my mother sending her regards. Dr. Pfau smiled "softly". That is the only way to describe her smile. It "softly" spread from her mouth to her eyes. "How is she?" she asked. "Pretty well" I replied. "Brave lady, your mother" she said. "We got on so well". I told my mother what she had said when I got back. She was touched by Dr. Pfau's compliment and went on to describe the wonderful work she was doing and how we Pakistanis were not at all supportive of her efforts.

A few years later I read about the awards heaped on Dr. Pfau not only by the Pakistani government at the time but also other international organizations. I saw photographs of this small "angel" holding her award and looking somewhat surprised. She was that kind of a person. She was not doing it for the accolades or the praise or the publicity. For her it was all about serving humanity. She was "building" her 'house' or 'houses' in Heaven.

Come to think of it, isn't that what we all want to achieve too, except helping lepers doesn't quite figure in our efforts!

Moneeza Hashmi:	Dr. Pfau, a long time ago, in 1960, you came to Pakistan from Germany. Why did you choose us?
Dr. Ruth Pfau:	Well primarily, I didn't choose Pakistan; in fact I wasn't even fully aware of Pakistan's independence. I was supposed to go to India and I couldn't get my visa so I got stuck here. I really got stuck because as they say in Urdu, *"mera dil lag gaya"* (My heart felt at home). What could I do?
Moneeza Hashmi:	That was our good fortune then. Talk to us about your life in Germany before 1960.
Dr. Ruth Pfau:	It is difficult to talk about it. I had a happy childhood. We were six children at home so it was lots of fun. But early in my life when I was just four years old, Hitler took over. It was a time of great insecurity. When the war broke out I was just ten and when it was over I was only fourteen. This was a horrible time because we were occupied by the Russians. We were hungry and cold and our house was bombed out. It took me a long time to answer this question. I never really answered it. It took me a long time to come to terms with this question: why is life the way it is and what does it all mean? What does God want? The Nazis and Communists both thought God was something for our grandparents but not for us. They did not consider it modern or futuristic. It took me a long time to realize that there is more to life than what we can weigh or see or measure. Once I understood this, I found a way back to religion. I went the whole way. I went to church and got baptized, which for us is an entry into religion. I became a nun.
Moneeza Hashmi:	You took the vows?
Dr. Ruth Pfau:	Yes. It was tremendously important for me to do nothing by half measures, and to be free to serve people. It was my congregation that asked me to go to the third world, where development had just only started. They asked me to go to India. By this time I was a qualified doctor and I wanted to go somewhere I could serve humanity. Germany was picking up at the time. You could see after the world war everything was in ruins, everything was

just flat. We were at a point where we were rebuilding our country. It was quite clear to me Germany had qualified people. We knew what was required. But I had heard that there was a desperate dearth of qualified people in the developing countries so I thought it would be better to go where I was needed most.

Moneeza Hashmi: When did your interest develop in leprosy?
Dr. Ruth Pfau: When I reached Pakistan I thought leprosy was a disease that did not exist any longer, because it wasn't there in Germany. It was only when I was confronted with it that I could not sleep. I had to do something here and now. My first thought was to help and to do something structurally so that the misery could end. I think we were successful.

Moneeza Hashmi: Tell me about your first contact with leprosy here in Pakistan?
Dr. Pfau: It was here on McLoud Road, the Leper Colony, and it was unbelievably horrid. I had seen enough misery in my childhood and in my youth, but this was beyond everything I could have imagined. At the time people in Pakistan did not know that this disease was curable. And we had developed the drugs in 1942.

Moneeza Hashmi: But they had not obviously reached here?
Dr. Pfau: Well, the knowledge had not reached here.

Moneeza Hashmi: So you were attempting to get into a field that nobody would want to get into?
Dr. Pfau: Yes. At the time you could not possibly imagine anyone wanting to get into leprosy.

Moneeza Hashmi: Because one was afraid of catching the disease?
Dr. Pfau: I think it went further than that. People just denied reality. I remember when I went for the first time to the municipality and said you cannot let these patients just rot there. They said, "We don't have leprosy in Pakistan". I said, "Come with me and I will show you". They insisted, "Madam, we don't have leprosy in Pakistan". I thought why am I even talking to them? Let me first do something

	and then show them.
Moneeza Hashmi:	It was like moving mountains, wasn't it Dr. Pfau?
Dr. Pfau:	Luckily when you start off you are so busy that you only see the next patient. Looking back it seems unbelievable.
Moneeza Hashmi:	And you are doing all this alone?
Dr. Pfau:	No. I had a very dear sister in religion who had discovered this colony. She is still with us. She is a Mexican pharmacist and she also couldn't sleep when she saw this misery. She had written to our headquarters in Paris requesting a doctor. They wrote back that a doctor had been sent to India. But I could be a replacement if I wanted it that way. So that is how I got stuck here and then she prayed very hard for me to stay on!
Moneeza Hashmi:	She must have been one of the people who were instrumental in keeping you here?
Dr. Pfau:	Definitely.
Moneeza Hashmi:	How did you begin to raise awareness about leprosy in Pakistan?
Dr. Pfau:	At the time we were not thinking about raising awareness. It was a time when all we thought about was to ensure the patients who had lost feeling in their hands and feet were not eaten by rats at night. We needed very short term but very concrete objectives at that time. So we collected all the kids around and told them anyone who got a dead rat gets a one rupee gift. They immediately started hunting and brought dead rats in sacks. Because I didn't know anything about leprosy and I hadn't learned about it. I needed a monograph about leprosy to know what I should do professionally.
Moneeza Hashmi:	Explain to me very briefly what leprosy is and how it can be cured?
Dr. Pfau:	I don't know why after forty years of leprosy control people don't know much about it. I know that the better educated the less knowledge they have about leprosy. It is just an ordinary disease caused by bacteria which comes from the same family as tuberculosis. It is our

luck and the patient's luck we now have medication that kills the bacterium and thereby totally cures the disease. We still don't know how it is transmitted, most probably like tuberculosis by breathing and inhaling. And it is the least infectious one out of all the others.
It is difficult to diagnose because once the germ enters the body it can sleep for three or five or even forty years before it comes out and this is what makes it so difficult to eradicate it. Every year we get approximately two thousand fresh cases in Pakistan who are coming out of this incubation period.

Moneeza Hashmi: And of course they are curable?
Dr. Pfau: Yes of course, fully. If we get them in the first stage, it can be cured in six months. If the immunity of the patient is very low, then it can be cured in two years, but there is a hundred percent cure for leprosy.

Moneeza Hashmi: At that time Dr. Pfau, you worked without a team You then prepared a team. Did the team come to you or did you go to them?
Dr. Pfau: I understood very soon that a team wasn't ready made in Pakistan. You had to make your own. The first member I picked was a patient on the way to getting cured followed by the children of leprosy patients. Once we had floated the idea that leprosy is curable and we were going to do something about it. This nucleus team grew because their friends joined in. In this sense we have been extremely lucky to have found a team that really wanted to serve. There wasn't much money to be earned. At this time there wasn't even respect. So the first team was really thoroughly motivated.

Moneeza Hashmi: And now as you look back after 44 years in the field, what do you think you have achieved?
Dr. Pfau: When we started off we began from an old hut which the patients had themselves nailed together from crates. And we were busy killing rats at the same time.
Today, we have a *National Leprosy Control Program*. Leprosy is on the agenda of each health department in all provinces. Punjab is a little short, and we are

working with the medical universities. We have registered fifty thousand three hundred patients across the country. Everybody today is cured, except approximately two thousand, since annually we get a thousand new patients. Leprosy today is a patch. It doesn't really upset the life of a patient, except very rarely. We still have certain ethnic groups that think that leprosy is the absolute end of their life. You have to be very careful as you lead them into accepting a diagnosis but this is a very small percentage. Leprosy today is on the way out. Those whom we picked late, because we did not come in time, those who are deformed and are uprooted, even those people are alive today.

In the past fifty years we have seen about fifty thousand leprosy patients which of course means fifty thousand families, out of these about twenty thousand are quiet settled in society and on their feet. The other twenty three thousand we still have to work on and this is very important. Many of them, when they were children didn't get a chance to get an education. Many of them went down the social ladder facing difficulty to start again. And then, I can't say this often enough, there are twenty thousand individuals in Pakistan who are infected, but we can't diagnose them because it's hiding inside, but it will eventually surface. Therefore it is very important that we continue with the services that we are providing.

Moneeza Hashmi:	As you look back over these years spent in this country, and at the sacrifices made personally, and the sacrifices made on behalf of your team and their hard work, would you have done anything differently?
Dr. Pfau:	No. And I don't think that for anyone in the team either. We have actually filled our lives with eminent meaning and a lot of happiness, a lot of happiness. But also frustration: I avoid painting too rosy a picture, I mean we have been often very mad at times, I mean really very mad. When I look back, I would do the very same thing over again.
Moneeza Hashmi:	Today, how do you find this country and how has it

Dr. Pfau: changed?

It has changed a lot; there is absolutely no question about that. I mean, just you, and your mother are a proof of it. Women can now be heard in Pakistan. If this continues it will be very good for Pakistan. I wish it wasn't always only a certain social stratum that has a voice. We still have to ensure that women are heard through-out Pakistan.

If you make a comparison practically, where we once walked on foot two weeks at a stretch, we can now take a jeep or drive a truck. When I look at Pakistan, this is where being rich really matters.

I will tell you a story. I don't like to make big statements but I like to tell little stories.

I had a piece of Pakistani equipment that got out of order. I was upset when my leprosy technician answered, "This is only because it is made in Pakistan". This is what is bad! This is bad! If it would have been made in Germany, he would have said, "Wow, made in Germany!"

It is very important that we look at the beauty in the country. There is a lot of beauty here. We should not allow people to bury it. We have already cured about thirty three thousand leprosy and tuberculosis patients also. So we work with a lot of patients. You cannot work with such a large section of society without getting involved in human rights. These human rights cases are much more painful for me than leprosy. Leprosy we can do something about. What about them?

Moneeza Hashmi: When you settled here or by default settled here, there must have been people back home who must have said you were quite mad? There must have been some criticism.

Dr. Pfau: At the time there were a lot of things going on that were crazy and I was living in an age where I was allowed to do something crazy. I am just back from Germany, and there are awareness campaigns I keep attending. They keep inviting me because I am one of those rare westerners who have lived a happy life for over forty years in an Islamic country. They all say you must be absolutely mad because I continued living here even

after I needed to; by choice.
After September 11 especially, I was asked this question. After the Afghanistan war and the war in Iraq they just can't understand why I continue to stay.

Moneeza Hashmi: And for you this is home?
Dr. Pfau: It cannot be. You are a product of your soil.
But Urdu has beautiful distinction: this language allows you to have a place where your heart is and also a place of your birth.

Moneeza Hashmi: So where is the place of your birth?
Dr. Pfau: Germany

Moneeza Hashmi: And where is your heart?
Dr. Pfau: In Pakistan

Moneeza Hashmi: You've received many international and national awards. When you received the first Pakistani award from the Government of Pakistan what were your sentiments at the time? Do you remember?
Dr. Pfau: Do I remember? This was in Karachi at the time when Yahya Khan was the President. He walked in like a *gora sahib* (white man), and I thought to myself this is going to be an interesting award. I remember getting an award from a little girl. That's my recollection of it.

Moneeza Hashmi: Then of course you got many consecutive awards?
Dr. Pfau: I got rather fed up of receiving awards after a time. It meant preparing for it and getting new clothes stitched. I had a leprosy patient who told me that these awards may not mean too much to me but that they had a great value for leprosy patients themselves. This field of leprosy and its cure was beginning to get respect because of such recognitions.

Moneeza Hashmi: Last year you got an award in Manila?
Dr. Pfau: I was a little irritated with that one too. I had planned that I would for once go on a vacation, and then that one opportunity got shelved as well because I had to show up for this award. But receiving this particular

award was wonderful because it is given to those who kept their dreams and values alive despite the pressures on them.

Moneeza Hashmi: Do you want to retire?
Dr. Pfau: I have already retired. When I was sixty five I officially retired. But somehow in Pakistan you do it differently than we do it at home in Germany. I had retired and moved out of the hospital after installing my very efficient team to carry on the work I was doing. But the next day all of them were pestering me asking me why I had abandoned them? I explained that retirement means that you step out and someone else steps in but they refused to accept that. They explained traditionally the daughters move out of the family, the sons too can move out but if the mother moves out it is highly insulting to their sense of respect. So I ended up moving back again! At some level it is true I have much experience which the younger crew doesn't have just yet. They are happy and secure when I am around. Then there is also the problem of funding. Even now eighty percent of the funding comes from Germany. I help out there as well.

Moneeza Hashmi: So you are also an intrinsic part of the fundraising?
Dr. Pfau: Very much so but we must see Pakistan take over the responsibility which Germany has been tackling for the past thirty five years. When I started off Pakistan was poor. Today the government maybe poor but the people are not. Large sections of society can take over this cause. This is at the focus of our new awareness campaign. Here too we talk about the aspect of self-respect.

Moneeza Hashmi: Will you look back and say all the sacrifices were worth it?
Dr. Pfau: Yes. There is absolutely no question. I am one of those few lucky ones who look back and say it was all really worthwhile.

Moneeza Hashmi: No regrets?
Dr. Pfau: No regrets.

Moneeza Hashmi: Will you ever go back to Germany?
Dr. Pfau: No I won't. In our congregation we do have young Pakistani women who are dreaming of doing somethingsimilar. I have really only lived in Pakistan and that too, in the main part of Pakistan. I would really like to have some time to shift focus to the women of Pakistan. This is a group that is full of the future. This I will do as long as I can.

Moneeza Hashmi: You think that the women of Pakistan are now better?
Dr. Pfau: There are no "Women of Pakistan." It's all broken down into very different groups. There are women of Balochistan, there are women of Kohistan, there are women of Punjab. Everyone is different. In many ways their fate has improved a lot, but there are enough places where it is exactly the same way it has been for years. I was reading a newspaper report about a girl from a low caste who was gang raped. All this is constantly going on. There is another story where the mother of three died in police custody. They tell us the mother of three with the youngest who is eleven months committed suicide. These things make me absolutely mad. As long as this is going on I cannot leave. Perhaps one day I can join other human rights groups because there is still so much work to be done.

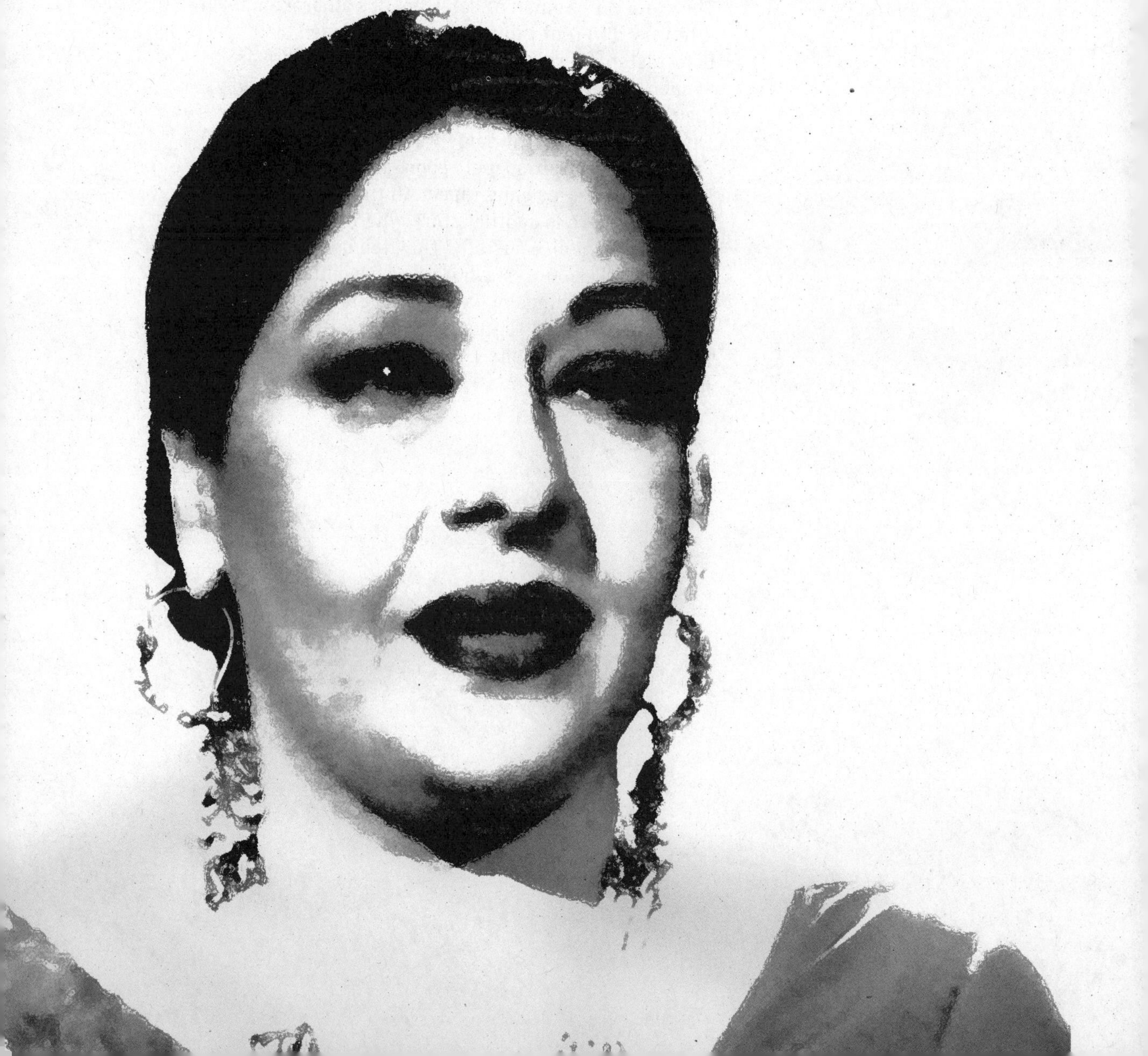

Place of Birth
Calcutta
Marital Status
Married
Number of Children
Four daughters and one son
Area of Personal Interest
Taking care of my children and meeting friends
Moment of Pride
When Faiz Ahmed Faiz would ask me to sing for him
Moment of disappointment
Being a witness to artists and performers struggling their entire life
A quality I am proud of
I do not lie
A trait I could do without
Reaching late at events
The first question I would ask myself
Why don't people reciprocate the affection I have for them?

FAREEDA KHANUM

September 1997. Despite her polite but very definite temper tantrums, despite her almost never being on time for rehearsals or recordings, despite her *'nakhras'* (difficult attitudes) with the audio balancing procedure, despite her sari *'pallu'* (edge) never hiding but rather enhancing her ample cleavage, Fareeda Khanum is most certainly a music Madonna who has reigned and dominated the ghazal singing domain for more than two decades in Pakistan. You could never get to talk to her on the phone. She would pick up the phone but pretend to be someone else. She would decide to become completely incommunicado whenever it took her fancy. No matter that there was an audience waiting in the studio. No matter that an audio shift worth thousands of rupees was being wasted. No matter that there were programme deadlines to meet. Madam would just virtually disappear and the frustration of the poor PTV producers was so pathetic to watch as they ran from pillar to post trying to either find substitutes or persuade the programme department for an extension of their telecast dates.

And then as suddenly as she had disaperared she would miraculously make an appearance; saunter in the PTV Lahore premises as if nothing had happened; deny all knowledge of any previous booking; smile and make all the excuses she had made many times before. She was unwell; she had guests; she had a bad throat; she had no transport; she had to leave town; a relative was sick and so on. She would twist and turn phrases to serve that occasion and set up yet another appointment for yet another recording date and sail out. No one would ever be sure if she would actually turn up the next time or whether it would be yet another 'repeat' performance!

But the wonderful end to all this drama however many times it was repeated was that when she did turn up and the song was recorded, it was a sheer delight to hear and see her perform. She would sing so effortlessly! She would glide over the notes like a waterfall flowing gently downhill in complete harmony with the orchestra. She would wrap up the show in record time and walk away the winner!

Fareeda Khanum was a household visitor and a name in our home as well as that of Sufi Ghulam Mustafa Tabassum. He was my father's teacher and mentor. As a child we were often over at Sufi Sahib's house along with my parents. Fareeda was usually there, the peacock in the middle, aware of all the attention she got from the guests present and preening herself left, right and centre. She was ravishingly beautiful and used it to her complete advantage. The evening always ended with Fareeda singing the poetry of Faiz or Sufi mostly without any instruments. Her throaty melodious voice could be heard in the verandah outside where I would be playing with the other household children. I remember well the applause and praise she would elicit from her listeners and smile coquettishly in response. She was quite the performer on and off stage.

She walked into my office a few days after I had returned from performing Umrah. How she found that out I don't know but she was carrying a huge bouquet of flowers. Following close behind was my office boy with a large cake. She embraced and congratulated me. Then presented me with her offerings and swept out as regally as she had swooped in. I was most touched by her affection.

When my producer told me he had set up our interview I had sincere doubts of her actually showing up. But there she was in front of me, dressed as always in her flowing chiffon sari, diamonds shining on her fingers and on her ears, vibrant red lipstick and toe nails to match, Fareeda Khanum was all ready to 'bare all'. I have always found most celebrities difficult to converse with especially the 'musical' ones. For them their lives and stardom is all about their singing. They live only through their music. They always find it difficult to articulate outside their notes and melodies. I was in for surprise with this interview. Fareeda was as lucid as they come! I got insight into her life as a young girl, her aspirations, her daily routine and how hard she worked on developing her voice and her career. She surprised me with her diction and vocabulary. She had me entranced listening to her description of her life as a young girl. She made me travel with her to another world, a world full of music, of creativity, of crossing boundaries of time on the wings of melodies. It was a magical world and I was blessed to have shared it with one of the maestros of our time.

Moneeza Hashmi: Did professional singing lead on from a personal hobby?

Fareeda Khanum: This was not my hobby at all. I was naturally gifted with a melodious voice, and there was a general agreement amongst my family members that my voice should be trained and not wasted. But that is where it stood. It was my elder sister who thought that I should be instructed in the field of classical music.

This art was then developed and nurtured in me by my parents through the same vigorous routine and discipline that one would give any formal education. In their opinion, the art of singing was an equally respectable and elaborate form of knowledge. So I was given a pre-determined and formal schedule of practicing music daily with my *Ustaad* as if I was enrolled in any school program. This education of music, and the accompanying training replaced my formal education. My childhood was a constant routine of music practice and more practice.

Moneeza Hashmi: Can you tell us how those days were spent and what they involved?

Fareeda Khanum:	Every morning at dawn I would be handed a music lesson to learn and sing. I was about eight years old at the time and like every eight year old I would rather go out and play or have fun with friends. However I was put on a tight leash and made to learn the given notes. I recall I would always cry, but my parents would entice and bribe me that if I reproduced my lesson well I would get to have fun in the evenings. My anger would fade when I would be given a prize in the form of a trip to a cinema or some other present. In the end, I would recite the lesson for that day and more often than not, I would get it right. And they would say: "Perfect."
Moneeza Hashmi:	What significance did music have when you were growing up?
Fareeda Khanum:	Music was considered to be a great form of art. People, who indulged in it or formed the audience, would also belong to a certain strata of society. They possessed a certain style and they expected nothing less than an exceptional performance from singers who had gone through the rigors of learning music formally from great masters of that time. There was a tremendous level of interest also from the listeners of classical music in those days. It is through that high level of expectation that I began this long journey of acheiving who I am today.
Moneeza Hashmi:	Did you have any ambitions other than being a classical singer?
Fareeda Khanum:	I always had an interest to pursue architecture and consequently a higher education in that field was a dream which did not realize. I was so inclined towards this field that in my free time, I would sit and draw sketches of houses with elaborate front porches and garages for cars, and entertain myself with those creative images. I was not allowed to go out and play so this became my next best alternative. I wasn't even allowed to go to a friend's house, unless my parents accompanied me. They were threatened by the thought of my meeting other kids and cultivating interests other than music.

They were very aggressively protective regarding my space and ensured I was exposed to only certain kinds of experiences and to certain kinds of people. There was also a fear that I would get so involved in other 'trivial' matters which would make me lazy or less motivated to work on my singing. So in the absence of any other outward activity I would just sketch my houses and often asked my younger brother to join in.
As I look back now I am certain I would not have been as successful in any other field compared to the recognition I have found in music. God has been especially kind in this regard. I didn't sing publicly as much as other performers, but I have still gotten a huge level of admiration.

Moneeza Hashmi: Do you hum or sing to yourself at home?
Fareeda Khanum: Yes. I often find myself singing a tune that I like. I also try and create different rhythms to songs that I have sung before. This has been continuing ever since I was a child. I am not sure why exactly I revert to this habit but I do sing all the time to myself. That is when my family realized that I did indeed have a naturally musical voice which should be professionally trained. That is how the cultivation of my art began to take root.

Moneeza Hashmi: Art requires patience, nurturing, love, attachment and much sacrifice. If I were to ask how much of that did Fareeda Khanum dedicate to her art, what would you say?
Fareeda Khanum: Sacrifice for me simply was forgoing a normal childhood. This was a forced sacrifice and not one I would have volunteered on my own. My elders would explain that this art required a supreme form of commitment and later on I would find respect and recognition. But it wasn't until I was about 12 years old, that I began to develop enough concentration to spend two hours daily on continuous practicing. It was then I realized that music and singing were indeed wonderful. I would get so involved in music that it would create an ambiance of wonderment and excitement and that in turn would spur me on without parental pressure.

Ustad Barkat Ali Khan was my one true mentor and teacher. It was his voice and the music he created that inspired me. It also gave me the incentive to learn the rules of his singing and try to emulate his form of music. I searched for that *alaap* (free style of singing) and wished I could achieve that level of perfection.

Later on however, I gave up singing pure classical music because I frankly couldn't manage to dedicate the time it required.

Moneeza Hashmi: Because of your domestic responsibilities?

Fareeda Khanum: Yes. I was a homemaker by then and wanted to have a settled life that did not involve too much distraction from external sources. I was also conscious about not creating any problems for my children. My daily routine all day revolved around them, picking them and dropping them to school, their other requirements as well.

Those were the days when my work was limited only to performing on the Radio. Since my domestic life demanded time and at that time I couldn't give my music practice the same attention it demanded, my performances on the radio also dwindled.

I sang until 1952, and there was absolute silence until 1956.

People would ask about me and protest about my prolonged absence and my turning down important invitations. What was I to tell them? There were certain domestic and family constraints. I would explain sometimes and their answer would be "What could possibly be so difficult that is preventing you from performing?" They would urge me to restart my career. I did perform for a few programs for television in those days where other great singers would also be featured. The prospect of meeting artists such as Ghulam Ali Khan, Roshanara Begum, Chote Ghulam Ali Khan, Umaid Ali Khan, Ustad Amanat Ali Khan, Ustad Nusrat Fateh Ali Khan made me very happy. Talking to them after a gap would motivate and propel me to find a way and participate too. Just being listed among these titans of classical music made me feel that I too had managed to sing well.

Moneeza Hashmi: When an artist has the passion and the talent to perform, and he or she cannot do so for whatever reason, surely there must be some sort of frustration or a sense of loss?

Fareeda Khanum: I would miss it. If I came to know of a grand event and I could not participate in it I would hum to myself at home all that day just to make up for it. I would try and use up my energy in that way. Sometimes I would console myself in thinking, who will take care of these little kids if I go? This would calm and pacify me.

My husband was not restrictive. He would not say "Do not go". He too loved music so there was some support that I got from his interest. I put restrictions on my self.

A few times there were invitations from abroad such as Kabul or London on a government paid trip. The thought of meeting so many artistes and singers would make me excited. Those were events when we would attend for the sheer thrill of being a part of the performances, without much caring for other consequences.

As the children grew up and needed less supervision and I did not have to worry about them so much I returned to singing in public. This was around the year 1957. By 1963 I was traveling abroad for performances in Russia and many other places, which largely made up for the time gap and my absence from the performance arena.

Moneeza Hashmi: I heard that you also acted in a film?

Fareeda Khanum: Immediately after partition there was an opportunity to sing for a film. This was a music genre I really enjoyed being a part of. There was also much charm and excitement in films. I wanted to work with established artists and act too.

I attempted to live that life of glamour and make believe but I soon realized there is far more hard work and time that went into a film career than what I had actually thought. So I gave up on that dream immediately. I felt music was something I should remain with.

In those days people who worked in the Pakistani film industry worked extremely hard. They would spend all day rehearsing and shooting films. People worked passionately and for weeks on end, sometimes getting to go home only for short breaks. It was very tough work.

Moneeza Hashmi:	When you sing a ghazal what do you look for before selecting the text?
Fareeda Khanum:	Ghazals have a world and a meaning of their own. I find a natural connection to a ghazal because of the way its words are expressed and how they sound to me. As I read the verses its beauty reveals itself to me and I connect with it. My next focus is to ensure that its composition would do justice to the words and expression of the poet. Converting a poem into a melody with a specific rhythm is an intuitive process and evokes in me only one desire: that I should be able to bring the words to life and be able to find the exact right mood. Primarily that I should do justice to the poet and his or her creativity.
Moneeza Hashmi:	Whenever you appear on stage to perform, you are immaculately dressed. Is this also a passion of yours?
Fareeda Khanum:	I have always loved wearing new clothes. Ever since my childhood, it has been a favorite indulgence of mine. I would try out my elder sister's earrings, shoes and saris. She would get upset with me for ruining her best materials. Way back then saris were art in themselves.
Moneeza Hashmi:	I heard the other day that you are often found singing to yourself. Is this true?
Fareeda Khanum:	When I am sad I sing. When I feel that I am neither performing nor am I practicing, which is very irresponsible of me, I sing on my own. I sing old ghazals and songs that I have sung before. I really enjoy singing Faiz Ahmed Faiz's ghazals in *aiman raag* (a classical melody). That is the way to lift my spirits and avoid whatever sadness is engulfing me.

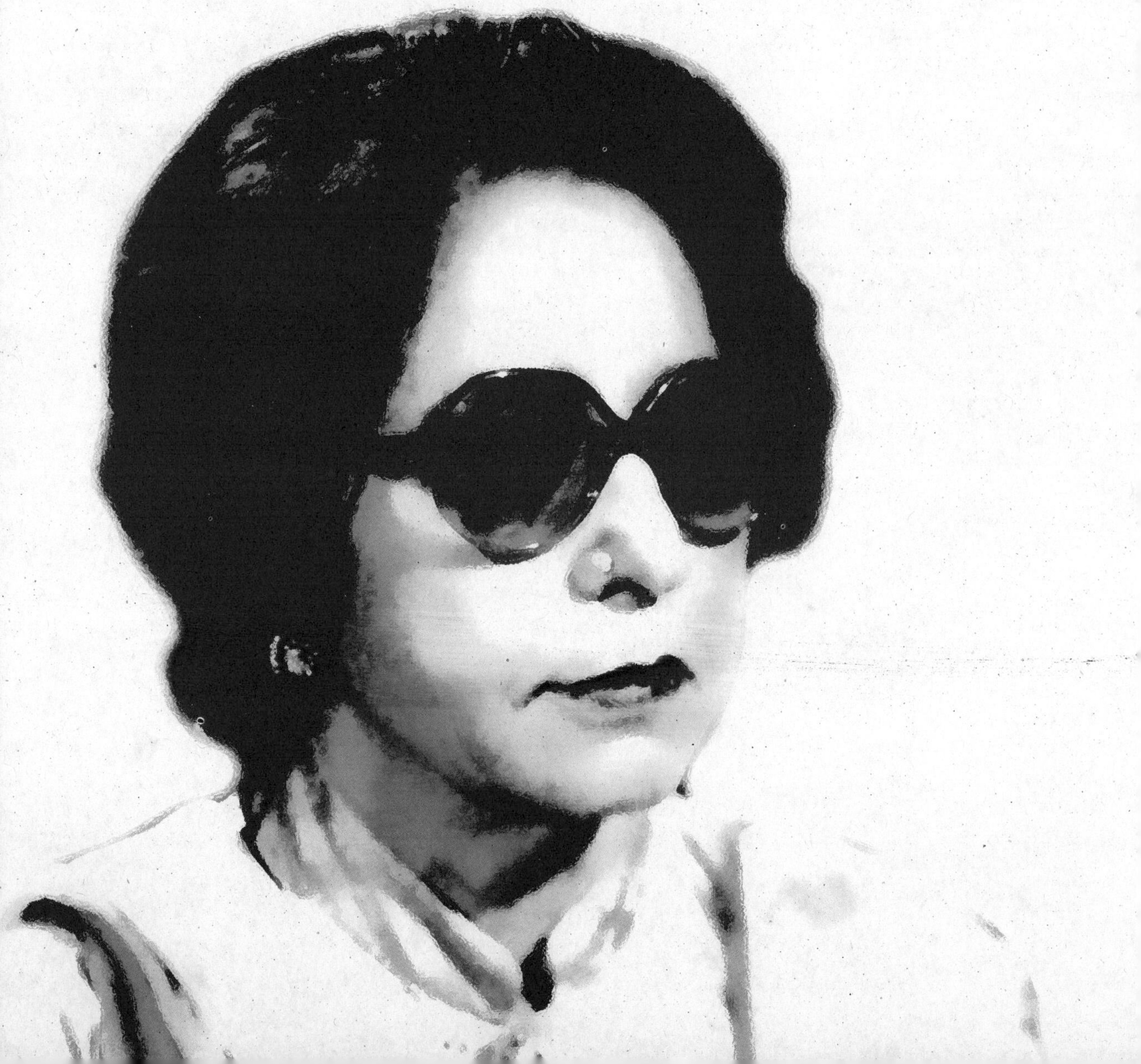

Place of Birth
Jammu
Marital Status
Married
Number of Children
Two daughters and four sons
Activities of Interest
Gardening and Embroidery
Moment of Pride
I have never held myself to be proud of anything
Moment of disappointment
Quite a few
A trait I am proud of
Honesty
A trait I am embarrassed about
Being honest and then facing many consequences as a result
The first question I would ask myself
What if it had happened this way and not the other way?

MALIKA PUKHRAJ

September 1997. I called her *"Masi"* (maternal aunt) although her affection for my father was no hidden secret or his admiration for her as a person and her singing.

When we would visit her home as a child I remember *'Shah Sahib'* her husband was a great host. He was a keen "shikari" (game hunter) a hobby bordering on addiction that was later inherited by his sons. *Masi* would serve us a typical Punjabi lunch or brunch: *makaiee ki roti* (corn flatbread), *sarson ka saag* (mustard seasoned spinach) and *lassi* (yoghurt drink with water). Shah Sahib would drag on his "*hookah*" (Pipe) while my parents and other guests enjoyed their hospitality and lounged in the warm sun-shine of a December afternoon. Peacocks and geese roamed about freely. Dogs were asleep under the trees. Deers looked sleepily at us from their cages. The *tandoors* (ovens) were bringing out hot *rotis* (flatbread) at astonishing speed. Masi was admonishing the women servants for their slow service. Her voice was low but commandeering. Her tinted spectacles hid her eyes from the world outside but were all observant. Her diction was amazingly graceful but her vocabulary was simple and direct. She was the typical *Chaudarani* (Head of the clan) wife but still carried the court aura around her, a token of her upbringing.

Interviewing her was perhaps one of the most difficult sessions I've had to do. Although I was at ease with her having known her all my adult life I knew her to be a woman of very few words. She would not mince her expressions nor be diplomatic at all in saying exactly what she thought and meant. She was a recluse of sorts so getting her to agree to come into the studio was a feat in itself But I knew I could persuade her and I did.

As the final touches were put to the production I observed her. Not a hair out of place, nails painted red as always, wearing a bright yellow outfit, shining under the studio lights, sparkling rings on all fingers, diamond solitaires shimmering on her ears. Regal in her stance. She sat almost detached from her surroundings. Watching silently from behind her dark shades she sat quietly as the lights went up or down, technicians yelled at each other, cameras moved around for angles, microphones were tested, photographs were clicked. She was utterly and completely at ease.

I was given the signal from the master control to begin recording and out of deference I asked "*Masi shuru karan?*" (Aunty, shall I begin?)

"*Bismillah karo*" (Begin in the name of Allah) she replied and I asked my first question.

Moneeza Hashmi:
Malika Pukhraj:

How did you spend your childhood?
My childhood was mostly spent studying, not studying in school but strangely enough in a shop. It was a paan (beetle leaf) and cigarette shop whose owner was also a *hakeem* (herbal doctor). I studied Urdu and Farsee (Persian) from him. He didn't know any English unfortunately. In those days there were no schools. Tents were set up and children studied sitting under those tents. There was no concept of any formal education. Compared to that

situation the shop where I would learn to read and write was a better option. I spent all day at the shop because the owner was also a distant relative of mine.

Moneeza Hashmi: When did you start singing?
Malika Pukhraj: Barey Ghulam Ali also lived in Jammu as did Allah Bux who people said had gone slightly mad. He was from the Patiala family I believe. He could always be found at our home and was very fond of me. He loved singing, but he only sang when and if he felt like it. People said there was no greater singer alive than Allah Bux. Barey Ghulam Ali had a great voice, and by that I mean the way his voice sounded. He introduced me to music and by the time I was 4 or 5 years old I had learnt to sing well.

Moneeza Hashmi: Did you enjoy singing?
Malika Pukhraj: I was too young to know at the time. When the month of *Muharrum* came I would want to recite *marsias* (odes of tragedy). I learned them from my teacher at the shop who was a *Shia* (A Muslim sect). He taught me all the melodies he knew. During Muharrum I would be asked to recite marsias. If I recited well I would get more *niaz* (sweetmeat). That was my entire motivation at the time.

Moneeza Hashmi: What does music mean to you?
Malika Pukhraj: It is my life and blood. I recognize the entire universe through music. What would life be without any sound? When sounds and noise synchronize in harmony it becomes music and is one of world's most beautiful creations.

Moneeza Hashmi: What was your daily routine as a singer?
Malika Pukhraj: I didn't believe in hard work and long hours of practice. Thankfully what I lacked there I made up for in courage and perseverance. So when I did practice I did it with a lot of intensity and sincerity. People liked the quality of my voice and my singing was appreciated.

Moneeza Hashmi: You married into a *Syed* (descendents of the Propht Mohammad PBUH) family. Did your husband's family accept your profession?

Malika Pukhraj:	There was no objection at all. They treated me as one of their own.
Moneeza Hashmi:	What is the difference between good and bad music?
Malika Pukhraj:	Good music has a finger on the pulse of the public. Good music will definitely be loved by the audience because it outlives generations and goes beyond its time. Bad music is like a bubble which stays on people's tongue for a few days and then fades into oblivion.
Moneeza Hashmi:	You are also a wife and a mother. How did you adjust this with your professional career as a singer?
Malika Pukhraj:	My husband played a very supportive role in my domestic life. I was very methodical when it came to raising my kids; I took them to school and brought them home. After coming back from school I would spend an hour or so checking their school work. In the event of my having to leave the house my husband would take care of that for me. Today all of them are well educated and serving on important posts.
Moneeza Hashmi:	Did your husband ever object to your schedule?
Malika Pukhraj:	Not at all. On the contrary, when I was to perform he would bring me morning tea earlier than usual and insist on my being punctual. Sometimes when I had to travel outside the city to perform, I would hesitate. It was always he who insisted and convinced me to go.
Moneeza Hashmi:	What was your own reaction to your popularity?
Malika Pukhraj:	Which ever song I sang would become popular by the grace of God. Particularly, *Zahid Na Keh Buri* from *Diwane Aadmi*. I once went out to buy some wool for my embroidery. The shopkeeper put the wool aside and said he wanted to tell me something. "Please sing that song *Pagal Aadmi*". I was confused. "What song is that?" I asked him. He said the one that was broadcast the night before on the radio. Then I realized that he was talking about *Diwane Aadmi*. People who didn't even understand the meaning of the poetry still loved the music.
Moneeza Hashmi:	Do you see a future for music in Pakistan?

Malika Pukhraj: The future looks very bleak. There are hardly any good teachers left. There are even less interested students. Singers have two hit songs and claim they have arrived. They neither believe in hard work nor in disciplined learning from any teacher.
The teachers are lost and the students are no longer there.

Moneeza Hashmi: Have you instructed anyone?
Malika Pukhraj: Yes there have been many girls who came to learn but the moment they got married, I would never see them again.

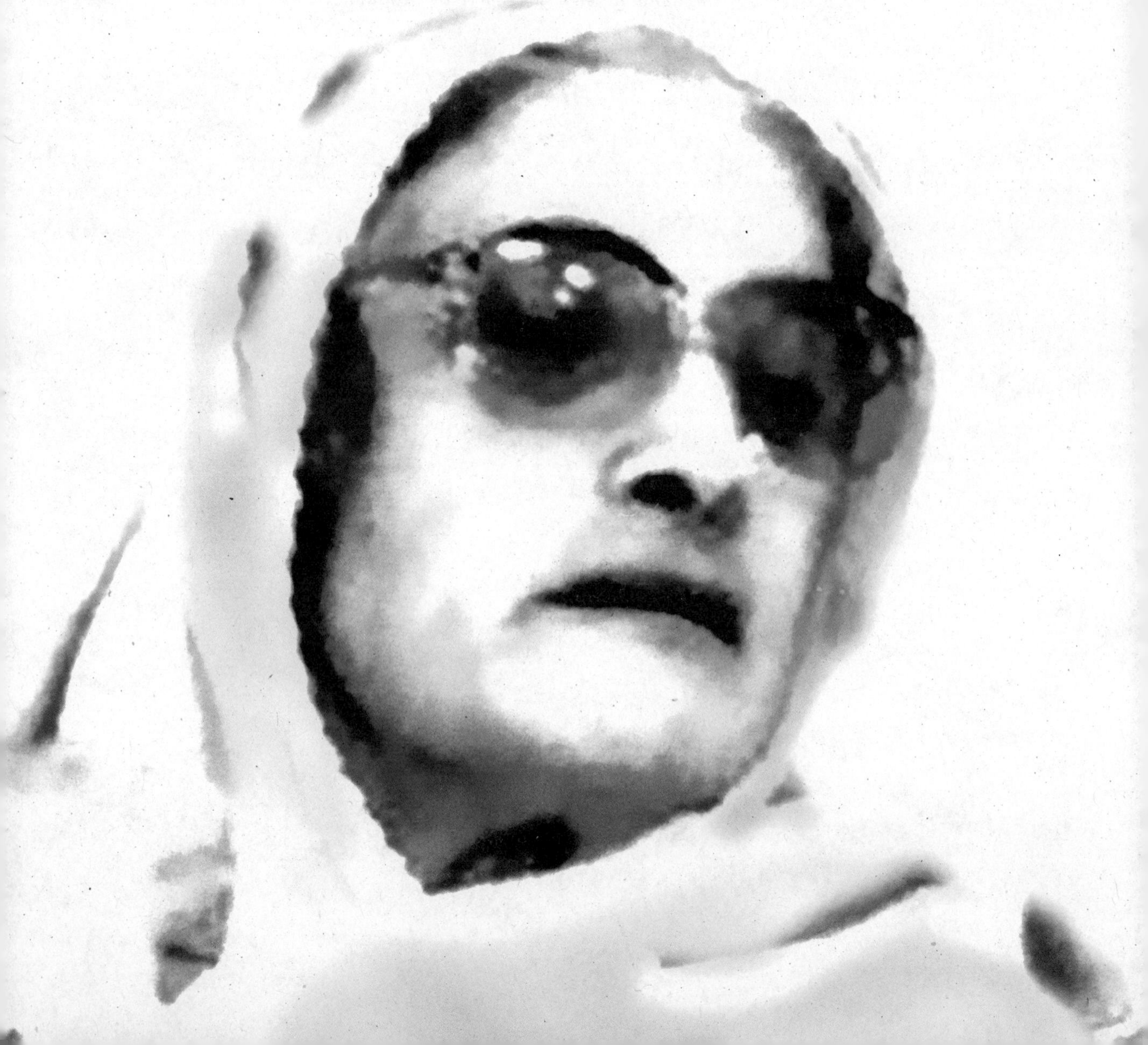

Place of Birth
Hoti
Marital Status
Married
Number of Children
Two sons and three daughters
Activities of Interest
Renaming the province of Sarhad
Moment of disappointment
That is forbidden for me
A trait I am proud of
I am a Pakhtun woman
A trait I am embarrassed about
I don't consider my decision once I have made up my mind
The first question I would ask myself
In the interest of the party, I sometimes behave roughly with the party workers. Later I feel bad about it and I question my behaviour

NASEEM WALI KHAN

November 1997. I was in total awe of her. A woman politician from NWFP (as it was then called), and in active politics too mind you, who belonged to one of the most influential and well known families of the area, a woman known for her courage and strength whilst facing the wrath of a military dictator, a woman who suffered the agonies of victimization both socially and politically, whose immediate family members were imprisoned and tortured for speaking their minds freely. What does one ask such a person? What question can give me an insight into her eventful life? Was I even qualified to seek an interview?

The car sped on to Charsadda and I knew it was too late to be beset with such doubts. Very soon I would sit opposite Nasim Wali Khan and I had better start 'putting my house in order'. I watched the road ahead and thought about all of what I had heard regarding the Wali Khans in the past. Their contribution in framing the political scenario of the province was well known. Their leaning away from the radical conservative fundamentalists was quite common knowledge. Their challenging the establishment time and again which landed the men in jail periodically was also a documented fact. They were a "red" party, their party workers were volatile fire brands and their leaders vocal in their criticism of the "powers that be" as well as being pro democracy.

But what of the women in the party? Where did they get their strength from? Who supported them in this conservative province? How difficult was it for them to be active politicians in an over predominately male political scene? Did anyone give any importance to their opinions and views? Did anyone actually listen to their opinions? Were they discouraged and told to stay at home? What was that inner "calling" that made them break those domestic boundaries and venture out? All these and many more questions crowded my brain as the miles rolled passed.

I would not be telling the whole truth if I did not mention my nervousness and apprehension as we approached the house of Nasim Wali Khan. I was treading on unfamiliar ground, in an unfamiliar territory, meeting an unfamiliar person, discussing an unfamiliar subject. I did not feel comfortable at all as I entered the house. As a rule we never start to set up the equipment on location until we have received permission from the owner(s) hence we waited for someone, anyone to make an appearance.

A servant came in with drinks but did not speak Urdu. We waited some more. In walked Begum Sahiba. I stood up as a mark of respect. She gestured for me to sit down. I asked her permission to get the tech team moving which she graciously allowed and while we sipped our drinks the boys got busy.

I made small talk with her as we waited to begin the recording. I found her easy to talk to. Quite unpretentious. Not the firebrand I had imagined nor the 'dragon' I had envisaged her to be. But certainly someone with a fire burning within to change conditions for the better.

"Madam, Ready" said a voice from somewhere. I requested her to move to the other side of the room. We started getting wired up and I quietly mentioned my father's name. Immediately she responded with a smile and compliments to his memory.

It never fails! After that it was smooth sailing through out.

She walked us out to the car, wishing us a safe journey back and stood waiting until the car left the premises. It was my first and probably last meeting with her. She may still be the only female of that province to influence the National political scene for a long time to come.

Moneeza Hashmi: What were your aspirations for yourself while growing up?

Naseem Wali Khan: I wanted to become a doctor. I belong to a traditional and "primitive" family so I was unable to turn my dreams into reality. As a child I liked to read books. I really enjoyed reading Naseem Hijazi's novels. In those novels the character of a woman would stand before a crowd of men and address them bravely. I used to wonder whether I could ever do the same.

Moneeza Hashmi: Why did you use the term "primitive"?

Naseem Wali Khan: It's a strong word. Our family is an old family, and old families are very particular about hanging on to traditions. The same is true of *purdah*. By *purdah* it meant complete segregation from men. I was not allowed to go and study even at the girl's college in Mardan. Although I had my father's full support to complete my education but he was in jail at the time. So his influence on the rest of the family at the time did not carry much weight.

Moneeza Hashmi: Having a father in jail must have been a very difficult time for you?

Naseem Wali Khan: Today people go to jail like going to the *Bari Imam Mela* (festival). Back in those days jails were very tough places to be in. My father was a member of the party which had revolted against the British. Interestingly, he was imprisoned after we had won independence in June 1948 until late 1954. Our entire assets were seized, our furniture and everything else in the house was confiscated. We survived those 6 years only on our mother's strong faith, courage and fortitude.

Moneeza Hashmi: Tell us about your mother.

Naseem Wali Khan: My mother was a very simple woman who could survive on limited resources. She was married at 13 and half years. She understood and lived by the rules of a joint family system. When I was young, my mother carried the entire responsibility of running the household by herself. My grandparents had passed away and she faced her challenges with courage and determination.

Her strength was what was later reflected naturally in our personalities. She would always tell us "No matter how long the night lasts, morning will come". After 6 years of long nights that morning did come and our father was released.

Moneeza Hashmi: Did you visit your father in jail?

Naseem Wali Khan: Initially it was disallowed but later they would let us visit. My younger brother, Azam was about 5 and half years old when he first went to visit my father in jail. They did not recognize each other. You can only imagine how strange that was. Only few people know how tough it is to actually live the life of an orphan even when your father is alive.

Moneeza Hashmi: They say girls are very close to their fathers. Were you close to yours?

Naseem Wali Khan: I was and I am proud of the fact. We were five sisters, yet everyone including my mother and sisters knew that my father and I were particularly close to each other.

Moneeza Hashmi: How did you enter politics?

Naseem Wali Khan: My entry into politics was purely accidental. I was brought up in a political family and also married into a political family. I consider myself fortunate in a way. Politics is in our blood. Traditions however forbade me to participate in practical politics. During the Bhutto era, both my husband and my father in law *Baccha Khan* were imprisoned. My older son *Asfandyar* was sentenced to 19 years imprisonment. My only brother was accused of instigating 50 blasts and had to take refuge in Afghanistan. People said *Baccha Khan*, his party and his political life was over. Without a patriarch in the family, I stepped into politics. It was all accidental and this "accident" continues.

Moneeza Hashmi: It is one thing to decide to come into politics and

	quite another to survive the expectations levied on a woman.
Naseem Wali Khan:	Initially I had a lot of issues. When I appeared publically in other provinces my fellow party members had no objection but in NWFP it was a problem.
Dealing with this province was difficult because I had no one to guide me, no husband, no father no son, no father in law and no brother. The only person who was really there for me was my brother in law, my sister's husband, Lala Yar Khan.
The party almost broke up because there were those who wanted me to come into politics and those who didn't. Lala advised me to join mainstream politics.
I have this intrinsic belief that whateverneeds to be done must be done well and to perfection. It is this very determination that has made me survive so long in politics.
Moneeza Hashmi:	Once you got into practical politics was it at all enjoyable?
Naseem Wali Khan:	For me it was a new discovery. When my husband returned from jail I told him that it seemed as if God's hand was leading me the entire way. I never felt bogged down with difficulty.
I have no hesitation in saying that my closest allies were very forthcoming with me. They were very supportive. The older generation of politicians blessed me and told me they had stood by my father in law, and my husband and now they were with me. This made my determination stronger. As days went by I became personally involved in this momentum. My days would start at 6 am and go on till midnight. I had no idea what tiredness was, what sickness was and what rest was. These words were lost on me.
My involvement gained so much momentum that even if I tried I wasn't able to get out of it. Every day was a new challenge for me. I would look at each day as a set of goals which I had to achieve and once done would stack up more new goals for the next day.
Moneeza Hashmi:	Can politics be taught?

Naseem Wali Khan: Politics can be taught theoretically in books but being successful in practical politics is God's gift. I didn't learn politics from anyone.

Moneeza Hashmi: How did you learn?
Naseem Wali Khan: I learned from my environment; first from my father then from my in-laws. People would crave to be with Baba (Abdul Ghaffar Khan). I was fortunate to have spent 35 years in his company.

Moneeza Hashmi: Can you elaborate about the learning process of your politics?
Naseem Wali Khan: I was mostly secluded, and oblivious to the outside world. My only window to it was the conversations that took place in our drawing room between men. There were some people who I did not observe purdah with and so used to hear them speak and gradually this listening turned to speaking. I would form opinions and judgments of my own and share them.

Moneeza Hashmi: You must have also faced a fierce opposition?
Naseem Wali Khan: Yes. I faced a lot of opposition, not just from my party but also from my own family. My uncle was one of my greatest critics. My own family is far more orthodox than my in laws. They opposed me and tried their best to ensure I wouldn't step out of the house. But I refused to give up.

Moneeza Hashmi: How would you assess your gains and losses?
Naseem Wali Khan: You lose some you win some. To gain something you have to let something go. That happened to me. I had to let some things go.

Moneeza Hashmi: You are a mother and a wife. Politics demands a lot of sacrifices. There must be some corner left unattended by yourself. It's not possible to be everywhere all the time
Naseem Wali Khan: I tried my best to keep up with my traditional roles and duties. I would go to weddings and funerals, network with my relations but at the end of the day I would have very little hours left in the day for it. I tried to do justice

	to this role but quite honestly I couldn't.
Moneeza Hashmi:	Tell us more about this side of your life.
Naseem Wali Khan:	I couldn't do justice to my home, I couldn't do justice to my family, or my children who needed me so much given that their father was absent, I just couldn't manage that. I couldn't create the environment I wanted to have in the household. But my utmost effort did go into instilling a set of values in my children. They understood my responsibility to politics and did not demand too much attention.
Moneeza Hashmi:	Politics is also a very dangerous game. Were you ever afraid?
Naseem Wali Khan:	I was never afraid. Only two years ago I was attacked. It was at 8:00am in the morning, four men with Kalashnikovs attacked my jeep. I say my morning prayers in the car, and was in *sajda* (prostration) at that exact time otherwise I would have been dead. The bullets pierced the headboard. After that episode the little fear that I had, vanished. The aggressor is not larger than the savior and those who disrespect life are not greater than the giver of life. No. I have never been afraid.
Moneeza Hashmi:	Did you ever wish you had become a doctor?
Naseem Wali Khan:	I am very content now with what I have acheived. If I had become a doctor I perhaps would have served humanity better than what I am doing now. Politics nowadays doesn't allow you to serve people like you should or want to.
Moneeza Hashmi:	What are your expectations from your children in politics?
Naseem Wali Khan:	Two of my children are in politics. My daughters saw the damage politics did to their father, their home life and they considered the price paid to be too high. They don't approve of politics. When I was arrested after one of the protests in which I participated, my older daughter had to step out and fight for me. My sister also stepped out. When my sister and daughter were put under house arrest, my younger

daughter stepped out and protested. They can keep denying politics all they want but it is in their blood. People often ask me what I have done for women'srights. I tell them first let the men get their rights and then will be the turn of the women. Rights should be ensured equally for both men and women. The party I belong to is a progressive and secular party. I believe only those societies are successful where women and men progress equally and in sync. In Pakistan, socially, economically and in terms of geopolitics we are stunted. We should have been far ahead than where we are at present. We need to fight ignorance and illiteracy. Controlling our population growth is the most important thing for us as a nation right now. We are growing exponentially and along with that so will our problems. There is no system of increasing our output. Industrialization is not happening at the rate it should happen. We are left with little land and more mouths to feed.

Moneeza Hashmi: How do you find you have changed?
Naseem Wali Khan: I have changed for the better. There is so much to learn and absorb in this world. Because my education was left unfinished I have always tried to learn more and more from the people I meet and inter act with. One learns as long as one lives.
Years ago the perception, the depth and the ability that I have now was not there.

Moneeza Hashmi: When you come home at the end of a tired day how do you relax?
Naseem Wali Khan: Before I came into politics, I was a very domestic woman, a home maker. I would stitch, knit and do embroidery. I would cook. Nowadays, I pick up my knitting and sit in front of the Television.

Moneeza Hashmi: Are you a successful wife?
Naseem Wali Khan: My husband has never complained.

Moneeza Hashmi: A loving mother?
Naseem Wali Khan: This again my children would be able to answer best. But yes, they have always said I am a good mother. I love them

and they love me.

Moneeza Hashmi: Do you want to change anything in your life?
Naseem Wali Khan: God has been very kind. I have got all the happiness and satisfaction I could ask for. If I had the Hindu belief of reincarnation I would ask God to give me the same life over again.

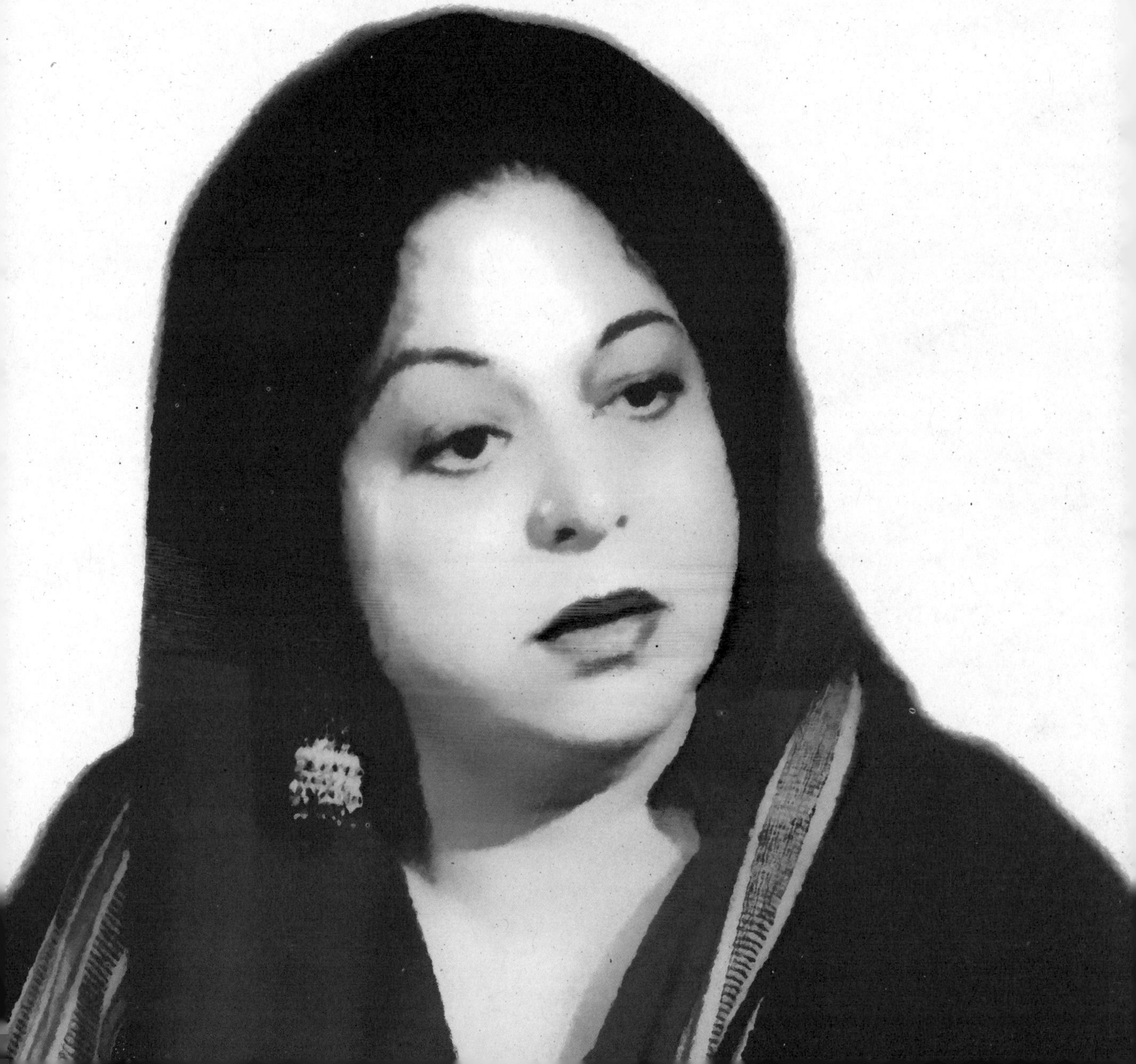

Place of Birth
Gujrat, Pakistan
Marital Status
Married
Number of Children
One son and two daughters
Area of Expertise
Acting
Area of Personal Interest
Reading religious books
Moment of Pride
When I married Syed Musa Raza and had a son
Moment of disappointment
When I lost my husband
A trait I am proud of
I always tell the truth
A trait I could do without
I cannot control my temper
The first question I would ask myself
Why did I have to abandon my education?

SABIHA KHANUM

July 1997. What usually attracts you to someone?
Looks?
Personality? Voice? Appearances?
How they speak or interact with you?
Do they make you feel special?
If the answer to all of the above is 'yes' then you have Sabiha Khanum right in front of you.

I watched almost all of her movies as a teenager. Her round full face, button black shining eyes, a long plait which she swung to and fro as she sang and danced, curls framing her broad forehead, a full figure without being overtly buxom or vulgar, she was a charmer from the word go. As a young heroine always on the 'receiving' end but always ending up with the hero as her prize she portrayed her characters with poise and grace. Whether she was the ever suffering 'poor relation' or the wronged 'bhabi' (sister in law) or the girl next door Sabiha Khanum was never out of step either with her audiences or with her co-stars. Throughout her film career she was untouched by scandal or gossip. Her reputation was unblemished throughout the more than three score years she dominated the film scene of Pakistan.She was referred to as Sabiha Bhabi (sister in law) or Sabiha Apa (elder sister) by every one on set. After her marriage to Santosh Kumar, the green eyed handsome hero who dominated the screen in the 60's alongside her, Sabiha's position as top heroine was stamped loud and clear. This husband and wife double billing was a sure shot of the film being a commercial success. But for me the fascination was neither her stardom nor her fame or cheerful disposition. I was curious to know how she had agreed to become a 'second wife' when she was at the pinnacle of her film career. A top star, the film world at her feet, adoring fans, she could dictate not only her roles but the terms of her film contracts. And then she suddenly decides to intertwine her life with a man who was not only married but also had children! It was all beyond my comprehension. I had to know why. Did she fall so recklessly in love with Santosh to throw all caution to the winds? Was she honour bound for some reason? Was there a financial game plan lurking in the shadows?

I had decided on the offset when I began this series of interviews that I would not intrude into the personal lives of my guests. I was not going to use this opportunity to embarrass or put them on a spot just to further my own popularity. That was never my intention. Hence it took me some time to wrestle with my 'principles' about whether I should or should not put the second marriage question to Sabiha Apa. We sat across each other while the technical crew got busy with last minute details. She was making light conversational remarks in her usual amiable and charming manner. I was squirming within myself trying to make up my mind.

"Ready Madam" and we were on record. She smiled her sweet smile and we got talking. The conversation flowed effortlessly. She was one of the easiest persons to talk to. Uninhibited, with heart and soul open wide to read. Honest, transparent, willing to share her life with millions of viewers across the world.

How and when the actual question popped up I don't recall. Without missing a beat she described her relationship and her acceptance of Santosh's marriage to another woman. She had nothing but praise for Jameela his first wife. When they decided to get married Sabiha

described how Jameela accepted her as 'the other woman' in her husband's life and they did all 'live happily ever'.
It has been several years since I recorded that interview but Sabiha Apa's grace and dignity have stayed with me throughout. She had even then begun to suffer from an eye 'twitch' which badly affected her facial expressions as well as her concentration. She became extremely conscious about it and preferred to avoid being seen in public. I am very very grateful to her granting me that interview despite her physical affliction. I particularly saw to it that the camera angle did not expose her weakness and the result was certainly worth the extra effort. We talked on about the film world, the professionalism which kept her so enthused about films, the directors who made her the actor she finally became, the audience who gave her so much love and admiration, the husband who let her continue her profession and her own passion to excel in her craft with every passing role.

Years later I was in conversation with Agha Taalish, another great actor of his time. I asked him to identify which co-star he felt 'at a loss' to face. "Sabiha Bhabi" was his reply. "She would present a new interpretation of her dialogues with every take", were his comments.

For me her mischievous swirling around Santosh trying to elicit a smile or trying to make Waheed Murad behave responsibly as the elder Bhabi or prancing around the fields as a village lass are lasting memories of one of the greatest legends of the Pakistani film scene.

Moneeza Hashmi: Tell us about your childhood.
Sabiha Khanum: My childhood was spent in the village. Even now when I travel to Gujrat, our lands there remind me of my childhood. When I see the trees that I had planted as saplings as a child it gives me much joy. I spent my childhood eating healthy vegetables and fruits. This is a lifestyle recommended by doctors today. Possibly this could be the reason I am strong enough now to deal with so many illnesses.

Moneeza Hashmi: Your family was a conservative one. How did you get to choose acting in films as your profession?
Sabiha Khanum: I was a spoilt child and everything I demanded I received. My father had actually fought a court case to win my custody from my mother. He was extremely affectionate towards me and let me have my way all the time. After I went to live with him, he fed me meat as a special treat.

I immediately got unwell as I was not used to that kind of diet. He took me to consult a doctor who was connected to the film industry at the time. We also took a tour of Radio Pakistan. There I saw women reciting *naats* (verses in praise of Prophet Mohammad PBUH). I had a good voice. So I asked if I could also participate. They agreed. Before I knew it I was being auditioned and performing live on radio. Later we went to see a theater performance. I told my father I could act better. I was auditioned and got selected in a play immediately in the lead role! I looked older than my age because I used to eat a lot of butter and sweets. That is how I joined the acting industry. But the maternal side of my family who were extremely conservative warned me that if I as much dared to even come close to their village I would be killed. They were all *maulvis* (religious leaders) who recited the *Azaan* (call for prayer) in the local mosque. So this kind of activity was "*haram*" (prohibited according to Islam) in their views. I tried to convince them it was like going to school. I told them I would even cover my head with a *dupatta* (scarf) but they wanted nothing to do with it.

Moneeza Hashmi: Who was your role model?

Sabiha Khanum: A mother is that person in every one's life who is remembered at every step of your life. In times of difficultly one thinks of one's mother. But I did not have that support. I later got so wrapped up in my new life and in the desire to be independent that I stood alone. However I got a lot of support from fans and colleagues in the film industry.

Moneeza Hashmi: Your marriage to Santosh Kumar was an iconic one. When you first saw him what did you feel?

Sabiha Khanum: My heart would beat faster every time I would see him. His family and mine were close friends before partition when we were living in Delhi. I would play with his sisters when we were all children. I didn't know him that well because he was studying at the time in Hyderabad. He was a wonderful person and a great artist. We were really good friends. He would praise me and say I was a great performer.

Moneeza Hashmi: How was it acting opposite your husband? Was it ever awkward during the love scenes?

Sabiha Khanum: It actually helped. Your face expressions show your true sentiments. That said, I never let our relationship get in the way of my acting. If anything compromised my performance, I would protest. People told me I should be courteous because he was my husband but to me my profession always came first.

Moneeza Hashmi: Did you take your work home?

Sabiha Khanum: No, once we were home, we would forget about work. We had experienced our success in a flash. Our first film was a huge hit but we never let it go to our heads. We were the same two friends when we reached home. I was a very dutiful wife. I served him well. On any typical day I would wake up at 6:00 am and get his things ready by 9:00am and then leave for my work.

Moneeza Hashmi: When both spouses are in the same profession, is it easier or harder?

Sabiha Khanum: There can be a lot of difficulties. If you are not honest with each other then jealousy is bound to creep in. There was a time when he had discontinued his work but I was still acting. The conversation in those days would get sarcastic. He would sometimes comment, "You are a very busy woman". He would tick me off when I would forget to do something or when something he liked wasn't cooked. I always told him I would rather work for him than continue to act. But he would respond that he did not want to deprive me of my calling. We had our ups and downs but all said he was very accommodating and an excellent life partner.

Moneeza Hashmi: You married him knowing that he was already married?

Sabiha Khanum: Actually, I was his first wife and she was the second. Don't read this literally, but I mean judging from a mental wavelength perspective. He and I were in love before he married her. Somehow we never really had the courage to tell each other how we felt. When I received his wedding card I was very upset and though I didn't say

it to him then, I thought he had lost his mind.
He belonged to me, and eventually what was mine came to me. It was fate.

Moneeza Hashmi: Was it a compromise marrying him knowing he already had a wife?

Sabiha Khanum: You could call it a compromise but the image I had was of me and him together. That was clear in my mind and nothing was going to change that image.
If you really love someone you don't see anyone else. Even if he had 10 wives, I would still have married him.

Moneeza Hashmi: How old were you when Santosh Kumar died?
Sabiha Khanum: I was a young widow.

Moneeza Hashmi: Our society doesn't allow women to live as single woman and especially as single mothers. How did you cope?

Sabiha Khanum: At first I didn't understand what happened. I was in a state of shock. In fact this problem (twitching) I have now with my eye started in those days when I was under tremendous stress after his death. Doctors told me it was because of the trauma. I just didn't know what to do. I was cut off from my family after I joined films. So I was alone. Santosh Saab's brothers were still very young. They could not have supported me. I didn't work for many days. There were films which I left half completed. The person who got me to stand up again was Moin Akhtar. He came to me like an angel. He would recite Quranic verses and blow them on me. He is such a great human being. He would say that I needed to get my courage back and take responsibility for my family, regardless of the fact that I was a woman.
It was difficult to return to work but I did make the effort. I didn't work for money, I worked for my profession. I could have earned more, but the work I chose to do was for a good performance.

Moneeza Hashmi: How did you make the transition from heroine to character roles?

Sabiha Khanum: People think a heroine is all about being young. A heroine is a person who is the pillar of a story. It is not about age or looks. Let me tell you about an incident. I am a very conscientious driver. I was stopped by a policeman at a traffic signal who asked to see my license. I apologized and told him I had left it in my makeup box. He finally recognized me and let me go.

There are many incidences when people have shown much love. When I shop in *Anarkali* (shopping area) and *Icchra* (shopping area), I am recognized and obliged by the shopkeepers. I have always felt all these people are my relatives. It is because of this love and respect that I always have to watch my step. I never want them to be disappointed in me.

Moneeza Hashmi: You have been described as being a very good "reaction artist."

Sabiha Khanum: That is true. My timing in scenes where I had to react was always very good. My co-actors would hide in corners and rehearse, because I would perform flawlessly. Those who were not prepared were intimidated by my thoroughness. An actor who reacts well also assists the other performer. As a good reaction performer I drew the attention away from my own counterparts especially when actors have tried to dominate my performance. When I was new, I had to work with many seniors who would try to overshadow me. I would respond by reacting superbly in my acting. And they found out they were not dealing with an amateur!

Moneeza Hashmi: What is it about films that makes you want to go on working?

Sabiha Khanum: I still need to work. I have to provide for my family. My youngest daughter has just gotten married. I have also got used to working hard. Once you're accustomed to that type of lifestyle, you cannot stay idle.

My craft of acting has become polished over time. I am giving this cumulative experience back to the younger generation.

We are all rounders - we can bat, we can ball. We know all the tricks of the game!

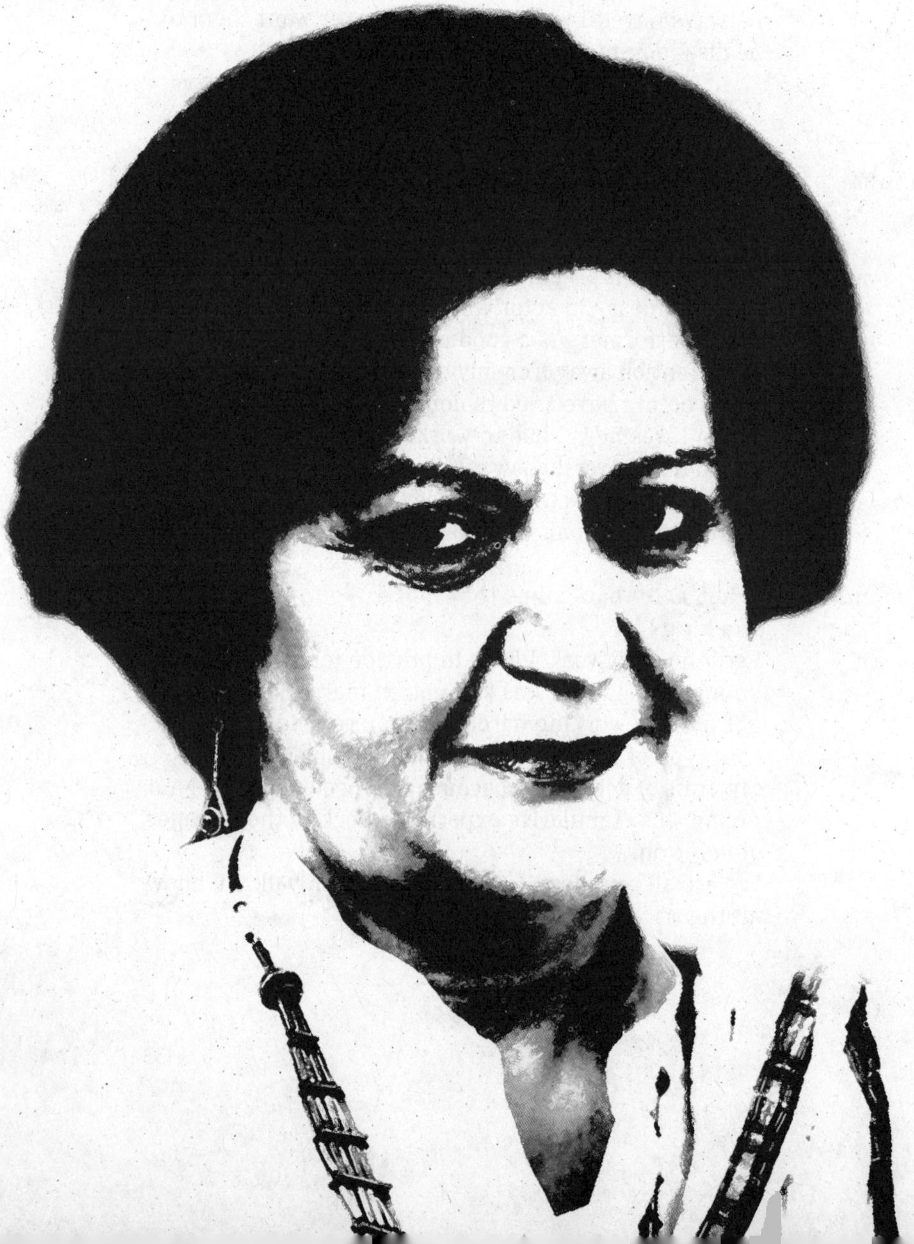

Place of Birth
Delhi
Marital Status
Married
Number of Children
One daughter and one son
Area of Personal Interest
Film, theater and music
Moment of Pride
When I stood first in my matriculation examination
Moment of disappointment
There were many such moments in life, but they can't be mentioned
A trait I am proud of
The ability to smile in the worst of times
A trait I could do without
There are many such traits
The first question I would ask myself
What is going on here?

SALIMA HASHMI

September 1999. How does one go about formally interviewing one's sister in public?

That could have been the one reason that made me postpone this episode for longer than necessary. However, there was no getting away from the fact that she was a major player of the Art scene in Pakistan hence her presence on this programme series was essential. Once face to face it wasn't so difficult or awkward at all. There were so many facets of her personality which I gently probed as the conversation progressed and I came way finding a multi-layered personality in the garb of my sister!

I had always accepted her in the role of an elder sister, far more talented than I was, in a field that I have never dared to either approach. It has always somehow been a world where I have never attempted to enter. I can view any painting and appreciate the images, the colours and the technique. I can be moved by the physical appearance of that piece of creation but beyond that is actually beyond me. My sister and I have shared a few laughs about my *jahalat* (ignorance) and total lack of regret about it and left it at that. I think one of the reasons for our understanding has been a respect of the other's space. We have allowed each other to be different. To be proud of our work and each other at the same time..

I knew my questions would basically revolve around two aspects of her life; her achievements as an artist and her unique position as being the eldest daughter of Faiz Ahmad Faiz. To live in a glass house, under constant scrutiny, subjected to standards set by others, putting responsibility of public service beyond personal gains or wishes, are all tall orders to be fulfilled in one life time. Yet she has done that and more.

She opened up and spoke honestly about the challenges of trying to balance her professional and personal life. She was forth coming about the sacrifices that had to be made when living under the shadow of a great legacy. She discussed the inspirations, aspirations and frustrations in relation to her work.

I may not have included all of what we talked about in the final cut but it was an illuminating and highly informative interaction with one of Pakistan's leading female painters

Moneeza Hashmi: There are merits and demerits of having famous parents. The positives are that you get to be respected and famous and the negatives are that you have to face jealousy, competition and the requirement to live life according to a determined legacy. In your life what were these influences and to what degree did they affect?

Salima Hashmi: I haven't really thought about the negative aspects that much, nor have I taken them seriously. Perhaps the reason for this could be a part of what I have inherited from my father. He had a gentle temperament. My nature is also not to laud my own personal achievements. The positives are many. There are many people who have given me tremendous affection and respect.

They have also given me a sense of ownership where they let me become a part of them and them a part of me. This is far more than what my own stature deserved. I do realize the respect I have from people is far greater than my own acheivements. In that sense the positives far outweigh the negatives.

Moneeza Hashmi: When you talk of your ancestral assets, do you think one inherits creative capabilities?

Salima Hashmi: Creativity in my opinion is not passed on. I remember being quite irritated at questions I have faced as a child when people would inquire if I also wrote poetry. I would feel like telling them, how dare I?

However, there are certain subtleties that do become a part of one's system, such as the ability to take pleasure in mundane details of life, to feel from within, from the heart. I am not sure if these would be classified as inherited but they would be certainly part of the ambiance that was created by the kind of people who would visit our home; the artists, writers and other creative people. Therefore it seemed but natural for me to pursue creativity as well. All this made me want to create art.

Moneeza Hashmi: There is an ongoing debate whether talent is inherited or learnt. Which argument holds more depth in your case specifically?

Salima Hashmi: My childhood was spent in the backdrop of partition between India and Pakistan. We came to Lahore in 1947. Those memories are marred by curfew nights when my father would ride home on his bicycle from his newspaper, *The Pakistan Times*. There was as much fear as there was passion to set things right. I also witnessed his imprisonment.

There was so much to learn from those times. You tend to feel things more if you're sensitive. When your father isn't home life's happenings have more of an effect on you.

I have also witnessed my mother's strength as she protected us from financial burdens. I also saw many friendships which she cultivated in those difficult times

and which saw her through tough times. However, there were also friends that looked the other way when we faced difficult times.
All these things stay with you and become part of your personality and who you are inherently and eventually show up in your work.

Moneeza Hashmi: In this day and age people wish for sons. Did your father ever wish or say that he would rather have had sons than daughters?

Salima Hashmi: This was an often discussed topic in our household. My paternal uncles had daughters as well. My paternal grandmother would have no qualms displaying her long sighs and through them her pain because she had only granddaughters. However, because all the girls in the family were quite vocal when we would tell her we are no less equipped than boys!
I think largely the world today is proof of the fact that women are equal in their ability to men. I also believe very strongly that the next generation is the generation of women. When people say that they would rather have sons, there is a background and history linked to that wish. There is a popular consensus that there are certain tasks which only men can do, but that difference is slowly becoming irrelevant.
We have seen this in our lifetimes. There are roles women now do which were considered purely a man's job and they do them perhaps even better. Just pick up the news paper and look at the examination results in Matric, BA, MA and PhD and you'll find women are scoring better. There is no competition anymore because men have lagged so far behind.
Now people would or should dream about having a daughter!

Moneeza Hashmi: How much of an influence did your father have on you?

Salima Hashmi: There is a very deep effect on me which continues till this day and it did not diminish after his demise. In fact I believe that connection deepens because you tend to emotionally analyze it more. When I was much younger,

he was mostly away from home, fulfilling his work demands. If I managed to see him for a few brief minutes I would insist he sat down to tell me stories.
There was this one night which I remember distinctly. It was the eve of Eid and I was listening to such a story. I recall I was torn between going on the rooftop with the other kids to see the new moon or stay with my father and have him complete the story he was telling me. I decided to listen to the story instead. When it was over I said I wanted to go see the moon, but by then, it had already disappeared.
That happened in my early childhood. When I started going to school, it was a different era. I absolutely loathed going to school, for which he would always support me. I would come up with all sorts of excuses from headaches to stomachaches and he would tell my mother to let me stay home. My mother was very strict about going to school, without which she'd say I would get nowhere in life. But he supported me in dodging school.
When he went to jail that was such a prolonged period. When he came back the relationship was never the same. We were no longer father and child. He became a friend.

Moneeza Hashmi: When did you start to paint?
Salima Hashmi: This was something I had been doing since my childhood. I was inclined towards drawing pictures as a kid but even more than that I loved to "play" teacher. Eventually I got to be both a teacher and an artist.
The other day I was going through some old files and came across drawings I had made as a 4 year old which my mother had saved. I never really knew for certain I would become a painter. I enjoyed more than anything the company of artists and the wonderful and enlightening conversations which went on between them. The profession later developed through formal education in the field.
When I got the opportunity to teach that was an extraordinary opportunity which I enjoyed.

Moneeza Hashmi: Is painting also taught or a natural talent?
Salima Hashmi: It can be taught. Some of it is of course part of your

natural talent. As in music you either have a good voice or do not have the right voice. But still there are many things about music which you can learn. Many of my students that had me believe that they had no natural talent have consequently proven me wrong.
This was when they got an opportunity to create art in the studios and classroom. While working with instructors and classmates they had conversations and debates that revolved around art. They developed an ability to see a different point of view and then there would be this magical development! The same young girls or boys who I didn't think had it in them, became great artists! Then there are also people who have a God-given talent but they do absolutely nothing about it. They don't value it. In a manner of speaking they demean their talent. That behavior is more painful to witness.

Moneeza Hashmi: In Pakistan very few women have gotten recognition in the field of art as compared to the likes of Sadeqain, Shakir Ali, Saeed Akhtar. Why is that?

Salima Hashmi: That was a different age. Only Zubaida Agha was painting at that time. This is a different time. Now when I look around I see more women. Women such as Jamila Zaidi, Naseem Qazi, Ana Molka Ahmad, Abbasi Abidi and Anwar Afzal were all art teachers because that is how they chose to express their art.
Many of these women taught men the art that they later got famous for. The upcoming generation of women is the generation where most of the women artists are going to make their mark.

Moneeza Hashmi: If one were to look at your paintings would it immediately stand out that it was the work of a woman?

Salima Hashmi: There has been a lot of debate about this for the past 20 years. I have always instructed my students that before creating good art you first have to identify with who you are. That entails the gender which is a large part of one's personality. I ask them to probe a little deeper in terms of their own identity. I believe only then can they make a complete piece of art which will reflect them as a person. There has been a study of creative world products. This study focused on creations by men and by women and the iconography linked to both. They are certainly different. Although you may not be able to pick out the difference using a set formula but there is a difference that can nonetheless be spotted.

Moneeza Hashmi: What process do you follow when you are painting?
Salima Hashmi: Many different processes. Sometimes it can be a personal trauma or a political event or even the environment around me that gets me thinking. At times a single word can be an inspiration: happiness, sadness or anger. All these things which make up life are the fabrics of my paintings.

There are times when one can ponder endlessly about something but still not be able to put it together in a frame. Other times a single moment becomes a definitive part of the painting. It's hard to tell what could be an actual inspiration. There are times when the most mediocre and off-beat matters become a reason to put color on a canvas. Someone may say a word, or tell a joke or a phrase and that would be a start for the process. But between the beginning and the end there are a few patterns it could take. Sometimes the texture of the canvas and the feel of spreading paint over it becomes the reason to keep on with the craft. Yet there are times when there is a pre-set destination that a painting will move in. The motions that one makes with the wrist also become a means to complete the painting.

Interestingly each artist has a separate vocabulary. Some like to see their painting in their heads before they start. Others have conversations with their paintings and their pictures keep evolving as they move on.

Sometimes you don't even know when a painting has finished. An unfinished piece looks good and you say to yourself "This is where I'll stop". There are also those odd times when you go on adding so much to a painting which was already completed a while back. Then you begin to undo the extra parts until it feels right, until the original inspiration re-emerges.

The bottom line is that there are no formulas to painting.

Moneeza Hashmi: This work requires peace of mind, silence and commitment. Women generally hardly have such moments.

Salima Hashmi: The oddest things happen when I am in the middle of a painting. The launderer shows up or the cook asks me what to make for dinner. I feel like telling her to fry my liver!! This is indeed a problem for us women.

I have been lucky though. If anyone has stopped me from working it has been I myself. I have felt guilty. All women feel guilty, especially if they are wholeheartedly involved in their work. I have often joked about the fact that my art is in competition with my husband, Shoaib Hashmi.

When you take time out for your work you feel you have stolen it from somewhere it was needed perhaps more. This is very difficult to reconcile to.

I feel that women who are artists need to determine very early in their lives that this is one of their basic needs. Just as they have to eat and drink and wear clothes they have to paint without which they would be incomplete. If she is incomplete then the people around her, including her children, husband and family will immediately realize she is not happy. It is in their best interest that they realize this and support her. They have to make a contract in their minds for this to happen. This is the key to happily coexisting. Giving space is that important.

Moneeza Hashmi: Artists often claim that during their creative urges they go through strange external stress. What happens to Salima Hashmi when she paints?

Salima Hashmi: There is not any set process with me. Sometimes I put on some music, specifically *Raag Bhatiyar* (a classical music Raga) which I love listening to or *Subha ka Raag* (Morning Raga) which has a lot of longing in it. When I like a piece of music, I tend to listen to it in a loop which often irritates people around me.

When there is silence then I am often found talking to myself. Sometimes I want to complete the painting in one stretch. Other times I want to get away from the painting after adding a few strokes to it.

I have experienced all sorts of feelings when I paint. At times there is so much pleasure in it that I feel like laughing out loud. Sometimes a lot of pain... lots of it and then there are times when one has a feeling that I haven't created anything of value.

Moneeza Hashmi: Artists have battled with society's predetermined norms. As a painter have you felt the same constraints of not being allowed to express what you really wanted to? And then when you compromise, how do you satisfy your inner self?

Salima Hashmi: This is not a problem unique only to painters. It is something every creative person has to face that he/she can only create within the boundaries of what society permits him/her to. Every age had an issue of the artist trying to push the boundaries. Regardless of the kind of creative work, an artist has to also cultivate the ability to convey the message through his/her medium while staying within given boundaries. It is harder for women because women have more limitations placed on them. But I also feel women know how to use these limitations to their advantage and work in spite of them. In fact they know how to do this even better than their male counter parts. They do this by developing a very subtle vocabulary shrouded with such innocence that it becomes palatable and beautiful even if the message demands change.

There is a unique charm associated with saying things out loud or sloganeering but that will last only until it is being heard. The things that are expressed more delicately, more subtley have a more long term impact.

Moneeza Hashmi: If Salima Hashmi chose not to be a painter what would she have been?

Salima Hashmi: I believe that it is important to first become a good human being. Once you do that, whatever follows is irrelevant.

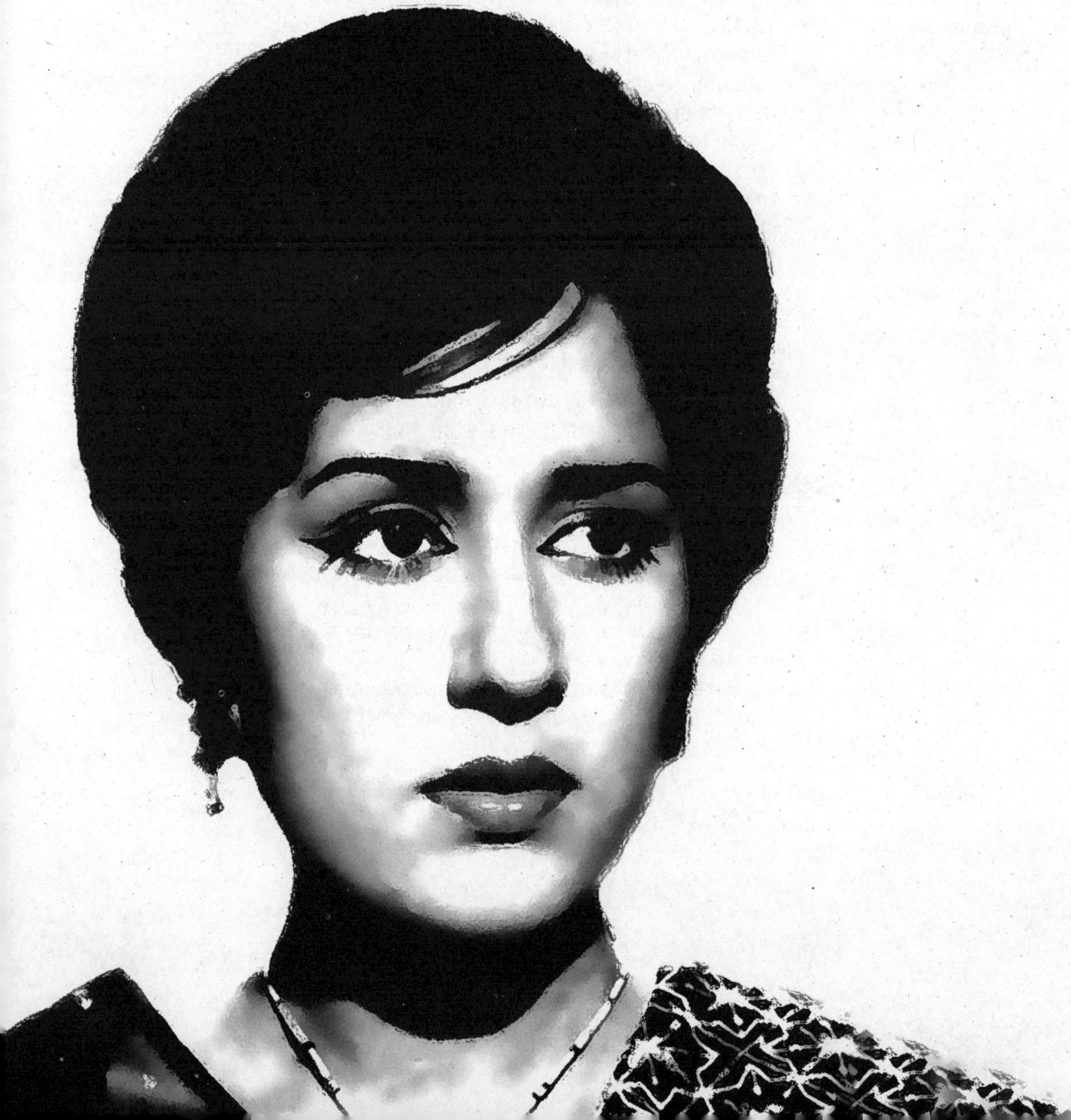

Place of Birth
Aligarh
Marital Status
Married
Number of Children
One son
Area of Personal Interest
Reading books, traveling, watching films
Moment of Pride
When I got an award in 1961 for my film," Saheli"
Moment of disappointment
When I lost my mother in childhood
A trait I am proud of
I don't get angry
A trait I could do without
People have lots of weaknesses
The first question I would ask myself
Why did I have to become an actress?

SHAMIM ARA

October 1997. She was perhaps the one "star" I had never actually met or got to know before we were sitting facing each other in the PTV studio for this recording.

That does not mean I did not know of her, admired her, had not seen many of her movies, watched her from afar at many a film "do", read about her and had also been a firsthand witness to her short one day marriage to Film Director Fareed Ahmad who was a close and dear family friend. For many months Fareed or *Sami* as he was fondly known to us would share all kinds of anecdotes about this actress with whom he was utterly and hopelessly in love. According to him, those feelings were reciprocated by her as well. Evening after evening he would come to our house after a long day of shooting at the studio and tell us of his day's activities in which she fared up front. I got to "know" her through his eyes and since I was extremely fond of him as a person I obviously was "on his side" as he recounted agonizing incidents of her "stand offishness" or her grandmother keeping them apart and so on. I found myself at times being most critical of her behavior towards Sami. Just why did she not marry him if she loved him as much as he said she did was a question that continued to haunt me until she did finally one day but divorced him the next! He was heartbroken and frustrated and angry. He blamed her grandmother for her "turn around". And I being his staunch supporter never quite forgave her for this cruel act of playing with the emotions of her suitor. Was it a publicity stunt? What goaded her into the final act of exchanging vows one day and retracting the next? How can you submit to your heart one day and change your mind after 24 hours? What kind of a fickle person would play with their reputation and their lives so irresponsibly? After all no one was holding a gun to her head or were they?

These and many other questions faced me as I watched Shamim being wired for the conversation. She was a good actress, a top one too. She had been most successful throughout her career although no one could ever call her glamorous or even beautiful. She had a sort of sultry look, a willowy figure, a graceful demeanor, an endearing soft voice. She played the "suffering victim of circumstances" characters to the hilt. She wept and whined most charmingly. She suffered violence and mistreatment from mothers in law, sisters in law, brothers in law, neighbors in such a believable manner that she held the emotions of the audience in the palm of her hand making them sob into their handkerchiefs and come back for another doze in her next film. She swayed to the musical melodies of Khursheed Anwar and Firoze Nizami with her long plait twisted around her neck like a swirling snake. She flirted with her male heroes on screen without offending her female fans. She had the "girl next door" image but dominated the screen for many years before calling it a day and moving into a more challenging field of Directing.

As one of the first female directors of the Pakistani film world Shamim Ara has several successful movies to her credit. She was the voice calling the shots for other super stars and at the time was a well respected professional in her own right.

As a movie buff I remember watching her in many films. Although now I would find those characters somewhat removed from reality, submissive, weak and irritating but back then Shamim Ara's portrayals of *Saiqa* and *Naila* were perfect.

Moneeza Hashmi:	How were you introduced to the world of film?
Shamim Ara:	My experience is somewhat different but parts of it may sound similar. I was visiting a friend where I met Mr. Najam Naqvi who is a notable director. He wanted to cast my friend in a role for his film but ended up deciding that my face and height complemented the role better. It was his selection that launched my career and I set off on this journey.
Moneeza Hashmi:	Wasn't your friend upset?
Shamim Ara:	She was disappointed but who can fight fate? You get what is destined for you.
Moneeza Hashmi:	Kawari Bewaa was your first film. Was it successful?
Shamim Ara:	It did terribly at the box office, but it made me into what I am today. I kept getting more opportunities from there on. I acted in a couple of films before I made "Saheli" which was a huge success. Unless your film does well at the box office your future is dark.
Moneeza Hashmi:	When your films did not do that well did you think of giving it all up?
Shamim Ara:	No, I never thought like that. The person who brought me up was my maternal grandmother, my Nani because my mother had died when I was very young. After two of my films had done badly she told me that I was not fated for this career and should bid it farewell but I refused. It became a matter of pride for me. I was adamant to continue until I made at least one hit film. "Saheli" did really well at the box office and that paved the way for more successes.
Moneeza Hashmi:	You defined the process of getting selected in films as very simple. But it's usually not like that. Most often families object to young girls acting in films.
Shamim Ara:	My family agreed because they saw my level of interest in wanting to do this. My Nani would agree to everything I wanted. No wish was left unfulfilled. God has been kind enough to grace me with a successful life since then. I am very grateful to Him.

Moneeza Hashmi:	Do you remember the first shot or your first scene?
Shamim Ara:	Of course I do. I remember it to every detail. When I first had my audition, the studio was completely new to me. I had no experience of how a film shooting was done. Studio lights made the atmosphere so intimidating that I was initially extremely anxious. I got very nervous because of the atmosphere and tried to grasp what exactly was going on. First I was asked to stand before the camera while the lighting was checked. Then I was given a dialogue to speak. I don't remember the line exactly but I was supposed to tell a friend about a dream I had had. I rehearsed it a couple of times. I had a few sips of water and did the shot in one take.
Moneeza Hashmi:	The first colored film for Pakistan was *Naila*. What kind of excitement and concern did that bring about clothes and lipstick shadesetc?
Shamim Ara:	It was a happy moment to find out that whichever lipstick or eye shadow shade or color outfit we would wear would actually appear as is. There was much excitement all around. Mr. Agha Gul had taken us to a festival in Indonesia for shooting of the film Naila. On the way back we visited Hollywood. He took me to the make up company Max to get my makeup professionally done. My complexion isn't very fair, as you know. Mr. Agha was concerned how I would look on screen with my wheatish complexion. The professionals at Max told us that my darker color would appear far better on screen than any pale white complexion! So he and I were glad my being dark wouldn't naturally end my film career.
Moneeza Hashmi:	Was every color under the sun used on set?
Shamim Ara:	In one scene even the horse's reigns were all colors of the rainbow! Just to make sure the message was conveyed that it was a colored film.
Moneeza Hashmi:	Did you find it strange that there were songs and dances in our films and you had to perform them?
Shamim Ara:	Yes it was odd at first. There was great difficulty in

synchronising words with the sound of the music. Sometimes what we would perform would turn out totally different from the song played on screen. It needed a lot of practice. I would practise singing along with the song when it would be played on the radio to get more control over the process. The directors would give us homework to practice synchronising the songs over and over again.

We would follow the instructions of the directors diligently. Now actors do not care much about the instructions they receive. Back in those days we would really be responsible and passionate about our work. We would be terribly embarrassed if there was re-taking of a shot or we did not get it right the first time.

Moneeza Hashmi: Who taught you to get better at acting than your peers? There is no academy or institute where this is taught.

Shamim Ara: Some people have this God given gift and confidence. You have to learn and practice no doubt, but unless you have the capability inside, no matter how hard the director tries, top quality of work just does not happen. If an actor is intelligent, he/she can pick instructions quickly and reproduce them well. For example remembering to pause at the right time or speed up at the appropriate time or raise the voice tone or suppress it at precise moments.

Moneeza Hashmi: You've mostly performed roles in the genre of tragedy?

Shamim Ara: I have done tragic roles more and as a result got pushed and shoved around a lot in the film. I was getting tossed out of my home. I got slapped around a lot. I was mostly playing the role of an oppressed character.

Moneeza Hashmi: Were these the only kinds of films being made in those days or was it because of your timid appearance?

Shamim Ara: I always wanted to perform a variety of roles but got type cast in such roles. Maybe I looked kind of pitiful! But it was also true that back then mostly the films being produced were family dramas and tragedies, and I was the first selection.

I have also played romantic characters. But people appreciated my tragic performances more than my romantic ones.

Moneeza Hashmi: Creative work is often likened to a pain in the heart, constantly reminding you that something should have been done better. After returning from your shoot did you also feel you could have performed better?

Shamim Ara: Yes and that would be a constant thorn in my side. On the way home I'd be thinking about if I had perhaps looked in a particular direction or lifted my arm a little higher in that scene it would have made the shot so much better.

I doubt if an artist is ever content or satisfied. Rarely were there shots when I would really feel that they could not have been done better. Most of the time I would think if I were to do it again, I would do it better.

Moneeza Hashmi: Your performance in the film *Lakhon Mey Aik* was perhaps your best. Would you agree?

Shamim Ara: In that film I played the role of a girl from a different religion. That in itself was a very new experience for me. It will always remain my favorite. That film also had really good music. It had so many variations in mood and tone it appeared to be at first a light hearted film, then it became a romantic one and then came tragedy with a beautiful end.

Moneeza Hashmi: Acting was something you learned on the go. Later you went into producing and then directing films. Direction is a different ball game; you have to check so many aspects of the final product. How and where did you learn to direct?

Shamim Ara: I learned some of it through observation over a very long period of time. I also worked with so many good directors. I would of course focus on my acting at the time but also focused on what else was going on around me. I would observe the lens being changed of the camera, and would wonder why. I would question the cameraman about lenses and shots.

Because I had paid attention to the craft it became relatively easier for me to learn direction. You get to learn a lot from different directors. I had worked in more than 100 films. So I had worked with approximately 30 directors. If I learned just one thing from each one of them, that in itself would be 30 things about direction. Whenever I had free time I would wander into the labs and talk to Mr. Pyarey Khan and pick at his brain. He would be pleased to see me and tell me everything about processing and developing footage. He told me how some colours were more distinct than others. Back then we worked on the lily system; color correction back in that day would be done one color at a time, by reducing the intensity of certain colors and increasing those of others.

Moneeza Hashmi: One day you were on this side of the camera and the next day you were on the other side of the camera. Did you see a difference in perspective?

Shamim Ara: There was a lot of difference. When I was in front of the camera we were learning, and when I was behind the camera, I was teaching. I would direct the actors to tilt their head a certain way and to look in a certain direction; I would ask them to lay stress on certain dialogues and to say other lines quicker.

I used to get a lot of satisfaction by improving the performance of an artist. I would teach them how to walk, stand, talk. Knowing how to act yourself is a huge advantage which comes into play as a director-actor. You know what you are talking about. And so do they.

Moneeza Hashmi: What role does an actor, a director and a story have in making a film successful?

Shamim Ara: I think the most important thing in the film's final result is the story first followed by the director. With a good director you need a successful producer and a good actor who does justice to the story. In our kinds of films you need good music.

Films can only be made with a good team. If a director is good, he/she selects a good team and all is well. If the artists fit the bill, then nothing like it. And lastly you need God to grant you that success and honor.

Moneeza Hashmi: Is Shamim Ara a hot headed director or is she gentle?
Shamim Ara: I am certainly not hot headed, I hardly get angry. When I do, it passes away in a second. The worst I could say was "Where were you and why couldn't you show up on time?" I remember there was an actor who exited the frame in the wrong direction and I asked him why he didn't die in the direction he was supposed to?

Moneeza Hashmi: Do you listen to other people's advice?
Shamim Ara: I would listen to anyone giving me the right advice. I even listen to my servants at home. When I am directing a technician should point out a mistake; provided I think he is right, I will listen to him.

Moneeza Hashmi: You are also a mother. You have a son. Would you like him to make films his career?
Shamim Ara: Not at all. My son is not interested in films. He has just returned from UK after getting his MBA. I don't want him to be associated with a field he does not want to be in.

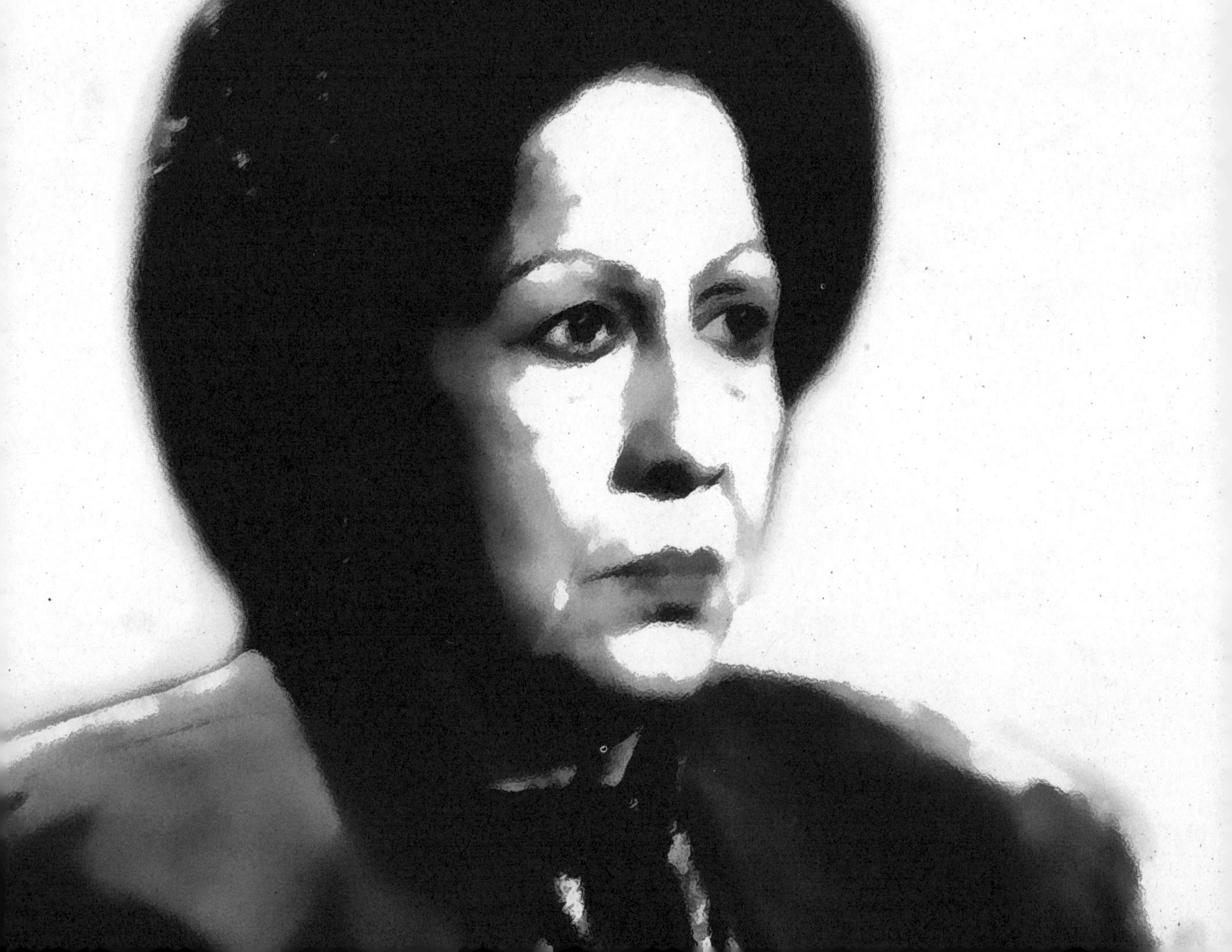

Place of Birth
Rawalpindi
Marital Status
Married
Number of Children
One son and three daughters
Area of Interest
Raising my children
Moment of Pride
When I gained fame and respect in the film industry
Moment of disappointment
When my young daughter passed away
A trait I am proud of
I am honest and punctual
The first question I would ask myself
None

SWARAN LATA

Feburary 1997. She had a sort of *do not disturb* sign around her. I cannot claim to have known her personally or closely but her face did carry a haughty "Please respect my privacy and keep your distance" look. In the 30 or odd years when I was organizing and arranging PTV events which needed glamour celebrities to dish out the awards or generally grace the audience or stage I do not recall a single instance when Madame Swaran Lata was present. She was invited but always declined gracefully but definitely. I used to be intrigued by her desire to remain aloof from the world of "lights and camera" which she had been associated with for so long. I never saw her socially either at other events in Alhamra where many stars did show up (hours late needless to add) but they were always there, preening and twirling for the cameras, smiling artificially but smiling never the less. Not her. If she was ever present she was hardly ever on stage or giving sound bites to TV crews. This lady was different. That was for sure.

Her two daughters were junior to me in college. I also remember their very aristocratic looks, their dark luminous eyes, and straight shoulder length hair. They too were different like their mother I guess. Then one of them died tragically at a young age. Barely in her thirties. A young mother. Some claimed it was due to doctor's negligence. The fact remained that she was dead. I remember thinking at the time of Madam Swaran Lata. How awful it must be for any parent to bury their child in his or her prime. I remember feeling extremely sad about the whole affair.

I asked my assistant to call and request her to come for the interview. He came back looking crest fallen. She had brushed him off politely as expected. It was time for me to move in and try my persuasive powers but to be honest, I was not too sure of how I would fare either. She gave me an afternoon time to visit her home where I arrived somewhat nervously. She lived on Ferozepur Road near Icchra, behind a school which was probably built on her property and leased out. It was an oldish house; certainly nothing like the mansion one would expect housing a top heroine of the film industry. I was shown into a room at the back which looked like a verandah converted into a room. It was dark, probably cool in the summer and even cooler in the winter. Not elaborately furnished. Simple middle class furniture. She walked in. I stood up. My first impression was again of a *"no nonsense"* person. Upright. Small boney frame. Receding hair line. Classical face features. Piercing black eyes which missed no details. Alert. Slightly disapproving expression. I had to get this over with and fast.

We had a cordial conversation. She heard me out. Perhaps my coming over helped soften her stance. I did mention my being in college with Tallat. Not deliberately. It sort of slipped out. There was no immediate reaction. She knew my ancestry. Her own *'samdhi'* (daughter's father in law) was Noon Meem Rashid and so I guess Faiz was in her dictionary. We agreed on a mutual day and time. I walked away with a huge sense of achievement.

On the day of the recording she arrived on time. Her bouffant hair style in place. I took her into the studio and looked into the affairs of the recording getting under way. I noticed how she was watching quietly all of what was going on around her. The light men were getting frenzied and shouting instructions at and to each other. Sometimes an odd cuss word would float our way. Cameras were being aligned and wheeled into place. Audio batteries were being checked and rechecked. My collar mike kept up the tradition of "dying" as soon as I started doing a voice check. "*Madam abhi cell change kiya hai*" (Madam I just changed the cell) the usual excuse was given by the engineer as he leapt to replace it in case I yelled at him. The set designer was looking at the set alignment through the camera view finder and messing around with a vase rearranging flowers. And of course the studio sweeper was swinging the wiper diligently, making absolutely no difference to the dust around. The studio supervisor was spraying the entire set with that horrible scented air freshener with flies still buzzing around, waiting to sit on my nose just as the camera honed into a close up. My assistant was running around like a headless chicken shouting "stand by for recording" not particularly making any difference as everyone kept up whatever they were doing at their own pace. The studio photographer was worming his way into our faces getting shots for publicity and insisting "*Madam idhar daikhain please*" (Madam look here please). It was always so embarrassing as he would take more photographs of me than the guest in the studio. I suppose most of the time he had no idea of the person opposite me and I was his direct boss anyway! I have a huge collection of such silly shots of myself gathering dust in my house which are of no particular use to me now. All of this was happening around us as Swaran Lata watched quietly and intently. I would see her eyes darting around taking in all the action. She would tilt her head to watch her face light being adjusted. She sat up to get her collar mike tested and then gave a voice test. She dabbed her face with Kleenex to take the extra shine off her nose. I felt the tension slowly ease out of her body. Her shoulders became a little more relaxed. Her face softened somewhat. Her eyes looked interested. She cleared her throat confidently. And I immediately sensed what was going on in her mind.

This seemed all so familiar to her. She was in an environment where she knew what to do. A studio with lights, cameras, microphones had been her 'second home' for decades. She was comfortable.
I asked her permission to begin. She nodded and turned her face towards me. Her eyes were now gentle. The frown on her forehead had virtually disappeared. Her professional side had taken over. She was ready.
So was I.
I asked my first question.

Moneeza Hashmi: You belonged to an orthodox Hindu family. What was it like before you got into films?

Swaran Lata: It was a very simple household where I was under many restrictions. I was not allowed to use creams or powders. I had to cover my head with a scarf. We were middle class people from an orthodox religious family where my father was very strict. If my brother's friends came over and I served them tea, my father would disapprove. Comparatively my brothers were very liberal minded. They encouraged me to see the world for myself and learn its ways.

I was only one year old when my mother died. We were five siblings and my elder brother was about 15 years old at the time. It was my brothers who raised and took care of me. My father had remarried and understandably there were a lot of crisis at home. For the youngest child (myself) these issues left lasting impressions on my young mind. Everyone was worried who would be responsible for taking care of me. But somehow I was raised by the Grace of God.

I acted in my first film called *Ishara*, and went on to become a film star. The film industry has a sort of intoxication that makes it difficult to leave.

Moneeza Hashmi: What was it like in the film industry back then?
Swaran Lata: Back then films had a lot of story value. One was cast because one was suitable for a certain role that fitted the character. I somehow got stuck with tragic roles. I really hated that. I insisted that I wanted to try lighter roles and finally got an opportunity to play that character in *Ratan*. That role had no hint of tragedy and the film did splendidly well. It was a film with a completely new cast. A distributer in Delhi, Jagat Naryain, who was a cinema owner, was asked to buy the film, because no one else wanted it. When we went to see the film he had already left the cinema saying this film is "not Ratan, it is rotten". That was a horrible thing to say and we were all devastated. He was however convinced by the producer to run it for a week. The first week was ok, the second was better. By the third week all tickets were sold out. That film eventually played for a whole year.

Moneeza Hashmi: Are you a serious person in your personal life?
Swaran Lata: I keep my distance with people. This is my nature. I mostly keep to myself, and I can't help being like that. I think your personality has an influence on the kinds of roles you are stuck with. Tragedy is something you have to feel from your heart. When I would act a

tragic scene, I would ask everyone to leave the room. I would remain silent for a few moments before so that I could actually feel the pain of that character.

Moneeza Hashmi: Did you rehearse?
Swaran Lata: I would conserve my energy and emotions for the final take. This method has helped me a lot in my career.

Moneeza Hashmi: When a woman begins a new career she finds more critics than supporters. Was it the same for you?
Swaran Lata: I didn't have many critics, because I was known to be a harsh and serious person regarding my career. I once signed a contract with *Mr. Vias*. Back then I didn't know much about dressing up or putting on makeup. When I met him I was wearing a white sari. He looked at me and thought me to be a very simple person, someone who would agree to whatever he said. One day he asked me to report to the office from 10:00 pm to 5:00 am. I took a taxi, got there and asked him what did he need me for throughout the night? I told him that I am an actress and will come to do my shoots at whatever time is required but I don't report to him personally. I returned his check and told him I didn't want to work for him anymore. He tried to cajole me. I made it clear to him that I am not the kind of person he thought I was. After that he was very careful with me. If someone wanted to come see me on the set he would caution them to keep away.

Moneeza Hashmi: You seem very disciplined. Am I correct?
Swaran Lata: Yes, I am. I inherited that from my parents. Later I also inculcated this in my household. My daughters are successful because of this discipline and so are their children. This is now habitual and I cannot change it. Dinner time at nine means dinner will be served at 9:00 pm and everyone should be present.

Moneeza Hashmi: Is Swaran Lata your real name?
Swaran Lata: Yes. When I joined the industry I was asked to change it but I refused. When I married Nazeer Sahab I changed my name to Saeeda Bano. Without that there would have

been no *kalma* and without the *kalma* there would be no marriage. Many people also know me as Saeeda Bano.

Moneeza Hashmi: How would you spend a free day if a shoot got cancelled?

Swaran Lata: I would devote that time to my children. Even during shooting breaks I would come home at least twice to check on my little ones. I did not neglect my family.

Moneeza Hashmi: Did you ever think of suggesting to them to enter the film world?

Swaran Lata: I don't consider films a bad line of work but I didn't want it for my children. Films are not a career. My sons in law are very successful in their careers. My children are focused on making careers that supplement their education.

Moneeza Hashmi: Is acting a difficult profession?

Swaran Lata: It is a very difficult profession. There is so much to learn when one is in it. There are a lot of sacrifices to be made. One needs to tolerate getting yelled at on the set. Our recording experts and even our cameramen had the authority to tell us off. Despite that we respected them tremendously.

Moneeza Hashmi: Give me an example of a time when you were yelled at.

Swaran Lata: I was working in the film called *"Ishara"* and playing a tragic scene. The director was very strict. Somehow that day I couldn't get the scene right. The director started yelling at me about how I was wasting his film with retakes. I started to cry. He immediately got the cameras rolling and asked me to say my lines. After I completed the scene he swept me off my feet! He was so happy with my performance.

Moneeza Hashmi: Why did you leave (the film industry)?

Swaran Lata: I was not happy the kind of environment it was becoming. Why should any person be in an unhappy situation? I want to stay happy in these last few years of my life. I want to be free of the he-said she-said business.

Moneeza Hashmi: You also retired from public life.
Swaran Lata: I felt there was no seriousness and commitment in it anymore. I am totally occupied with my children and their future and the future of their children. When you socialize, all you hear about are clothes, fashion and jewelry. Then there are get-togethers and clubs. I can't deal with all that any more.
I want to be free to enjoy the simplicities of life, of laughter and the joy, of not pretending to be someone I am not.

Moneeza Hashmi: You didn't have a mother growing up. Was there a void in your own life?
Swaran Lata: Yes I always felt something was missing. There is no greater relationship than that of a mother with her child. There will always be this sense of deprivation in my life, because I didn't get a mother's love. That kind of love cannot be given by anyone else.

Moneeza Hashmi: A personal question: When a woman loses her husband it is a huge tragedy, but even more tragic is when a woman loses her child. You have gone through both. How did you cope?
Swaran Lata: God has given me patience. I don't know where this patience comes from. When my husband died, I had to face many challenges, but I did. One doesn't die with their loved one. I don't believe in perishing in grief. I told myself that I must come out of this grieving process and I did.
When my daughter died at first I did not understand how this could happen to her, to me. When you have 20% burns on your body you do not die. She died because of the anesthesia dosage and the sheer negligence and incompetence of the doctors present. I saw her at the hospital and left. But was called back and in a few minutes they declared her dead. It was a huge shock.
I didn't cry. I sat with her all night and people talked about how brave I was, sitting there. Right in front of me lay my dead daughter.
Sometimes during family events like Eid, you remember and then of course there is no shame in tears.

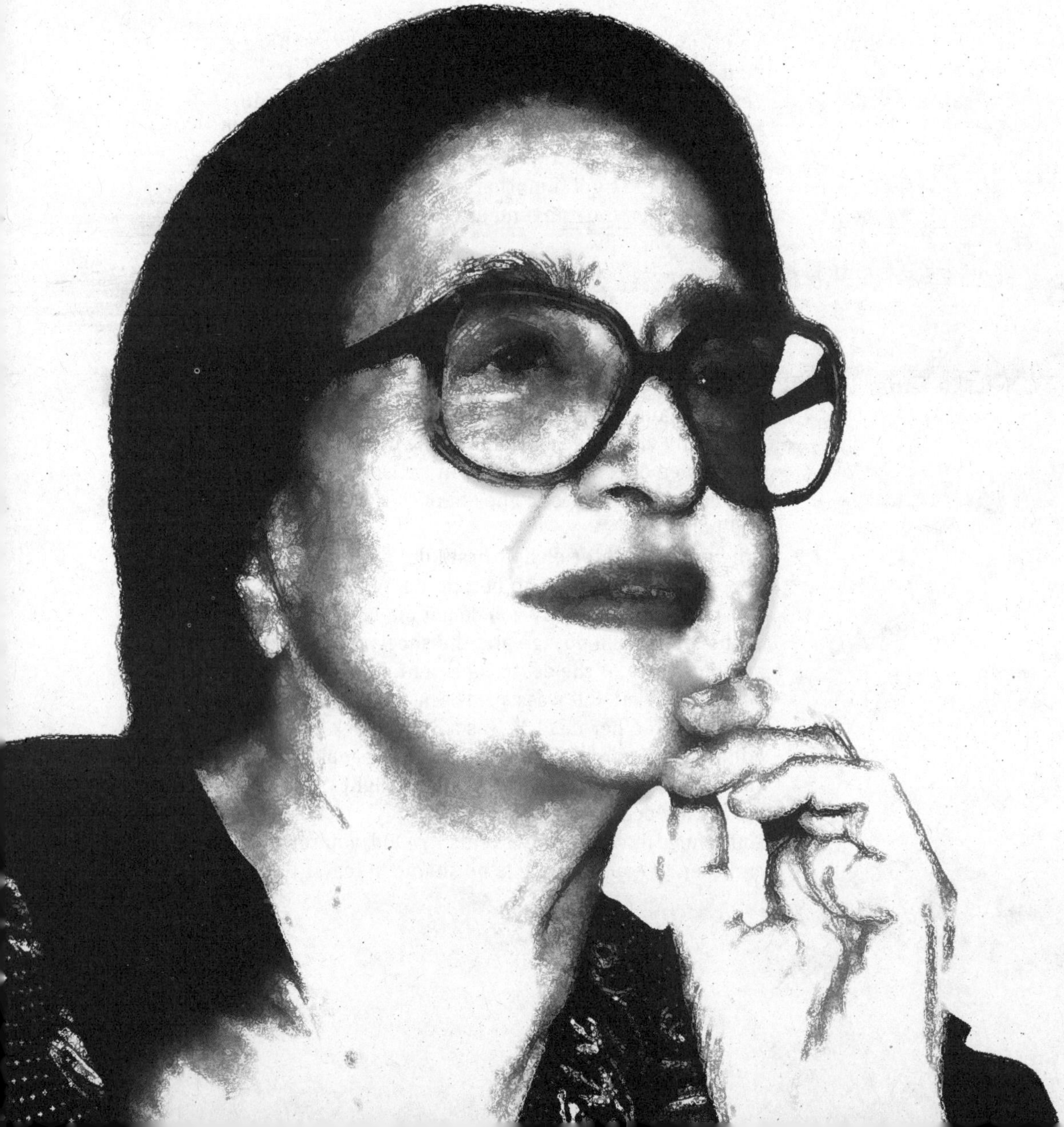

Place of Birth
Wah, Rawalpindi
Marital Status
Widowed
Number of Children
Two sons and one daughter
Activities of Interest
Trekking in the mountains and international travel
Moment of Pride
When my son, Tariq Ali became the President of Oxford University Union
Moment of disappointment
When the offices of Pakistan Times was closed down
A trait I am proud of
My work with women's rights and the trust I have gained from those women because of it
A trait I am embarrassed about
My overeating and the consecutive weight gain
The first question I would ask myself
Have I done anything meaningful in my life?

TAHIRA MAZHAR ALI

April 1997. Aunty T as I have known her all my life has been one of my inspirations and mentors for as long as I can recall. Topsy, her daughter Tauseef Hayat and Tariq Ali her son were my play mates while I was growing up. The

Mazhar Ali's were a part of our extended family. When Aba and Mama were working in *"The Pakistan Times"* we would spend countless Sundays playing in their upper flat on Nicholson Road.

Aunty T was my mother's closest friend and confidante. They would argue and disagree on almost every issue. Aunty T would call my mother "Memsahib" (Madam Foreigner) with both affection and disdain depending on what issue was being discussed. They however agreed on their passion and vision for providing a better world for the working and down-trodden women of Pakistan. The duo worked endless hours tirelessly in promoting the cause of peace across the world. They were leading rallies and marches down the Mall road, facing police squads, courting arrests, surviving lathi charges, shouting slogans, holding banners denouncing fascism and army dictatorships, motivating slum dwellers to walk with them, shaming "elite" citizens into action out of their drawing room politics, singing revolutionary songs. They were quite the odd couple both of them.

But there was another amazingly feminine side to Aunty T. I have seen her countless times at formal dinners dressed in the most beautiful chiffon sarees, hair in a bun secured with a large hair pin at the nape of her neck, a single necklace strand of pearls and diamond droplets in her ears, her sleeveless blouses causing quite a stir, her perfume swirling around her as she moved around the room. She was quite the belle of the ball where ever she was invited. She was also an "outdoor" person. Swimming and playing tennis kept her body fit and supple. We would all go to Nathiagali for the summers back then. Those were some of the happiest days of my teenage life. Aunty T would organize the long hikes up *Meeranjani Mountain*, pack picnic lunches and be up at the crack of dawn getting us all ready. She was always ahead of us all as we huffed and puffed up the steep climb. The kids would wander here and there plucking daisies, getting stung by nettle leaves, picking wild berries. We would slow the group down and get a "talking to" by Aunty T who did not like delays. We had a schedule to follow and she made sure we did. She was a great stickler also for time. Her dinners were early. Her breakfasts were almost at the crack of dawn. She was an early riser and went to bed accordingly. Inviting her over for a meal was quite an ordeal. She wanted to know what time would the dinner be served and make her entrance accordingly. If it was a late dinner she would eat at home and arrive. No one was allowed to mess with her schedules. She belonged to the "old guard" of principled and disciplined people, who never compromised, never gave up hope, never took orders lying down, never bowed down to pressures or political pressures, never asked for favours, were never afraid of speaking their mind no matter who asked the question, and most importantly were always ready to serve the needy and work with them side by side.. I went with her to Moscow in 1987 to attend the World Congress of Women. The leader of our delegation was Begum Zari Sarfaraz. That whole trip was an eye opener for me. I was probably the youngest in the group and totally in awe of all the "heavy weights" in the group. I was totally amazed at the reception Aunty T got from the Soviet government representatives. She was obviously very well respected in that country. She spoke her mind with candour and confidence and mingled with delegates from all over the world with ease and cordiality. Not a very religious person herself I remember, I went to pay my respects to her when I was going on Haj. She chuckled and said "*Kyun 900 choohay kha liyay hain?*" (Have you eaten the 900 mice?) I asked for her blessings and she laughed and said' Why me?I don't think my prayers will be of much use!"

Her astonishing faith in the women of Pakistan and their strength has always inspired me. Once I asked her if she was optimistic about the future of us women. She remarked "When you look at it in reference to days or weeks it certainly looks static. But when I look over my shoulder and view the years gone by I am certain we are progressing. Slowly but surely moving forward". For her the glass would always be half full, never half empty.

She was so proud of my achievements and was one of my staunchest supporters when I was appointed General Manager of PTV Lahore. She came for a recording and saw the cleanliness all around and said "Only you could have done it! I tell everyone she is one tough lady!"

Sitting across her formally as we started recording the interview, made me nervous. How and where do I start?Actually I knew so little of her political upbringing and family life before she got married that after the first question I was just intrigued to know more about her life. I was bowled over to know how she got married. Uncle Mazhar was such a strict laced person I recall. Could he have eloped with his young cousin barely out of her teens? But who could have resisted Aunty T I thought... If she was such a dynamic person when I knew her in her middle age she must have been a fireball when she was younger!

Moneeza Hashmi: Tahira Mazhar today has political astuteness, she raises her voice for women's rights, she opposes oppression in whichever and however form she sees it. I want to know of Tahira in her childhood. What were you like when you were a young girl?

Tahira Mazhar: I was aware of what I wanted to become very early in my life because I was growing up during the peak of the anti-imperialist movement. I developed an understanding in school that the people who were a part of this

movement were worthy people. They spoke to us of freedom. At the time I was about 13 years old.
But my main influence at the time was Mazhar, (my cousin and later my husband) because he was the President of sthe All India Student Federation. My older cousins would praise him a lot. We would argue about this movement with my father, because he was against it. It was however one of those movements that involved an active participation from women.

Moneeza Hashmi: You probably should have been playing with dolls and day dreaming in those days.

Tahira Mazhar: Doll weddings were very much part of my life then too. Syed Maratab's daughter, Sarwat once had a bash for 100 people when her doll got married. There used to be wedding bands and all of that stuff. However, immediately after this phase I knew that I would get involved in politics.

Moneeza Hashmi: What kind of values were you brought up with?

Tahira Mazhar: I was taught to respect elders, to respect all religions. There was much diversity and tolerance in those days. I was friends with Sikhs, Parsees, Hindus and Christians. Also there was to be no talk that would infuriate anyone about their personal religious beliefs.
Ramazan in our household was a time of great festivity because we would invite everyone over for *Iftari*. We competed with our relatives about who cooked better food. We'd wake up for *sehri*, regardless of whether we were fasting or not, and we'd just talk or go for a drive. It was loads of fun.
We are not *Shias* but we respected the sect so much that there was no music in our house for the first 10 days of *Muharrum*. That atmosphere is not present anymore. The other thing in terms of values I remember is that in our house no one ever discussed how much money was being earned. I recall when my father got up from the dinner table we would all rush to wash his hands. No one does that now. Even when elders walk into a room, the youngsters remain seated. I thought those were charming times wen younger people stood up as

	an adult walked in. It was respectful. I do this even today
Moneeza Hashmi:	Your family has been a political one. Your father was united Punjab's Chief Minister. There must have been politicians and political talk in your house constantly. You've also met Mohammad Ali Jinnah and Jawaherlal Nehru. Was that why you became so interested in politics?
Tahira Mazhar:	The exposure to our politician guests certainly helped. For instance when Mr. Jinnah would come to our house my father would ask me to join them at the dinner table. My mother however, was in *purdah*. Interestingly in our household the girls got more attention and preference than boys. When guests came, they knew us girls by name but not the boys. It made me feel very proud to strike conversations with Mr. Jinnah. Mr. Nehru likewise was a good conversationalist.
Moneeza Hashmi:	Why did you become a politician, why not a doctor or a simple housewife?
Tahira Mazhar:	We all knew how to do some cooking so I suppose we were partly all housewives to begin with. I was married when I was 17 years old and since I was marrying a political man; my life would be a political one. That was for sure. And this politics would be the kind I approved of politics of and for poor people;
Moneeza Hashmi:	This is incredibly demanding work. You need to be on the move constantly, meeting people and persuading them to think a certain way. How did in you overcome clashes at home if there were any?
Tahira Mazhar:	We were not very financially stable at first. We lived in the village after we got married. Mazhar was leading the peasants committee. I wasn't too active then, but I gradually started to interact with their wives and listen to their voices. Mostly my support was for Mazhar. I would help him prepare for his long trips, sometimes overnight and sometimes two days. At that time I learnt a lot about how to deal with people. Later it became a relatively smooth process for me to

	represent the peasant and down trodden women because I knew their language. I was very comfortable with them.
Moneeza Hashmi:	Were there any restrictions from Mr. Mazhar?
Tahira Mazhar:	Yes. He expected me to be home when the children returned from school. I then scheduled all my meetings outside that time. The moment he was out of the house and the kids were in school, I would get on my bicycle and visit areas like *Garih Shahu* and *Dharampura* for my work.
Moneeza Hashmi:	On one hand you were the daughter of the Chief Minister, and on the other you were cycling on your own to meet these workers. Quite a contradiction wouldn't you say?
Tahira Mazhar:	That gap closed when I married Mazhar. He was very close to the communist party. My father cautioned me that life would be very tough because I had been brought up in a home where we had all luxuries. But I knew who I was from within and knew I could face those challenges. We survived on very little money. We grew our own vegetables and mangoes and didn't have money to spend on other kinds of food. We ate *saag* almost every day, and if we wanted a change, we cooked *daal* instead. My son Tariq was about one and a half years old by then. For him we would chalk out a very balanced diet of eggs and fruit, but for us, we stuck to saag. People who came to stay at our house would go back yelling they did not want to eat saag again ever!
Moneeza Hashmi:	When were the times when you felt down and out?
Tahira Mazhar:	We were down and out a lot, but mostly it hurt when they started oppressing our children. *Tariq* was 15 or so years old, when he made a comment about democracy. This was during Ayub Khan's regime. He was expelled from school and barred from taking his exams. I was appalled. This was a country where no one was safe, where even children were not allowed to express themselves. In a dictatorship, your differences of opinion with the government were not allowed to be expressed. If you spoke your mind, you were considered an enemy

of the state. They confined you and your thoughts. The other infuriating thing was the thought that we must put an end to this revisionism of history. If someone had contributed, give them credit, regardless of how much you liked them or not. And again if you believed in something, then you had to fight for it. You must fight for what you believe in. When it is a question of the improvement of your country, you have to take decisions bravely.

Moneeza Hashmi: Pakistan's politics changes faces and values. One tends to give up on it after a while. But you never gave up?

Tahira Mazhar: Our politics was different. It wasn't power politics to get us into important positions. It was issue based and focused politics. We starved but we never played power politics. I wouldn't mind having power, but that power should be able to do something for the people of this country. To stand with the people in the same row and put their demands forward is my kind of politics. Power is not for me to construct two more houses for myself. That's what it's like in Pakistan: I want to be an MPA and I want a couple of houses.

Moneeza Hashmi: You made the first organization for women in Pakistan called the Democratic Women's Federation. This organization worked towards the welfare of women. What kind of work did you accomplish under this organization?

Tahira Mazhar: We have worked very hard with Trade Unions. We got 600,000 signatures for peace to a conference in 1952. That was a campaign against the atom bomb. We were recognized internationally as the country with the most signatures. Peace is still on my agenda. I work for this cause even today.

Moneeza Hashmi: You travel and meet women in remote areas. You communicate and educate them about their rights. Does the average Pakistani woman have that capacity to understand what is good and bad for her? Tahira

Mazhar: You will be surprised how aware they are about their rights. They don't want to be half witnesses, they want equality. They are far more aware now than they were before, but it is still not at a satisfactory level. This will only happen when this awareness is brought into the curriculum. I have conducted a survey in the northern areas, particularly Nathiagali. This is a place where men walk in front and the women behind. Here if you take a picture of a woman they confiscate your camera. I went to a village and asked them what they wanted most for themselves. They said they wanted schools for their daughters. I was amazed at their ambitions for their girl children. The women asked for gas cylinders, so they could stop cutting down trees to use for firewood. These women were extremely confident. They knew what they were talking about.

The younger boys who had completed their FA degrees said they wanted a medical college in Abbotabad. They wanted to study there and come back to their own areas and practice. The peasants and farmers said the government had once given them a loan of Rs. 10,000 when floods damaged their houses. Now that loan has grown to Rs. 30,000. Their children were holding onto my legs and weeping asking; how they would repay the loans since their father had died. I told them to write a letter to the government. What else could I say?

Why is it that rich people get millions written off in loans and poor people are dragged through the mud to pay back? The entire area had a loan of only about Rs. 600,000. We did manage to get at least the interest waived off. That is why I still work, because I hate to see any kind of injustice.

Moneeza Hashmi: Your grandchildren are now working with you in this field. Don't you want to retire?

Tahira Mazhar: I will retire when I am in my grave. When I cannot work anymore I will retire. I can however, never retire from politics. This is an area in which you continue to work till your last day.

I have faced so many disappointments. We all have. We had big dreams for this country. We wanted to make Punjab and Lahore particularly the Switzerland of the

East. The first two months of Pakistan's creation was full of euphoria. People worked with such passion. Only two months later we all discovered how this country was full of corruption.

People encroached on land that was not lawfully theirs. Now corruption is very blatant.

Our struggle is to highlight this wherever and whenever we can. And for this we are unfortunately called "unpatriotic".

Moneeza Hashmi: It must be very difficult to work under these circumstances?

Tahira Mazhar: Indeed it is. However the people I am working for makes it easy for me. When people tell me I have been a support to them throughout their lifetime, there is no greater satisfaction for me.

Moneeza Hashmi: Do you feel that something was left undone while you worked for this cause?

Tahira Mazhar: No, I paid complete attention to my home side by side. I gave my children enough attention too.

Women need to take time out for their children, especially women who work need to specially prioritize between their professional and domestic lives. Women need to be at home and be that nurturer for the kids. I cook for the pleasure of feeding my children whatever they loved to eat. Some women think that this part of life should not exist. They should realize these are the small pleasures without which there is no life.

And without these pleasurable experiences, there is no real happiness.

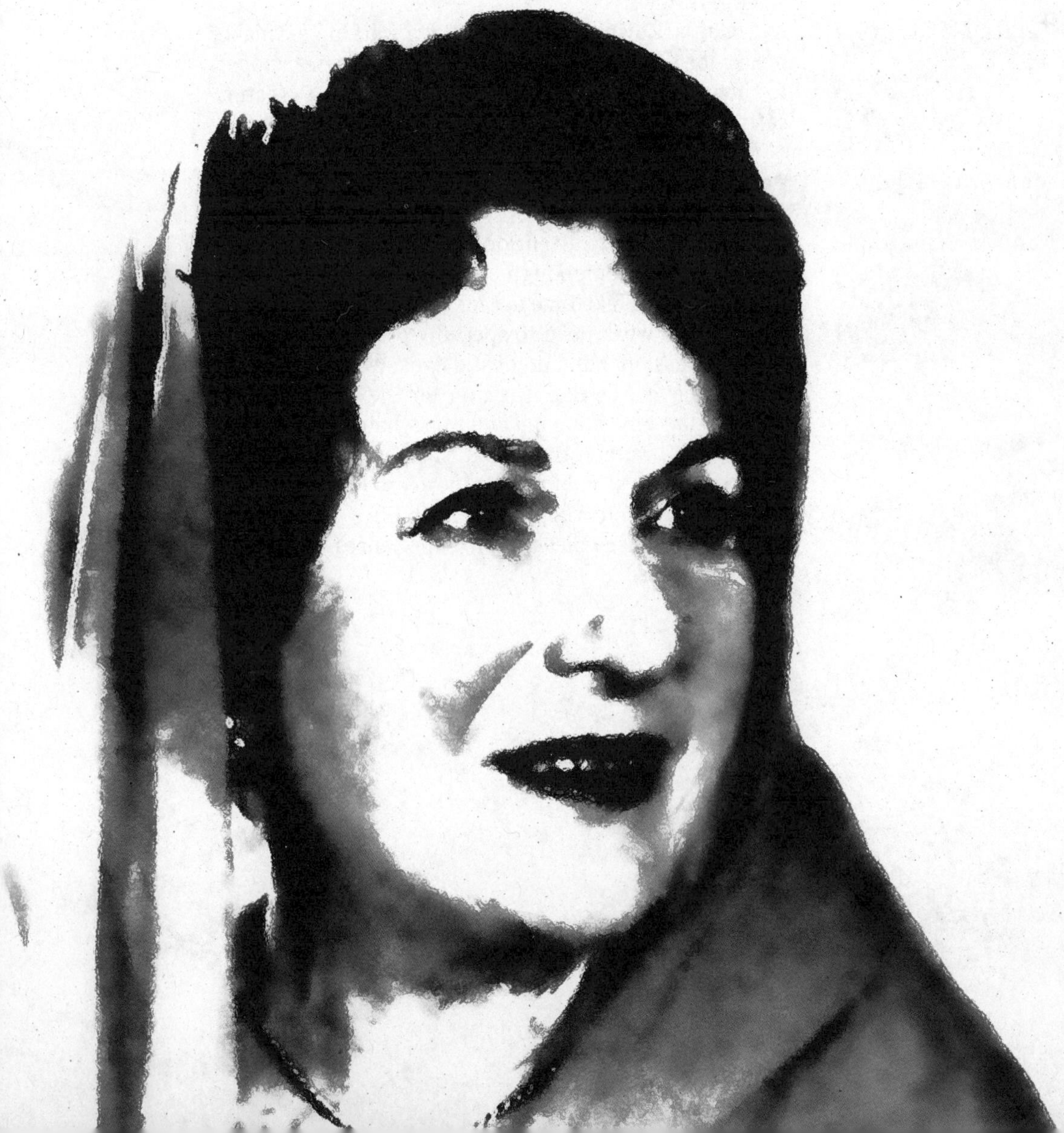

Place of Birth
Austria
Marital Status
Married
Number of Children
None
Area of Personal Interest
Hiking, Painting and Reading
Moment of Pride
When I got the Nishan-e-Haider from President Ayub Khan after working for the earthquake survivors in the mountains
Moment of disappointment
I do get sad but try to keep busy in doing something or the other
A trait I am proud of
I am a very objective person
A trait I could do without
I do not concentrate on any single one of my talents
The first question I would ask myself
Sometimes I feel depressed at not having done enough for other people.

VIQAR-UN-NISA NOON

January 1998. As a child I can remember her red chestnut short curly hair, bright shining eyes, flowing chiffon sarees in gorgeous bright colours, rings sparkling on her fingers and her smile! That was most clearly etched in my memory and still is. It captured your attention immediately because it was warm, genuine and so cheerful. When she entered a room, Aunty Vicki completely took it over! She flitted from person to person, smiling, joking, giggling! Her perfume floated alongside her as she moved about. "Darling, how lovely to see you again!" was her pet phrase for all and sundry! My mother would be quite amused watching the reactions of the wives of the "*darlings*" as Vicki moved about the room.

I lost touch with her for years after the 60s when we moved first to London and then onto Karachi. Even after my parents spent a few years in Islamabad before moving back to Lahore I never ran into her although I believe she was in the capital as a Minister of Tourism.

After I decided to record an interview with her and set it up through PTV Islamabad I was not quite sure how I would approach her or to tell you the truth how I would find her after all the years in between. I remembered her as a warm and loveable person, easy to be with and talk to. No pretences. She never put on airs. She was not highly educated and most definitely not apologetic about it. She carried herself with grace making up for all her shortcomings by using her feminine charms and those she had plenty of! She was no "fluff". I was told by the persons she worked with that she could be very gentle but most persuasive. She was no "push over". She meant what she said and stuck to her guns politely and with grace. She never threw her weight around nor flaunted her family connections in public.

Once the equipment was set up I asked the servant to inform Begum Sahiba of our presence.

The door opened and she swept in. Her bright blue chiffon sari twirling around her. A huge shining brooch pinned on her shoulder to keep the "*pallu*" (sari edge) in place. Eyes twinkling. Auburn hair with curls in place, freshly shampooed and set. Diamonds glittering on her ears. Bright red nails neatly manicured. And her smile! Still in place after all this time. Cheerful and welcoming as always.

"Darling" she said, "How have you been?" as if we were meeting after only a short separation. The years just disappeared. Aunty Vicki had bowled me over yet again!!

We sat down in her very elegant drawing room to begin our conversation. As we were being wired she was smiling and "cooing" at the technical staff. I thought to myself," Heck! Other than knowing her as "Aunty Vicki" I don't have a clue what to ask her!" I have had these blank moments several times before but somehow have still managed to pull off a pretty reasonable discussion. It was too late in the day now anyway so I decided to let Vicki lead me. And lead me she did. An excellent conversationalist, an amicable personality, a polite, cheerful demeanor, and a pretty face, Vicki had them all. The hour was over before I knew it!

Moneeza Hashmi: How did you end up in this part of the world? I know I am not the only person who would like to ask this question!

Viqar-un-Nisa Noon: I met Feroz Khan Noon when he was the Indian High Commissioner in London. I was very young at the time. I remember I was very impressed by his personality. He was charming and good looking. And he happened to be in a very high position. I will be very honest and say this combination impresses most people, especially young people like me. We met at an ordinary tennis party, nothing special. He went home on leave and when he came back after a few months he got in touch with me. I think I had made an impression on him. From there things speeded up. We became very good friends. I was only 19 years old at the time and very shy and nervous at the thought of marriage but I was encouraged by a very beautiful woman whom I worked with in a canteen in London. I was working of course like all other teenagers at the time. She was a beautiful actress called Virginia Chel who knew the *Mahraja of Jaipur* very well.
She said to me 'Vick' "if you ever got the chance to marry this man, for God's sake do so because it will be the biggest adventure in your life. It is going to be a life full of adventure" and she was absolutely right!

Moneeza Hashmi: What were your first impressions about this part of the world?

Viqar-un-Nisa Noon: I once made a very stupid remark when I landed here. I said "My God there are so many Indians here!" Only afterwards did I realize how silly a remark that was! But I was lucky. I came to live in a place which at that time was the imperial city of Delhi. It was an easy place for me to live in and easy for me to get used to. We socialized with mostly very high powered Europeans and Indians. I found I could talk to and had a lot in common with them. There was a lot to learn from them which I did. The women who were my husband's colleagues were very kind to me. Instead of ignoring me they took me under their wing and directed me how to sit, where to go etc.
I was very fortunate that my husband being very liberal

and worldly wise would be highly amused person when things didn't go right. He never stopped me from doing anything I wanted to.

He was my guide and my philosopher and I learned a lot from him. And in his company. I thank God that He was so good to me to bring me into contact with this wonderful man who married me. We were together for 25 years until he died.

Moneeza Hashmi: You were here in the subcontinent when times can be described as "very exciting".

Viqar-un-Nisa Noon: Those were indeed very exciting times but I did not quite understand what was happening around me. I wasn't a very intellectual woman, but I came from a group of left wingers in Bloomsbury.

When I arrived I heard people talking about a state built on a religion which in those days was not understandable. Today you can understand it but we were very different those days in the 1940s. Today the world has become quite different. Back then it was "middle-aged". I couldn't understand how you could build a state based on a religion. You see before you a Vicki Noon who had to work herself through with the help of one the greatest leaders of that time, Mr. Jinnah himself. I was very lucky that I got to know him well. He came to visit Feroz frequently because Feroz was a Muslim Leaguer and he was in Government and he was Jinnah's man.

People don't realize how important it was for young people back then to talk to Mr. Jinnah. He had come to know that he would not live very long. He also realized that the youngsters he was going to talk to would be the ones who would be speaking about him 50 years later as I am doing now. So he took the trouble of talking to me. He was very kind and very charming. He was also a very patient man.

Moneeza Hashmi: Then Pakistan was created and you became the wife of the Prime Minister.

Viqar-un-Nisa Noon: I was the wife of the Governor. I was the wife of the Chief Minister and then I was the wife of the Prime Minister.

Moneeza Hashmi:	It must have been a very enviable position.
Viqar-un-Nisa Noon:	You really think so?
Moneeza Hashmi:	I don't know. You tell me, wasn't it?
Viqar-un-Nisa Noon:	No. It was not an enviable position. In fact for me it was a ghastly position, because I didn't have the hide of a rhinoceros. If you are in politics there is a lot of nastiness that comes with it and a lot of people accuse you of things which are absolute lies. That is politics. And I was not made for that. I am one of those people who if I see two people on the road I will try to avoid them rather than be curious about what is happening. I am not the kind of person who is interested in any kind of *tamasha* or drama. I almost had a nervous breakdown. I was always very worried. I was so upset when people said nasty things about my husband. Of course he didn't mind because he was a politician, but I minded. It was not a happy time for me at all.
Moneeza Hashmi:	Do you feel that you may have got more opportunities because you were the Prime Minister's wife or the Chief Minister's wife?
Viqar-un-Nisa Noon:	It started when my husband had nothing. I worked with Mr. Modi during the war (at the Red Cross Society). We were engaged in a war at that time. We were making simple outfits. I was just a cog in the wheel. Later when we went to East Pakistan, I still wanted to continue doing what I had been doing. They asked me to become the Chairman but I said no. I would rather be a member I said. So for a good year and a half, I was just a member of the committee though my husband was Governor there.

They wanted me to be overall incharge but I deliberately refused. Firstly because I was an importation, not a local and then I also had to get to know the place and the people first. Later Noor-ul-Amin came to my husband who was the Governor and asked him to allow me to take over the Red Crescent Society. We need her and want her to iget on with it he said.

It is the Governor who nominates someone for that position. That was the reason my husband wasn't recommending me, but when the Chief Minster asked him to do so, only then I became the Chairman of the East Pakistan Red Crescent Society or the Red Cross Society as they called it at the time.

I was able to do quite a lot I must say. I don't want to hide my light under a bushel because that is one thing I really did well. I really organized the Red Crescent Society, East as well as West Pakistan.

Moneeza Hashmi: If I was to ask you where lie your strengths, what would you say?

Viqar-un-Nisa Noon: I am a good administrator. I am objective and I know priorities. Those are not qualities all administrators have and could be reasons for their not doing well. It is no use to help Mrs. X or Mr. Y. You have to help institutions. You can't just work with personalities. I always tried to build the institutions.

I will give you an example. A girl came to me when my husband was the Chief Minister of Punjab and told me both she and her husband were government servants and were posted far away from each other. She wanted to be posted at the same station as her husband. I pleaded her case on principle and it was accepted. Sometimes individuals with their complaints, and worries and needs give you very good ideas.

I often joked with my husband and told him I am your best informer because it is I who goes to the child welfare centers and it's I who sees the women and talk to them. They tell me what the going price of wheat and rice is which I am not sure if your commissioner is telling you correctly.

It is actually very useful if a man in public service has a daughter or grandmother (it could be anybody) who works with the people and really knows what's going on. That is a great help.

Moneeza Hashmi: You became a relatively young widow...

Viqar-un-Nisa Noon: Yes. I was warned about that before I married him. My parents were very worried, and told me that I would be alone, because the age difference between us was 27 years. But he was so young otherwise.

Moneeza Hashmi:	You stayed on in Pakistan even after his death?
Viqar-un-Nisa Noon:	The most important time of my life came after his death.

Moneeza Hashmi: And how was that?
Viqar-un-Nisa Noon: I told you that I was unhappy with his positions. I never wore his mantle and perhaps because I didn't do that is probably why people still like me. After he died I was alone. I didn't know how I was going to face living by myself.

My husband often wondered if I would stay on in Pakistan. But I would tell him, "Darling where shall I go? My roots are here". He would say "Yes. I know that you have your Red Cross and your Child Welfare Council". Although we said all that in a joke, it was all true. When you give so much of yourself to an organization and work very diligently, it does become your family. I went to work at 9:30am. I was very organized and disciplined. Although it was all voluntary work, I believe that voluntary work must also have some discipline. I had a wonderful group of voluntary workers who supported me.

Moneeza Hashmi: Is it then the work that kept you here?
Viqar-un-Nisa Noon: The work kept me here and my roots kept me here. My roots are here. I couldn't possibly go anywhere else. What would I do? Just host coffee parties?

Moneeza Hashmi: What is it that you like so much about us?
Viqar-un-Nisa Noon: I am really in love with the country. That is it.
This is why I get sad when things don't work out as they should.
Even when I go out at night in the car, and the fruit vendor's shops are still open, it's like a thousand and one nights. People are bustling about and still buying fruit at 11 O'clock at night.
It's like you want to say I have been here before. Somehow there is a connection.

Moneeza Hashmi: Do you miss home?
Viqar-un-Nisa Noon: Sometimes I miss it culturally. I love the music. We have our music players and CDs and all, but you are not where the actual music is being performed or being played. I

miss all the other cultural events. Whenever I go to Europe I get into a taxi and go from one theater to the other. That is what I would do in the evenings when I am there.
I have kept quiet lately. Last summer I was very ill. You never know at my age what may happen. Every day is a gift.

Moneeza Hashmi: I see a lot of paintings around us which you've painted yourself.

Viqar-un-Nisa Noon: There are many people who are born with any talent but never have an opportunity to find out what they can actually do. It's like being a hero: How can you know that you are one unless you are given the opportunity to prove yourself?
Yes, these are all my paintings. I don't paint anymore because I am not strong enough. But I hope that I will be strong enough again and go on painting. I love it.

Moneeza Hashmi: As a busy person who was and is organized and disciplined, how do you spend your time nowadays?

Viqar-un-Nisa Noon: That thought sometimes hangs heavy on my heart and makes me feel very lonely.
I still have certain organizations I am affiliated with, but they are just being kind to me. I don't do much work. They keep me on as the President because they feel I still have some brains to help them. I do.

Moneeza Hashmi: You didn't have any children of your own?

Viqar-un-Nisa Noon: No I didn't. This is perhaps why I am so close to the children who are studying in my schools.

Moneeza Hashmi: As you look back, do you have any regrets?

Viqar-un-Nisa Noon: No, I had a wonderful time. I could have done better in certain areas if I had been more diligent, more hard working and not so lazy. I could have done better had I concentrated a bit more on any one aspect of whatever I wanted to do. But I am a jack of all trades and that's the trouble. Maybe it's nice to know that you can do so much in so many fields but in the long run it is not as productive as it would be if you concentrated on only

one area.
For instance if I had concentrated only on music or on my painting, I probably would have achieved more and done better.

Moneeza Hashmi: One last question, have you been ever made to feel that you were a foreigner, and this was not your country.

Viqar-un-Nisa Noon: It's very interesting that you should ask that question. Either I have been stupid and didn't understand, or it truly never existed. There are certain people I would call "grievance collectors" who go out looking for things to bother them all the time: 'She didn't look at me, they didn't get up to greet me," all that nonsense. I am not like that at all. If someone is deliberately rude, that I can understand very well, but if someone doesn't bother to talk to me or notice me, I don't take notice either.
I have never felt a foreigner here and no one ever let me feel that way or let me know. It was never conveyed to me. They may have thought that she doesn't have the right pigmentation or that sort of thing, but I don't know any of that.
I have never felt like a stranger here. It may have been my stupidity. Or it may have been actually so.

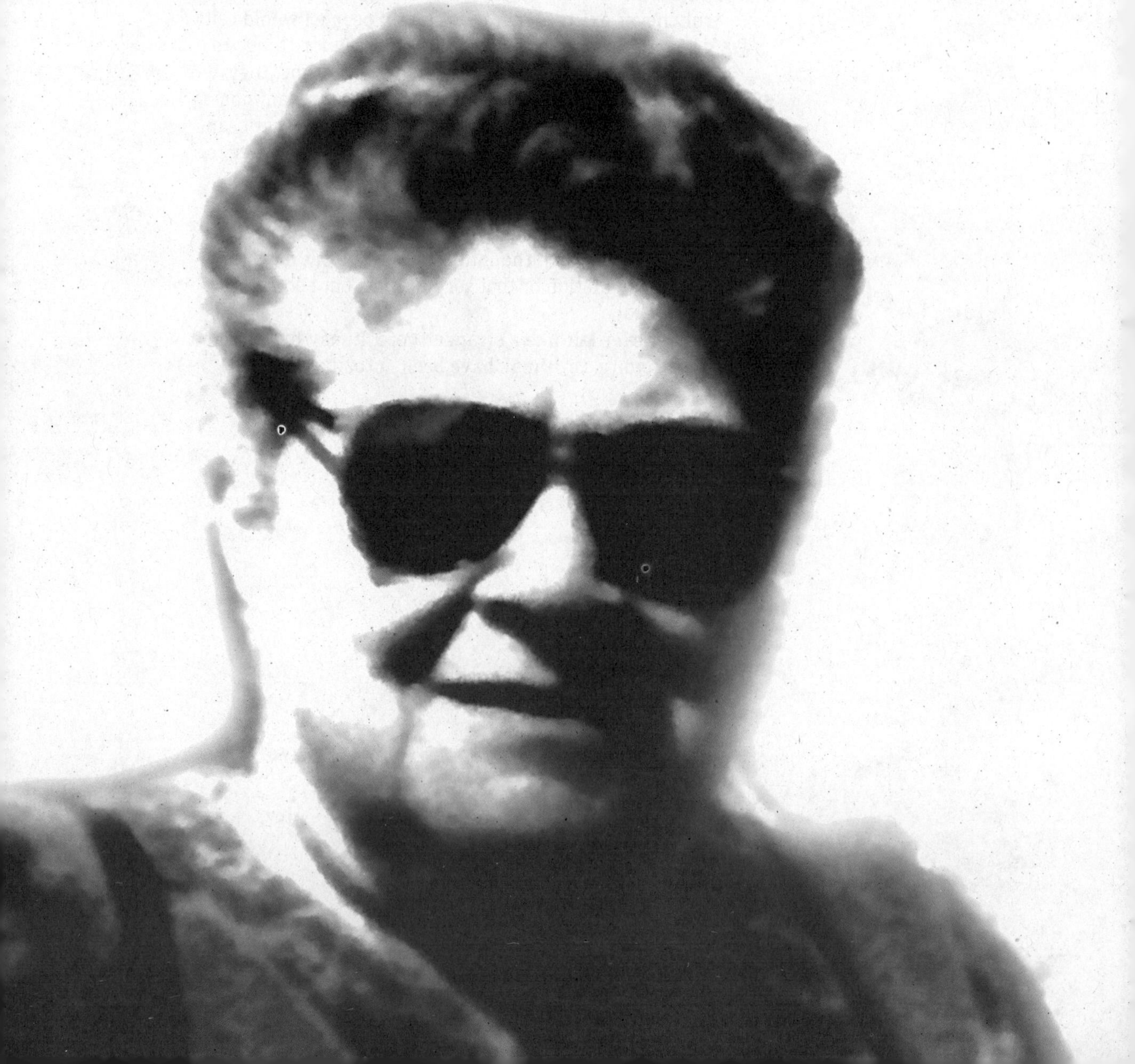

Place of Birth
Mardan
Marital Status
Unmarried
Area of Expertise
Social Work
Area of Interest
Gardening, Photography and Music
Moment of Pride
Being part of the Pakistan movement
Moment of disappointment
When Pakistan got divided
A trait I am embarrassed about
My conscience is clear
A trait I am proud of
I took part in the Pakistan movement
The first question I would ask myself
Have I achieved any purpose in my life?

ZARI SARFARAZ

May 2004. We followed her stout figure moving ahead at an impressive speed for a lady her age and weight. She was the leader of the delegation to attend The World Women Congress in 1987 of which I was also a member. Moscow was 'out of bounds' for most Pakistanis back then. Still known as United Soviet Socialist Republic (USSR) it took some courage to actually decide to take a 'peek' behind that iron curtain. For most of us (not me) this was a first ever visit to the USSR so there was a certain sense of apprehension as we gathered behind our leader of the delegation at the immigration desk. The official behind was completely masked by a dark shade. He (or she) could see us but for the person standing in front it was like looking at a black window. And yet as we all know this was defining moment when we would either be stamped in or asked to board a flight back. Hence each of us stood silent and waited trying not to look nervous or anxious which can be very difficult when no face is visible in front. Zari Apa as she was popularly known kept her face and body upright. She presented all our passports so we waited in line behind her. After a short while a stone faced officer waved us through. A visible sense of relief rippled through the group and the chatter came back. 12 women had kept quiet for too long. We just had to let go!

Zari Apa was a stern looking woman. She did have a permanent frown on her face that made her look extremely forbidding. Horn rimmed glasses. A deep voice. Always dressed simply and usually in cotton. Always in a *shalwar kameez*. Later in life she carried a cane for support while walking. Short curly hair tied at the nape of her neck with a clip. She had a complete 'no nonsense' look about her which made her a bit on '*Ustaniji*' figure. She would speak slowly, measure her words carefully, never beat around the bush but my goodness did she command attention! At the Moscow conference the Pakistani delegation was especially under scrutiny as Pakistan was still under Martial Law of General Zia ul Haq. The women of Pakistan were at their lowest ebb with the head of state ensuring that we were declared 'second class' citizens by all standards. Laws were passed to reduce our status in society. Punishments were meted out left and centre to degrade our image in our own eyes. We were hounded, made to feel pariahs, violated, gang raped, thrown into jails for crimes we could not even imagine let alone commit. Those were dark days indeed for the women of Pakistan. It was an act of sheer bravery to have undertaken the responsibility to lead this delegation and face the world congress of women and answer their hard hitting questions. But Zari Apa stood the test admirably.

I was in one of the sessions where she made an excellent presentation on the plight of her country's women. She pleaded their case of helplessness against traditions and tribal customs. She defended their lack of action. This was due to fear and total dependence on the men for their well being indeed their lives and the lives of their children. She was vocal in her criticism of the government in aiding and abetting the negative forces to suppress the rights of women. She was critical of the religious clergy for interpreting Islam 'their way'. She spoke loudly and clearly neither mincing her words nor camaflougeing her tone. She knew her facts having recently produced the first ever documentation on the plight of women across Pakistan. She knew what she was saying and why she was saying it. She highlighted many cases of courage and bravery across the country and saluted their struggles. The standing ovation at the end of that session was given not to Zari Apa but to the women she was representing, in recognition of their struggles. It was indeed an awesome moment to have a hall full of women from all over the world stand up and applaud. The mood was not of pity or sympathy but of solidarity and hope. Hope for the women of Pakistan to achieve their rightful status as equal citizens in the Islamic Republic of Pakistan. And this all happened because Zari Sarfaraz brought this to light as their champion.

I would feel somewhat intimidated in her presence. She was always most kind and gracious while addressing or talking to me. She had the highest regard for both my parents. She would praise my efforts to project a positive image of Pakistani women on TV. But I would still feel extremely small in her presence.

When we sat down to talk in her comfortable drawing room in Islamabad I wondered if I would be able to bring out all aspects of her character. She was not an easy person to talk to in real life. Her Pashtoon flavour somewhat made her aloof. She was no softie and did not open up easily. This was going to be a tough one I thought. So be it.

The next hour was an eye opener for me and also my viewers. I knew Zari Sarfaraz of today but the stories she told of how she got involved so deeply and committed to the politics in her youth were hair raising. How fortunate were these people, I thought, who were truly a part of that struggle for a separate homeland, who walked and talked with the great leaders and visionaries of those times who were actually moulding and building this country. I listened to Zari Apa humbly describe her contribution in raising an awareness in the purdah clad women of her province. I heard her relive the death of Fatima Jinnah. It was like going back in time, revisiting events which I did remember but only just. That interview of Zari Sarfaraz for me was a history lesson I will not ever forget.

Moneeza Hashmi: How did a young girl think about participating in the Pakistan movement?

Zari Sarfaraz: This story began in 1935. I was going to India with my mother. I met with Begum Tasaduq Hussain at a party in Lahore. She asked me what I was doing. I told her since my father had passed away I was working for our family business. My education had been brought to a halt as my mother wanted me to sacrifice my studies so my brothers could be educated.
Begum Sahiba told me she needed young ladies especially in the province of Sarhad to take the Pakistan movement forward. She offered me the chance to join the Muslim

League. I was a bit of a rebel, so I said I would think about it. I joined the party soon after by paying *annas* at the time and filling in a form. Two days later she asked me to accompany her and other party members to Sheikhupura. I packed some clothesand went to the railway station. In Sheikhupura speeches were made at a public gathering for women. There it was announced that a new member from Sarhad would now address the gathering. I was not prepared for this at all. I spoke whatever came to mind and returned home to Mardan soon after.That was my first induction into politics. After 6 months, I got a letter from Begum Tasaduq Hussain saying that women from all over India were collecting together under the leadership of Begum Nusrat Haroon. They wanted to form a branch of the Muslim League in Sarhad. She wanted me to help prepare for this conference.

This was impossible to do because women in this province only left their homes for weddings and funerals. It was a real challenge for me to think of a way to invite them to a conference of the Muslim League. There was hardly any awareness about politics among women at the time.

I told Begum Sahiba the only way the women would be able to attend this event in Mardan would be if they wore the *burkah*. If purdah wasn't observed the Muslim League would get a bad name. I consulted a few women who advised me to organize the conference at my home, because that would be the only place the women would be allowed to attend. In those days women would not even consider sitting on chairs. They only sat on *charpoys* (string beds).

Moneeza Hashmi: Was this part of any tradition?

Zari Sarfaraz: They considered chairs to be a western influence. Eventually I prepared everything at home. I had a stage made and laid out the charpoys. To my utter amazement about 500 women showed up. All these women were clad in white *chaadars* (head to toe cover). They had lunch and sat down to listen to the speeches.

The speakers were speaking in Urdu and these women

didn't understand one word. I ended up translating for them. That was the beginning. After that there was no looking back. We were all charged up to be part of this great movement.

Moneeza Hashmi: You said you had to abandon your studies for your brothers.

Zari Sarfaraz: When my father died one of my brothers was 9 years old and the other was 11 years old. I was about 16 years old and studying to become a doctor. At the time, land was given to landlords who worked on the land and paid the British. My mother wrote to the AC telling him that I would work in place of her husband. I knew the AC's wife. During the war we were given a supply of wool to knit scarves for the army. The AC asked his wife how someone who came from a very conservative family and was only 16 could manage the task of looking after acres of land. She convinced him that I was no ordinary girl and could do it. She asked him to try me out for a year. I thankfully managed all matters efficiently for that one year and our properties were not taken away. My education however ended.

Moneeza Hashmi: What was your family's outlook on education?

Zari Sarfaraz: My father wanted to send me to boarding school in Lahore. His elder brother convinced him about girls from our family should not go to boarding school. I had to unpack and change my plans. I was home-schooled after that.

Moneeza Hashmi: It's very interesting that you emerged from such an environment and later became part of such a historic movement.

Zari Sarfaraz: It was a challenge and I always fought hard to meet challenges. It started with public meetings and speeches. Later we went to stage civil disobediences. The Congress in Delhi sent me a new challenge. They said that women in Mardan have not come out in the streets to protest. I managed to get protests staged by women in Mardan. We started on 22nd February and ended on June 3rd when Quaid-e-Azam announced that there would be a referendum in the province of Sarhad and in Assam. Then from 3rd June to 20th July we worked for the referendum.

Moneeza Hashmi: Did you ever meet Quaid-e-Azam?
Zari Sarfaraz: I met him in 1948 during a Muslim League Council there was a reception hosted by him at the Government House. I asked Lady Haroon if I could get an autograph of the Quaid. He looked very exhausted and was reclining on a sofa. She introduced me and told him all of what I had done for the Muslim League. He said he was tired and could I give the paper to his ADC. He would sign it and send it back to me.
I had met him a few times before he came to Mardan. I had collected some money for the riots that took place between Muslims and Hindus and sent that money to Quaid-e-Azam. He sent the money back and told me to deposit the money in a Habib Bank account in Delhi. When I had deposited the money I got a letter from him. I still have that letter. He wrote that he was grateful to me and to the women of Mardan for their struggle for rights of the minority Muslim community.
Then I met him again on December 25th on his birthday at Sir Ghulam Hussain Hidayyatullah's residence. We sang a song for him at that dinner, *"Millat Key Liey Hey Ajj Tera Dumm Aye Quaid-e-Azam"*. (You live only for your people Quaid e Azam)
The third time I met him was in March 1948. He had come to Peshawar, and all the women who had participated in the cause insisted they wanted to meet him. He agreed. At that time I was the president of the Women Muslim League for the Province of Sarhad. I presented him with a garland of flowers. He was very tall so he had to bend down considerably for me to put the garland around his neck and our hands touched. All I could think of at the time was how cold his hands were. It was almost like he was dead. I then realizedthe gravity of his illness. I knew that he wouldn't live long. I really wanted to have a picture taken with him but because my thinking was very conservative, I couldn't dare ask. He told me that day: India has expelled Muslims

as if someone throws out a stone. You have a responsibility to settle and rehabilitate them. There is a lot of work to be done.
I met him in July again the same year briefly when he returned from *Ziarat* to inaugurate the State Bank. He looked even weaker then.
The fifth time I met him was after he had died. I was in Karachi. Lady Haroon woke me up and gave me the news of his demise. She asked me if I could drive her to the funeral. I agreed willingly. When we reached the governor house the ADC took us to Miss Jinnah. She was sitting with a lone lamp beside her. *Begum* Hidayatulah was with her. Miss Jinnah pointed me to an adjacent room. Lady Haroon sat with Miss Jinnah while I went inside that room. There was a nurse sitting there but there appeared to be no sign of the body. The nurse asked if I wanted to see the body. I said yes. She went to the bed and drew away the sheet. He was so emaciated that it didn't seem like there was anyone lying on the bed. I was overcome with emotion. Placed next to him were some chapters of the Quran. I started to read and cried at the same time. Before I left I noticed some medicines lying near the bedside. I picked them up as mementos. In the drawer there was a blank diary and a stamp of the Bombay High Court. I took those too. That was my last meeting with him.

Moneeza Hashmi: You still have these things with you?
Zari Sarfaraz: Yes, each one of them.

Moneeza Hashmi: Politics is a difficult field for a woman.
Zari Sarfaraz: It was particularly difficult for a woman in those days. But somehow I feel those days were better than today vis-a-vis acceptance of women in politics. During rallies no one would harass us by throwing stones or whistling or even clearing their throats. We would walk in the middle of the bazaars and people would watch in silence with respect.
Today how many women's rallies can pass peacefully through bazaars? There will be ridiculing laughter, lewd remarks and general harassment. People had more

character and a sense of values back then.

Moneeza Hashmi: Was there any opposition from your family when you stepped out in public?

Zari Sarfaraz: The family didn't protest and neither did anyone in Mardan. The feeling was when Sarfaraz Khan's daughter departs for a rally, our women will accompany her. The old and the young would be part of all the protest rallies I would arrange.

Moneeza Hashmi: That must have been a big responsibility?

Zari Sarfaraz: It was. And I was additionally responsible for getting the women safely back to their homes. Sometimes we would not be allowed to proceed forward by the police. We would have to push and shove our way forward. But it was all for a cause.

Moneeza Hashmi: You did all this based on your passion?

Zari Sarfaraz: I did. I also became a member of the assembly of the province of Sarhad, then West Pakistan. I left politics in 1960s because it had ceased to be politics. It was about thugs and goons running the show. I did not want to blemish my clean career. It was best that I made a respectable exit. After that I started doing social work.

Moneeza Hashmi: A commission was later set up for women at a time when it was difficult for women to walk with their heads high. You took that responsibility and headed that commission. You traveled all over Pakistan and wrote a detailed report on the situation of women in Pakistan. How did it happen?

Zari Sarfaraz: That is a very long story. We told the government that women had been an instrumental part of the Pakistan movement; they went to jails and faced *lathis* (batons). In the province of Sarhad they even lay on train tracks. We demanded the government should do something about their rights, especially their right to education. A commission more like a committee was formed under Justice Abdul Rashid, who was the first Chief Justice to take oath from the Quaid-e-Azam. He wrote a report which was shelved. However, later the Family Law

Ordinance was largely based on that report.
Then a committee called the Women Rights Committee was formed under Zulfiqar Ali Bhutto. I was nominated to work on this committee with Mr. Yahya Bakhtiar as Chairman. Again no action.

Sometime later I got a call informing me that I had been nominated by General Zia as Chairperson of the new Commission for Women's Rights. I wrote a letter to Salima Ahmed who was Secretary of Women's Division saying I wanted to meet the President and discuss a few issues. If my requests were accepted I would accept the position, not before. At our meeting I asked General Zia if he knew who I was and my past. I told him if he wanted a specific kind of report he would have to get it from someone else. I said I am a woman with a moderate outlook and that is what I want for the Pakistani woman.

He agreed.

Then I told him my conditions: I will not take a salary. I will not use government vehicles to travel and will take no travel money. I will not stay in a government accommodation, but just use the office facility. I told him I will cover my own expenses.

I did this because I knew the moment I accepted government funds I would be expected to fudge the report accordingly.

Then I asked to be made a Minister, so that my work would be hassle free. I told him I am not status conscious but the report demanded certain protocol. He agreed to all of that. I went to the Tribal Areas, to Dir, Swat, Balochistan, Turbat, Punjab, Azad Kashmir and Sindh. I interviewed both men and women. I recorded all the interviews on cassettes.

Moneeza Hashmi: What was the result of the report?

Zari Sarfaraz: General Zia asked me to give it to Mr. Junejo who had by then became the Prime Minister. The report was marked "Confidential For Official Use only". I asked for it to be distributed to members of the Assemblies so some work could begin based on its recommendations. The report was printed and distributed to members of the National and Provincial Assemblies. Nothing much happened.

During Benazir Bhutto's first term it was published in the National Gazette for public consumption. It is a now public document. What upsets me most however is that no recommendations from that report were ever implemented. We would be in a much better position had some positive steps been taken. Some however were implemented. For example the women's jail in Multan adopted some recommendations. Similarly when a Pakistani woman marries a non-Pakistani man she can apply for his citizenship. This too was recommended. When General Zia asked me what was my major recommendation I told him we must adopt primary education across the board for girls. This education should be co-education. According to our feedback from all provinces no one had an issue with coeducation until after class 5. We also recommended University education should be co-education as well because that is when students become most confident.

We also realized the only way to empower a woman was to give her economic independence. This was even more important than giving her an education. Women who could put even their thumb prints on checks would say their opinion was being taken seriously when making decisions because they brought in money. Two things empower women: education and financial independence.

Moneeza Hashmi: Is there a hope for a better future for our women?
Zari Sarfaraz: There is certainly hope. But the problems are far greater. These problems are not just for Pakistani women but women globally. I have traveled the world and almost everywhere problems are the same. A woman's greatest weakness is her children. If women were given guarantees that their children would not be taken from them that would solve half of their issues. We live in fear. No woman dare stand up against her husband in fear that he will take away her children. She lives in fear of a divorce.

Moneeza Hashmi: Do you miss being in politics?
Zari Sarfaraz: When I see members of the present assembly on TV I remember my time. I recall how much fierceness and strength I had when I spoke for the rights of the people and for bringing about a change. I would refuse to cast my vote if I had not been consulted on a bill or an amendment. I said I was not a rubber stamp. I had this conviction because I had no vested interest. There was no personal gain. I did not ask for ministries, permits, houses or favors. I wanted to work for Pakistan. I had the freedom of my voice and I used it. I made demands. I protested. I asked for whatever my country deserved to have. People can't talk like that now. They do not seem to have a voice. I don't understand what the reason is for such silence from our legislators.

Moneeza Hashmi: Have you ever thought you would rather have become a doctor?

Zari Sarfaraz: I still work with tuberculosis patients and do realize perhaps how useful it would have been for me to have become a doctor. My emotions can be read on my face when I visit a hospital. I want to run every hospital and help the poor get treatment. I work with patients but I have no knowledge about how to cure them. Yes. If I had been a doctor my life would have been different.

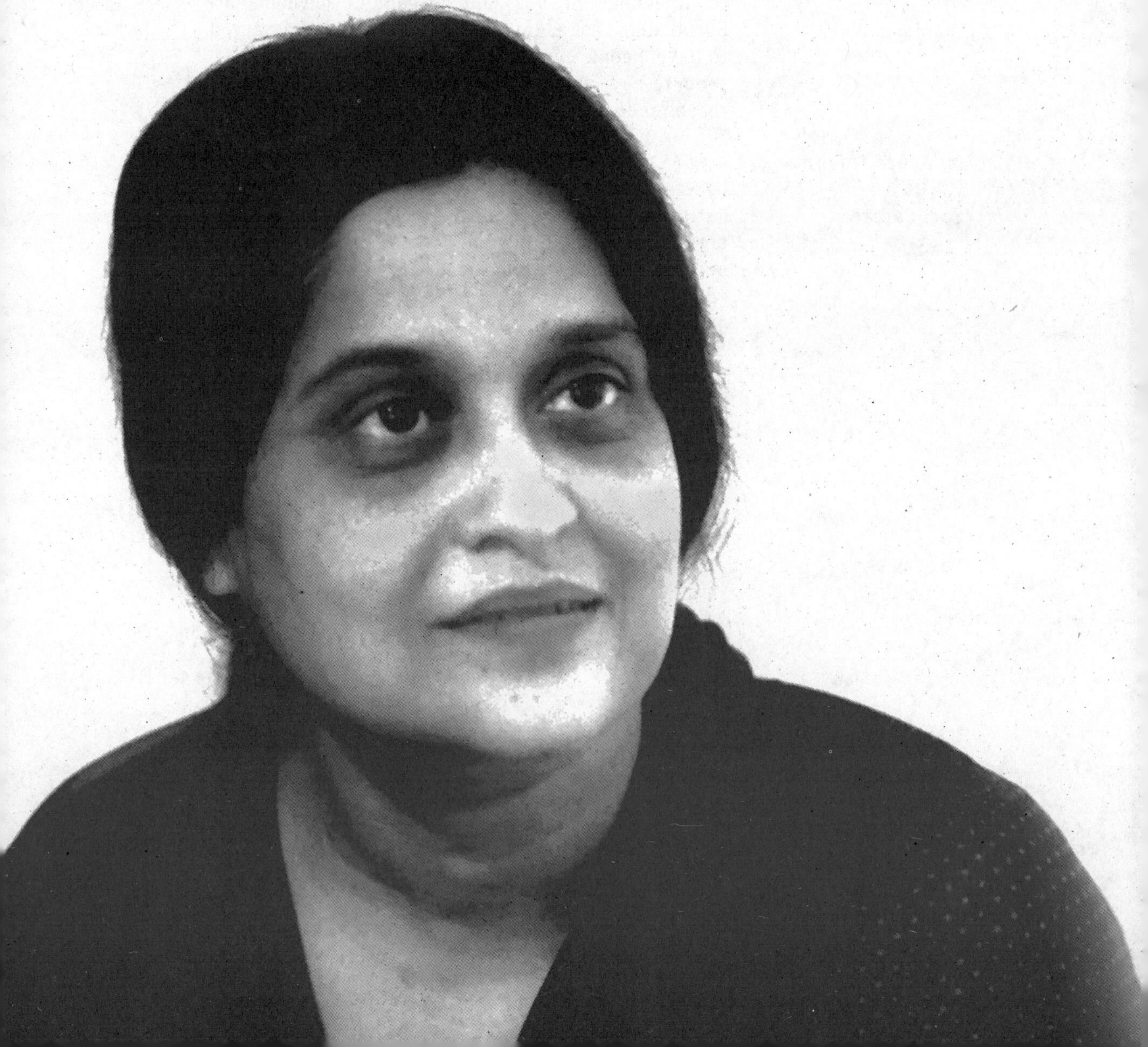

Place of Birth
Hyderabad, Deccan
Marital Status
Married
Number of Children
Two sons
Area of Personal Interest
Writing and Reading
Moment of Pride
The first time I recited at a Mushaira (Poetry Recitation)
Moment of disappointment
Many such moments in life
I am proud of
My kids, my siblings and my mother
I am not proud of
I should have written more than I did
The first question I would ask myself
Have I actually achieved something in life?

ZEHRA NIGAH

December 1997. Zehra Apa can only be described as 'extended family' when it comes to any reference to Faiz. I am not quite sure exactly when she came into my life per se but am presuming she became associated with my father and the poets 'elite fraternity' ever since she herself entered that magical world of words and expression. There were many names (and faces) that used to float in and out of our household and drawing room discussions which I would hear (and see) as and when I was around. Zehra Apa was one of them. She was around our lives for a long time before I met her formally. She was a distinct favorite of my father's. As I look back I can clearly see why.

Zehra Apa is a complete picture of dignity, genteel natured, polite, simple, almost lyrical in every way imaginable, a lilting melodious voice not just in recitation of her poetry but in general conversation, affectionate, warm-hearted and humble. Just the kind of person in whose company Faiz would be most comfortable in. Other than that she pampered and fussed over him. Again something he enjoyed no end! She was his 'younger sister' and 'guardian' rolled in one during his very trying lonely years of exile when he lived in their Knightsbridge flat for weeks on end struggling to find activities to occupy the days and nights away from family, friends and country. Zehra Apa has seen my father at his loneliest, his creativity level at a dangerous low, his heart breaking at not being able to go back to his wife and daughters, his eyes dull and sad. She along with her husband Majid Bhai supported him through those difficult days, giving him a home away from home, making him laugh, nurturing him like a child, giving him love to continue hoping. She was his anchor. I know all this to be true both from her and my mother who was not an easy person to win over. We both will remain indebted to Zehra Apa (and Majid Bhai) for this bond of love with the Faiz family that now continues with both of my sons.

Many years ago I got stranded in London when the 'roof' I was counting on suddenly evaporated and I was told to pack my bags and leave at a moment's notice. Why and how that happened best remain untold but I recall the panic at not knowing where to go as I still had a week or so before my flight back home. I called the Knightsbridge number I had and spoke to Majid Bhai. I told him I needed a place to stay and recall the lump in my throat. He called out to Zehra Apa who came the phone and without to much ado told me to get there as fast as I could. She opened the door and her arms and I knew I was safe. I was home. I spent the most wonderful week in their home, waited on hand and foot by their servant. There was always a stream of visitors coming and leaving. Some I knew. Some knew me as Faiz's daughter. The laughter and conversations went on late at night. Zehra Apa would be flitting in and out of the kitchen with snacks and food. Majid Bhai would be playing the perfect host. It was a 'happening' home if I ever saw one. I could now well understand why my father was so drawn there. Majid Bhai called it my *'mauroosi house'* (ancestral home).

I am a poet's daughter but my lack of understanding of poetry is not something I am proud of. I was never a literary person. I was (and still am) very practical. The mind for me was never a toy to play around with and create airy fairy images but an organ to exercise and fill with doable plans and to make them happen. I had no patience with wispy clouds floating around to capture and express in metaphors. I would go out to pick the daisies and make necklaces and wear them and be done with it. Poetry for me was a luxury I never had time for. But when I did read Zehra Apa's poems I felt an instant connection. Her language was simple. Her images were real. Her subject was women and their sufferings. She wrote with an understanding of the real issues.

I sat down to interview her in her tastefully decorated home in Karachi I was at a loss for words of how and where to begin. She was someone I had admired for years. But where do I begin and then a thought struck me.

Yes. I knew this elegant lady sitting in front of me.
Yes. I had enjoyed her hospitality many a time.
Yes. I knew her brothers and sisters.
But what did I know of her childhood, where she grew up, why she decided to express herself through poetry, what images came to her mind when she put a pen to paper.
Would the real Zehra Nigah please stand up?
'Madame we are ready' said the engineer in charge.

I replied, 'Roll tape'

Moneeza Hashmi: When did you discover you possessed the talent for writing poetry?

Zehra Nigah: It is the atmosphere at home which makes it possible to write or read. It is your mother, father, grandparents and everyone you know who take pleasure in reading and writing poetry. If poetry recitals called *mushairahs*, become a part of your identity in childhood you cannot but become a poet.

The one advantage I have is a good voice. I would reproduce in my own voice whatever poetry was recited in our home. In those days it was common for children to get a reward of five rupees if they succeeded in reciting a poem by Iqbal or any other classical masters of poetry. That would be tempting enough for us as children to memorize and recite long poems. By doing this we also learnt the delicate art of how to judge a good poem; we understood its structure; we put emphasis in the right places; we became aware about rhyme and balance. I learnt all this while I was growing up.

All these experiences helped in my becoming a poet. Although one's environment determines much of the sensitivity cultivated towards appreciating art and poetry, there is always of course, a natural talent which goes hand in hand.

Moneeza Hashmi:	Do you recall your first poem?
Zehra Nigah:	I don't exactly remember my first poem but I recall my elder sisters playing with their dolls and planning a wedding for them. They had bumped me off for being too small to play with them. Since I could think of no other way of becoming involved I planned on writing a poem about the wedding of these dolls. The sister who owned the groom doll or *gudda* was the one who was rude to me so in the poem I portrayed her as anold hag! Somehow I would blend words together and link as verses or stanzas of poems. Eventually my sisters started to take me seriously, and invited me to play with them. If nothing else, I would get the role of the *Maulvi Sahab* (preacher) who would conduct the proceedings of the marriage.
Moneeza Hashmi:	Do you recall your first recitation at a mushaira (public poetry gathering)?
Zehra Nigah:	I began my formal schooling after we arrived in Karachi. I had an Urdu teacher who would be very pleased (with me) because I did well in her class. She would encourage me to write and recite poems as farewells odes for teachers. One day she asked me if I wanted to attend a recital of women poets. I told her I had never recited at a public gathering before. She convinced me; got permission from my mother and off we went. It was an APWA (All Pakistan Women Association) event where I, for the first time, read my poem publically. That was a very interesting event. The men in the audience (attending this event) were segregated in an enclosed area whereas the women sat in the front listening to the recital. It was all very strange. The news of my participation reached Lahore. I received another invitation from a university to recite my poems. There was a lot of objection from various family quarters regarding how I could possibly attend a recital on my own, being a girl etc. I was fortunate to have my father's support. He encouraged me to go. He felt there was

absolutely no issue in promoting good art. But my extended family did not approve at all. They did not think it was appropriate for a girl to recite in public and that too with such enthusiasm and over excitement! My mother laid down a condition which said I could not attend unaccompanied. It was also decided that I was to wear a set uniform for the event. I suppose they wanted to ensure that I would not wear gaudy or bright clothes which could attract too much public attention. There was absoloutely no chance of my wearing any makeup at all. I was allowed to wear a white *kameez (shirt)* and *dupatta (head covering)*. The drill would be that I would arrive on stage, fold my hands, recite my 4-5 *ghazals* (poems) and leave immediately.

Moneeza Hashmi: Was there any rehearsal held at home before you left?
Zehra Nigah: No, but there was a clear understanding that the instructions given to me on what my expected behavior would have to be followed strictly to the letter. One particular such caution was issued by Jiggar Sahib himself. When Shaukat Thanvi announced my name the audience did not understand how a lady's name was possibly called. Since females had never appeared on stage to recite they wondered if I was just another announcer. When I started reciting my ghazals they were surprised that it was serious poetry! They sat electrified after the first recitation. Interestingly, their praise and encouragement were very loud and supportive. I have never got that kind of support after that from anywhere else. It turned out to be a superb experience. The year was 1953. I was later advised by elders to use a plural and inclusive expression in my verses such as, "we went and we said". They said it sounded more dignified than using the first person which I used to do then.

Moneeza Hashmi: What inspires you to write?
Zehra Nigah: Inspiration is present in the environment in which you are brought up, provided you have the intellectual capacity to grasp and understand that inspiration. What we experienced was very amazing because we saw

nothing less than a revolution at that time. A fourteen year old child witnessed a society that was uprooted and replanted in a new place called Pakistan. I am talking about the 1947 era and the migration that we witnessed. As kids we always imagined we had come to Karachi temporarily, on some sort of a picnic, and we would eventually return to our home in Hyderabad (India). Then one day our mother sat us down and explained that this was a permanent move and our new home and now our country. Our greatest asset at the time was "hope". There was a distinct belief that problems experienced today were not going to continue in the future. This is precisely the inspiration which sparked the creativity in me and brought out the same themes in my poetry:

A ray of hope
spiring for greatness
Found within the toils
Are life's ebbs and flows
Walk together, each step with care
Troubles are but gone
And just a few feet ahead
Lies the dust of our destination
Thoughts of this world
Of beginnings and ends
And what betrayals have we born
For our loyalty
What of love and care
Togetherness and the separation
When there is still a wanton need
Lingering for life itself

Now imagine this was the level of expression of a very young girl who was reciting poetry. It was considered very "avant guarde" at the time. There was also a seeming agreement among some people that my brother actually wrote the poems and I merely recited them. Women have been writing amazingly well. So much so, that people are actually now scared of their success.

Moneeza Hashmi: How would you actually write your poetry?

Zehra Nigah: It is a simple reality that if you are a poet you'll yearn to write poems. This situation was expressed to me rather articulately by your father. He said "Zehra Begum, one has to work hard, and working hard is an intrinsic part of this success." He would read to me a stanza of Atish which went: *"Shere kehna hey Aatish murashka-saaz ka."*

The fundamental fact of the matter is that there should be much that one wants to say, and all at the same time, it has to be backed by a passion to express one's thoughts. Only then can you fuel your intellectual faculties and get to work. It's extremely easy to write mediocre poetry. Writing a bad ghazal is even easier because at least in a good poem you have to work hard. This is why for the longest time I had absolutely nothing to say. And when I did, I published my book.

Moneeza Hashmi: If you have an image in your mind that you have to translate on paper, how would you go about that process?

Zehra Nigah: The creative process or the flow of creativity is brought into action through a personal and subjective method where each poet relies on his or her own devices. Once a lady invited me to her house because it had beautiful exterior with springs and mountains where she thought I would be inspired to write poetry. I explained to her that our country's most beautiful poetry has emerged from a small house where the noise and ruckus of the road was everywhere. Beautiful scenes and a beautiful ambiance is not a prerequisite for beautiful poetry. The only need is for you to have something to say: something that bothers you from inside be it love, a struggle, principles, a party line all these things blend into the need for you to say something meaningful. However the base of all these things is love itself from which all these other branches bloom.

Sometimes it would appear as if you've written four stanzas too soon. You are your best judge and critic. Something hits you right at that spot and you just know when you've written well. Similarly when you're working on commission, you immediately become aware of a betrayal of the self too. It does not sound right and then

you get to work editing that piece.
When a poet completes a piece of work that is worthy and beautiful, there is no feeling to express that satisfaction and elation.

Moneeza Hashmi: A woman who is a mother and a wife doesn't get the time or the opportunity to lock herself up in a room and work on her craft. How did you manage it?

Zehra Nigah: When I had two small children, the first thing I did was pack away my poetry books. I did not want my books, which were my assets, to weigh heavily on my children. I put the needs of my children first. Then there was the need to ensure that my husband was alright and everything else was in place. The act of not writing or the act of writing, are completely independent notions from the needs of your household, children or husband. One can take time out to write no matter how occupied you are. Writing is a kind of disease that has no cure. If you know how to write, there is a chance that the disease may distance itself for a while but it will certainly return.

Moneeza Hashmi: The caricature of a poet is of ruffled hair and a confused face, lost in a world of his own. What would you say about that?

Zehra Nigah: Dramatizing a picture of an intellectual is very easy. The first thing to emulate is messy hair, the second would be to stop showering, and then ripped clothes and then to surround one's self in a world of fantasy. You've seen your father. He was such a neat man. Mr. Qasm is another example. He led an immaculate life with everything measured. So many poets are like that.

Moneeza Hashmi: You've had an opportunity to meet many poets that are considered to be titans in this field. What did you learn from them?

Zehra Nigah: Many things. We were lucky enough to have an opportunity to be with Faiz Sahab, although he was in a league of his own. He told me to stop bothering about the small stuff in life. I asked him how was I to do that, and he responded, "Why don't you switch off?" Then he explained that a poet's mind is not supposed to be engulfed by the trivialities of life and must be saved from its disastrous banality by turning off that switch in the mind. I have since, learned the ability to "switch off."

Jiggar Sahab told me that a woman is a thing to revere. So I should stop stooping down to greet and thank people. But, I protested, that people who praise me would be annoyed. 'No', he said, 'they might be a bit surprised at first, but they would get used to it. And before you leave, nod slightly and acknowledge their praise'. These were invaluable small pieces of advice that have added so much to my style.

Then there was the common term of using the words mukarar /irshad (encore) to request a poet to repeat a verse or poem. I was advised by Jiggar Saab to read only the one that I wanted to repeat, otherwise not to repeat on every public demand.

In fact Josh Sahab once told me off for not acknowledging his praise. He said, "You should realize that big names such as us are praising you and you're not even listening to us". When I got to know Josh Sahab closely later I was enamored by him - there is a whole school of thought which follows him.

Those were the kind of people who should have been valued and prized by the people of this country, but unfortunately we have not done that.

Moneeza Hashmi: Your children are older now and settled abroad. How do you deal with your loneliness?

Zehra Nigah: I miss both Faiz Sahab and Majid (husband). Faiz Sahab had this habit of being quiet, especially when he got back from Beirut or London. He'd close his book and stare into space. I would then ask him if he got fearful of that loneliness that so often hangs around poets. He said, "yes and no," and he said that he had a trick to keep it at bay. I asked Majid about the trick Faiz Sahab mentioned. He told me Faiz Sahab actually enjoys his own company. What better companion can you have? If you can master that thought then there is very little loneliness can do. Of the few last things Majid taught

	me was not to sit and wait for someone to give me company. Now even when I am alone, I don't feel lonely. I am content.
Moneeza Hashmi:	Will you read for me?
Zehra Nigah:	There is a poem called *Raastey*

Abb talaq in nigahon mey mehfooz hain
Seedey Saadey vo veeran sey raastey
Apney humraaz, Apney shanasaa
Apney dukh, Apney sukh, dono pehchantey

Dekhtey dekhtey aik pull bangaya
Aur samandar ka paani, Samandar sey khichker
Phir Samandar bangaya

Dhoop sey taap key
Mitti ka geela badan phir jag utha, tan gaya
Ghair umakney lagey, Log bassney lagey
Phool khilney lagey, log hassney lagey

Abb kahi koi tanha sarak
Koi veeran raasta, ubharta nahi
Koi dildar saya bulata nahi
Koi ghamkhar raasta nikalta nahi

205

BIOGRAPHIES

Abida Parveen

Abida Parveen, today, is undoubtedly one of the world's greatest folk singers, specializing in sufi music. Born in 1954 in Larkana, Sindh, she grew up in a family which held the sufi saints in high regard, and therefore, their shrines and kalams formed the basic foundations of her childhood. Her father, Ustad Ghulam Haider, whom she calls "Baba Sain", was also a singer and had his own music school, where she got her initial music training. Later, Ustad Salamat Ali Khan of the Sham Chaurasia Gharana, became her mentor. A few years ago, she formally accepted the tutelage of Muhammad Najeeb Sultan, who she acknowledges as her spiritual master. One of the most revered sufi vocalists of present times, Abida Parveen sings mostly ghazals and kafis in Sindhi, Urdu, Punjabi, Saraiki and Persian.

Abida Parveen began her professional career in 1973 from Radio Pakistan, Hyderabad with a Sindhi song, "*Tuhinje zulfan jay band kamand widha*". She married the late Ghulam Hussain Sheikh, a senior producer in Radio Pakistan, who became her mentor and manager. Deeply religious, profoundly humble and quietly reserved, Parveen is known for her moving performances, whether in small shrines or the world's biggest concert halls, where she gives herself up to the music, enthralling her audiences.

She is the recipient of the President's Pride of Performance (1982) and the *Sitara-e-Imtiaz* (2005).

Babra Sharif

Babra Sharif is an actor, model and entrepreneur, who is as famous for her timeless beauty as she is for her incredible talent. Starting as a model when she was very young and moving on to become a reigning star of the silver screen, Babra Sharif has proved her versatility by rising to the top in every field.

Born in 1954, she was introduced to the world in a Jet Washing Powder commercial and a star was born. Later, her endorsement of 'Lux' as the beauty soap of stars sporting the tagline, "*Aakhir loag hamara chehra he to deikhtay hain*", raised her popularity to dizzying heights.

She worked in a super-hit television play, "*Kiran Kahani*" in 1973. In 1974, her first film, "*Intezaar*" was released and Babra Sharif became a household name. In 1978, she married a co-star, Shahid, however the couple divorced soon afterwards. Between the late 1970s to the 1980s, Babra Sharif ruled the silver screen in Lollywood, winning both critical and commercial acclaim. She worked with all the leading actors of her time from the Chocolate Hero, Waheed Murad to the legendary Muhammad Ali and Nadeem. She experimented with different roles, appearing in romantic films, comedies and action adventures, excelling in all of the genres. In her twenty three year film career, Babra Sharif worked in around one hundred and fifty films, winning the Nigar Award eight times for her work.

Babra Sharif was again in the media as part of the "Lux" 100 years celebration, astounding the public with her youthful appearance. Currently, she runs her own jewellery shop in Karachi.

Bahar Begum

Bahar Begum, formerly known as Kishwar, was introduced to the Pakistani film industry as a young actor in 1956 by Anwar Kamal Pasha, when she was just 14 years old. Pasha, an avid fan of horse racing, had a prized mare, Bahar, which won that year and, buoyed by the mare's success, he suggested this new name. Bahar Begum's film career spans many decades and she is said to have been associated with almost 600 films during this time. Her acting career is split into two phases, one where she worked as the heroine and the other when she played a strong matriarch. In fact, she played the legendary Sultan Rahi's mother so convincingly that the public actually started believing they were mother and son.

Known as the *Malika-i-Jazbaat* (Queen of Emotions), Bahar Begum married fellow actor and director, Iqbal Yousaf, and left the film industry in 1965, but came back after a decade to continue excelling in different character roles. Educated and eloquent, she speaks fluent English, Urdu and Punjabi, however, it is her portrayal of a loud, Punjabi village matriarch that she is most famous for. In 2012, she received a lifetime achievement award for her contribution to the Pakistani film industry by the Pakistani expatriate community in Norway. She works with various NGOs on different social welfare issues and projects.

Bano Qudsia

Writer, intellectual, playwright and spiritualist, Bano Qudsia is among the best Urdu novelists and short story writers in Pakistan. She has written numerous books, as well as plays for television, radio and stage. She writes both in Urdu and in Punjabi.

Bano Qudsia was born on November 28, 1928 in Ferozepur in India and moved with her family to Lahore after partition. A graduate of the Kinnaird College for Women, she wrote profusely for the college magazine and other journals. Later, armed with a desire to polish her Urdu language skills, she acquired master's degree, with distinction, in Urdu from the Government College, Lahore in 1951.

Raja Gidh is her most famous novel, which builds a story around the symbol of a vulture that feeds on dead flesh and carcasses, with the premise that indulgence in the forbidden leads to both physical as well as mental degeneration. Other works include *Aatish Zeir Pa, Adhi Baat, Aik Din, Amr Bail, Assey Passey, Bazgasht, Chahar Chaman, Dast Basta, Dosra Darwaza, Dusra Qadam, Foot Path Ki Ghaas* and *Haasil Ghaat*.

A celebrated scriptwriter, she has written many plays for Pakistan Television, most of them dealing with the plight of women and other socio-economic issues. In 1986, Bano Qudsia received the Graduate Award for Best Playwright, winning the same award three consecutive times in the following years from 1988-1990. She is also the recipient of the Taj Award for Best Playwright.

She was married to Ashfaq Ahmed (1925-2004), another renowned writer, playwright, intellectual and spiritualist.

Bapsi Sidhwa

Bapsi Sidhwa is one of the most recognized and prominent Pakistani novelists and the country's first English language writer. She was born on August 11, 1938 to a Parsi (Zoroastrian) family in Karachi who soon afterwards moved to Lahore. When she was two years old, she contracted polio and then was homeschooled till she was fifteen. Later she graduated from Kinnaird College for Women in 1957.

Her five novels, *Ice Candy Man* (also republished as *Cracking India*); *The Bride*; *The Crow Eaters*; *An American Brat* and *Water*, have been translated and published in several languages, as well as been turned into successful films. An anthology, *City of Sin and Splendour: Writings on Lahore*, was published in

2006. She also writes for the theater and her play, *Sock with Honey*, was staged in London in 2003. *An American Brat* was produced as a play by Stages Repertory Theater in Houston in 2007, playing to full houses and receiving much critical acclaim.

Sidhwa, who was on the advisory committee to the late Prime Minister Benazir Bhutto on women's development, has also taught at Colombia University, University of Houston, Mount Holyoke College, Southampton University, Rice University and Brandeis University. Among her many honors, Sidhwa received the Bunting Fellowship at Radcliffe/Harvard, the Lila Wallace-Reader's Digest Writer's Award, the *Sitara-i-Imtiaz*, Pakistan's highest national honor in the arts, the *LiBeraturepreis* in Germany and the 2007 Primo Mondello Award in Italy. Sidhwa says that it has been a long haul for her as a writer, but when she was inducted into the Zoroastrian Hall of Fame during the Millennium Celebrations in 2002, she felt the struggle had been vindicated.

Bapsi Sidhwa immigrated to the United States in 1983 and currently lives in Houston, Texas.

Benazir Bhutto

Benazir Bhutto, a politician and stateswoman, was the 11th Prime Minister of Pakistan and the first woman elected to head a Muslim state in 1988 and Pakistan's first (and so far, only) female Prime Minister. She was the eldest daughter of Zulfiqar Ali Bhutto, former Prime Minister of Pakistan and in 1982, when she became the Chairperson of the Pakistan People's Party (PPP), she also became the first woman in Pakistan to head a major political party.

Born on June 21, 1953 in Karachi, Bhutto was educated in some of the countryís best schools and later graduated from Harvard University with a degree in Political Science. She then moved to Oxford University, where in 1976, she was elected president of the Oxford

Union, becoming the first Asian woman to head the prestigious debating society.

Bhutto spent many years of her life in confinement, under house arrest, in jails or in exile. She married Asif Ali Zardari, a wealthy Sindhi landlord in December 1987 and gave birth to three children. When she had her daughter in 1990, Bhutto became the first modern head of government to give birth while in office.

Following the death of General Zia-ul-Haq, she contested the general elections and was elected Prime Minister in 1988. However, her government was deposed after just twenty months in office. Re-elected in 1993, her government was again dismissed after just three years in office amid various corruption charges and she went into exile in Dubai in 1998.

She returned to Pakistan on October 18, 2007, after reaching an understanding with President Pervez Musharraf under which she was granted amnesty and all corruption charges were withdrawn. She was assassinated on December 27, 2007 after leaving PPP's last rally in the Pakistani city of Rawalpindi, two weeks before the scheduled Pakistani general election of 2008, in which her party won a landslide victory and her husband became the first President to remain in office for a full term in the country's checkered history.

Her publications include Pakistan: The Gathering Storm (1983), *Daughter of the East* (1989), also released as *Daughter of Destiny: An Autobiography* (1989-03) and, at the time of her death, a third manuscript with the publisher, came out in February 2008 called *Reconciliation: Islam, Democracy, and the West*.

In 2009, Benazir Bhutto was named one of seven winners of the United Nations Prize in the Field of Human Rights.

To date, the investigation into her murder remains open and unsolved.

Bilquis Bano Edhi

Bilquis Bano Edhi is a professional nurse and one of the most active philanthropists in Pakistan. She heads the Bilquis Edhi Foundation, and together with her husband, Abdul Sattar Edhi, the charity runs many social services nationwide, including a hospital, an emergency service, and many orphanages and old people's homes in Pakistan. She heads the *"jhoola"* project, started by her husband in 1952, which consists of 300 cradles throughout Pakistan where unwanted children can be left. The project is credited with saving the lives of 16,000 unwanted babies in Pakistan.

Bilquis Edhi was born on August 14, 1947 in Karachi. In grade eight, a lack of fondness for academics, plus responsibilities in her home, led her to pursue a six month training program in midwifery and healthcare at the Edhi Nurses Training Centre, a subdivision of the Edhi Foundation at Mithadar, the old city district of Karachi. This was 1965. From here onwards, there was no turning back.

Her aim to help others in need took on a new life when she married Abdul Sattar Edhi, nearly twenty years her senior, at the young age of seventeen. The couple has four children who are all involved with the Edhi Foundation in some capacity and oversee the management of the Edhi Village, the ambulance fleet, the mental home, the orphanages, schools and offices in Pakistan and London.

According to records, every week one child is left at the gate of an Edhi centre. Bilquis Edhi personally interviews needy parents and has, so far, handed over 15,000 newborn babies for adoption. Apart from the financial matters, the rest of all the Foundation's work is monitored by her, particularly the women specific departments which include 17 homes providing shelter to 6500 destitute, mentally challenged and homeless women and about 10 nursing homes.

Numerous international honors have been awarded to her for her decades of humanitarian services. These include the Rotary Club Award, the Lenin Peace Prize and the *Ramakrishan Jeidayal Harmony Award*. In addition to this, the husband-wife duo has also received the 1986 *Ramon Magsaysay Award* for public service. Despite running the world's largest private charitable organization, the couple lives in a modest two room apartment in one of their orphanages.

Dr. Fatima Shah

Dr. Fatima Shah (1914-2002) was a noted social worker and educationist, who worked incessantly for the rights of the blind in Pakistan. She was the founder of the Pakistan Association of the Blind, which she set up in 1960, and served as its president for twenty five years. She was also one of the founding members of the All Pakistan Women's Association (APWA) and served as Health Secretary in the provincial and central cabinets. She was a World Council member of the Disabled People's International and organized the Disabled People's Federation of Pakistan to serve as its national affiliate. Dr. Shah played a significant role in the establishment of a global body called the World Blind Union and also became a member of the

Federal Council National Parliament.

Born on February 11, 1914 in Bhera, Dr. Shah was always an eager student. She received a gold medal in the High School examination from Aligarh University and then studied at Lady Hardinge Medical College for Women in Delhi where she was awarded the MacDonald Scholarship of merit. After receiving her MBBS degree, Dr. Shah worked as a house surgeon in Golanganj Hospital in Lucknow. This was followed by marriage and children.

In 1947, Dr. Shah came to Karachi and resumed her medical career. Plagued by problems with her vision, She left the medical profession when blindness overtook her at the age of forty. Around this time, Pakistan's First Lady, Begum Liaquat Ali Khan sent her to the United States to take a course. There, Dr. Shah found herself getting involved in social work, particularly self-help movements for the blind.

Dr. Shah made notable contributions for the blind nationally, like getting the government to introduce Braille, setting up of a Braille press, getting a 50 percent concession on both domestic and international routes on PIA for all blind persons, establishment of a Resource and Training Centre for blind women in Karachi, getting a 2.5 percent job quota for the blind approved by the parliament, and getting the health clause removed because of which perfectly healthy, intelligent and qualified people were being deprived of jobs.

Dr. Shah received many national and international awards in recognition for her services, including the Takeo Iwahashi Award at Gothenburg, Sweden, which she received for her outstanding national services in the field of organization of self-help movements of blind people and their progress and development, and an MBE (member of the British Empire) for her social services on the occasion of the coronation of Queen Elizabeth II. She was also bestowed the Medal of Merit for outstanding services in the field of blind welfare from the Regional Bureau of the Middle East Committee, Riyadh as well as unanimously elected as the First Honorary Life Member of the World Blind Union. On a national level, she received the *Tamgha-e-Pakistan* for her services in the field of blind welfare, a number of 'Woman of the Year' awards as well as the 'Golden Women of Pakistan' award on the occasion of Pakistan's golden jubilee. She also authored a book titled *"Disability: Self-help and Social Change"*, which was sent to all the libraries of the world.

Dr. Fatima Shah passed away after a prolonged illness in 2002 at the age of 88 in Karachi.

Farida Khanum

Farida Khanum is a renowned Pakistani Ghazal singer who hails from Punjab. She holds the title of "*Malika-e-Ghazal*" (Queen of Ghazal) as a tribute to her singing talents. Born in Calcutta in 1935 and raised in Amritsar, she migrated to Pakistan after independence. At seven years of age, she started learning *Khayal* from her sister *Mukhtar Begum* and later learnt classical music from *Ustad Ashiq Ali Khan*, the renowned maestro of the *Patiala Gharana*.

Farida Khanum's first public concert was in 1950. She then joined Radio Pakistan and achieved tremendous fame and recognition. However, after she got married, her career suffered a setback as she stopped singing. Then in 1964, Farida Khanum started singing publicly again. Her most famous ghazal is *"Aaj Jaane Ki Zidd Naa Karo"*.

In 2005, she was awarded the *Hilal-e-Imtiaz*, Pakistan's highest civilian honour by President Pervez Musharraf. Farida Khanum lives in Lahore, Punjab and performs only at select musical gatherings.

Malika Pukhraj

Malika Pukhraj was one of Pakistan's most famous ghazal and folk singers. Her contribution to music in the subcontinent is immense. She introduced the concept of ghazal singing in many different *raags*, based on her training in classical music. She also popularized the singing of free verse, which not many had done before her. Malika Pukhraj also promoted the *Pahari* music of her birthplace, Kashmir, by singing songs she had learnt from the people in Jammu.

Malika Pukhraj was born in 1912 in a small village, Hamirpur Sidhar, close to Jammu. When she was just three years old, she began a strict and rigorous musical training regimen with Ustaad Ali Baksh Kasuriya, the father of Ustaad Baray Ghulam Ali.

At five, she moved to Delhi to continue her training in music and dance (*Nirth Bhahu*) under the tutelage of famous musicians like Ustaad Momin Khan, Ustaad Mollah Buksh Talwandi and Ustaad Ashiq Ali.

When she was nine, she returned to Jammu to perform at the coronation ceremony of Maharaja Hari Singh, who was so impressed by her strong voice that he appointed her as a court singer. Malika became a gazetted officer and earned over Rs.500 a month as her stipend. She stayed there for another nine years. After partition, she migrated to Lahore, where she became associated with Radio Pakistan.

Among the many accolades and awards she received, some worth mentioning are the Pride of Performance (1980), Pakistan's highest civilian award and the "Legend of Voice" award (1977) which was given to her during All India Radio's Golden Jubilee celebrations. Malika Pukhraj also recorded her memoirs in a novel, *Song Sung True*.

She was married to Shabbir Husain Shah, a government officer and had six children. Her daughter, *Tahira Syed*, is a law graduate and a singer who has re-sung many of her mother's famous songs. Malika Pukhraj also had an avid interest in embroidery and gardening.

She died in Lahore on February 4, 2004 at the age of 92.

Nasim Wali Khan

Nasim Wali Khan is a senior politician and the former president and parliamentary leader of the Awami National Party in the Provincial Assembly of Khyber Pakhtunkhwa, Pakistan. She is also one of the leading members of the Pakistan National Alliance, a political alliance, and in 1977, she became the first woman ever to be elected from her province on a general seat in the elections. She was married to the famous politician Khan Abdul Wali Khan.

Although from a political family, in 1954, when she married Wali Khan, she had no inclination to enter politics. However, in 1975, the then Prime Minister Zulfiqar Ali Bhutto banned the Awami National Party and arrested her husband under treason charges. With the leaders in jail, ANP floundered. That is when Nasim Wali stepped in and resurrected her husband's party under a new banner, the National Democratic Party. Her emotionally charged national campaign attracted many and launched her political career. She joined an alliance of religious-political parties called the Pakistan National Alliance and made history when she won a seat in the provincial assembly. However, the military soon took over and all the political prisoners, including her husband, were released.

The second phase of her career started in the late 80s, when her husband retired from politics after he lost in the 1990 elections. Nasim Wali, however, won her own seat and took over as the provincial head of the party. She put forward a new vision of nationalism, completely different from her husband's. Later in 2002, Nasim Wali Khan was decisively defeated in her hometown which ultimately led to her ouster as the party's provincial president. Meanwhile, the party won a historic victory in the 2008 elections. Today, she is no longer active in politics.

Dr. Ruth Katherina Martha Pfau

Dr. Ruth Katherina Martha Pfau is a world renowned social worker, a German nun and a member of the Society of Daughters of the Heart of Mary who has spent the last fifty years of her life devoted to fighting leprosy in Pakistan. Due to her tireless efforts, Pakistan was declared to have controlled leprosy by the World Health Organization in 1996, becoming one of the first countries in Asia to achieve this goal.

Dr. Pfau was born in Leipzig, Germany on September 9, 1929 and pursued her medical degree at the universities of Mainz and Marburg. After her graduation, Dr. Pfau joined the Catholic Order of the "Daughters of the Heart of Mary". In May 1960, her congregation decided to send her to a mission station in India, but due to visa problems, she had to stop in Karachi. Here she was introduced to the leprosy work in the city. Dr. Pfau was so moved by the pathetic situation of leprosy patients in the city that she decided to stay and work to help them. She started medical treatment for leprosy patients in a small makeshift dispensary in the leprosy colony at McLeod Road behind the City Railway Station. With some funds from Germany, a leprosy clinic was bought in April 1963 in Saddar and the dispensary was shifted to the clinic. Today the Marie Adelaide Leprosy Centre (MALC) has over 157 control centres all over Pakistan with over eight hundred staff members.

In 1979, Dr. Pfau was appointed Federal Advisor on Leprosy to the Ministry of Health and Social Welfare, Government of Pakistan. In 1988, in recognition of her service to the country, she was awarded the citizenship of the Islamic Republic of Pakistan. On September 9, 1999, Archbishop Simeon Anthony Pereira of Karachi celebrated a Mass at St. Patrick's Cathedral to celebrate Sr. Pfau's 70th birthday.

She has authored four books in German, all of which are based on her work in Pakistan and Afghanistan. One of these books now titled, *'To Light a Candle'* is an English translation done in 1987 of her original work.

Dr. Ruth Pfau is the recipient of several national and international awards, prizes and medals. The Government of Pakistan awarded her the *Sitara-e-Quaid-e-Azam* in 1969, the *Hilal-e-Imtiaz* in 1979, the *Hilal-e-Pakistan* in 1989 and one of the highest civil awards, the *Nishan-e-Quaid-e-Azam* on August 14, 2010.

Among her many honours Dr. Pfau received the Order of the Cross from Germany in 1968, the Commanders Cross of the Order of Merit with Star from Germany in 1985, Damien-Dutton Award from USA in 1991, Ramon Magsaysay Award from the Government of the Philippines in 2002, the Jinnah Award from the Jinnah Society Pakistan in 2003, the Lifetime . Achievement Award from the Rotary Club of Karachi in 2004, Marion Doenhoff-Prize, Germany in 2005 and Lifetime Achievement Award from the President of Pakistan in 2006. In 2004 she was awarded an Honorary Degree of Doctor of Science by the Aga Khan University.

Sabiha Khanum

Sabiha Khanum was the leading star of Pakistani cinema in the 1950s and 1960s. She continued her acting career equally successfully on television and won many awards and accolades. Most of her films were with her husband, the late Santosh Kumar. The real life couple made a wonderful on-screen pair and enjoyed a huge fan following.

Sabiha Khanum was born Mukhtar Begum on October 16, 1936 in Gujrat, Punjab. She was brought up by her grandparents in a conservative rural environment. However, later she moved to Lahore to be with her father and that was when she got her first break when he introduced her to a leading stage drama writer and poet, Nafees Khaleeli. He offered her a role in the drama "*Buutt Shikan*" and gave her the screen name of "Sabiha Khanum".

She made her debut on the silver screen in 1948 and got an opportunity to work with all the leading actors of her time. However, her films with her husband, Santosh Kumar, are her most well-known and remembered ones.

Sabiha Khanum won the Pride of Performance from the Government of Pakistan and also won the *Nigar Award* for many of her performances. She is now settled in the United States.

Salima Hashmi

Salima Hashmi is an acclaimed artist, teacher, actor, writer and human rights activist. She is said to represent the first generation of modern artists in Pakistan. Her art work focuses on social and political issues, as well as women's struggle in a patriarchal society. In 1981, she co-founded Rohtas Gallery in Islamabad along with architect and friend, Naeem Pasha.

Born in 1942, Salima Hashmi is the eldest daughter of one of Pakistan's most famous poets, Faiz Ahmed Faiz. She studied art at the National College of Arts, Lahore. In 1965, she earned a Certificate in Art Education from Bath Academy of Art, Bristol University, UK and an MA (Honours) in Art Education from Rhode Island School of Design, USA in 1990.

Before taking up painting professionally, she participated actively in theatre plays. She was also part of Pakistan Television in its early years, and her plays with her husband, Shoaib Hashmi and other friends, like "Such Gup" and "Taal Matol" not only received tremendous praise but have acquired almost cult status in the comedy genre in Pakistan. Salima Hashmi was just eight years old when her father was imprisoned because of his political ideology. Later on when her father opted for self-exile under the regime of General Zia-ul-Haq she went through a difficult time, ultimately turning to painting.

Hashmi has taught at the National College of Arts (NCA), Lahore for thirty-one years as Lecturer, Assistant Professor and Associate Professor of Fine Arts. Later, she headed the institution for four years, simultaneously serving as Professor of Fine Arts. Currently, she is the Dean of the School of Visual Arts at Beaconhouse National University (BNU), Lahore where she is known to promote a unique intellectual perspective among students.

She was very vocal in her stance against the nuclear tests conducted by India and Pakistan in 1998. Her series of paintings, *People Wept at Dawn* was a direct result of the frustration she felt due to the stances of the two countries. She has been part of the human rights movement in Pakistan since the early 80's and was one of the founding members of Women's Action Forum, an organization dedicated to promoting women's rights. She is currently Vice-Chair (Punjab) of the Human Rights Commission of Pakistan (HRCP).

Unveiling the Visible: Lives and Works of Women Artists of Pakistan is Hashmi's labour of love encompassing the lives and works of about fifty women artists since independence. After years of extensively interviewing these women, she published the book in 2002. In 2006, she co-authored, with Yashodhara Dalmia, an OUP publication, "*Memories, Myths, Mutations: Contemporary Art of India and Pakistan*".

Salima Hashmi is the recipient of the President's Award for Pride of Performance (Art Education) 2000, Critics Prize for her documentary *The Song Remains* at the Kara Film Festival Karachi 1999, Fellowship, National College of Arts Lahore 2000, Academician, National Academy of Art, Kyrgyzstan 1997, Gold Medal 30 Years of Pakistan Television 1993 and Silver Medal Baghdad Festival of Arts 1988.

Shamim Ara

Shamim Ara was a Pakistani film actress, director and producer. She reigned on the silver screen in the 50s and 60s and later held the distinction of being the first successful female director in Lollywood.

Shamim Ara was born in 1938 to a popular dancer from Aligarh, India. She was named Putli Bai and started acting and dancing lessons from a very young age. In 1956, she migrated to Pakistan and by chance met Najam Naqvi, a prominent film director who was looking for a fresh, new face for his upcoming film.

Therefore, Putli made her maiden appearance in Najam Naqvi's "*Kunwari Bewa*" with the screen name Shamim Ara. The film flopped and she was left with the option of playing side roles until the film *Miss 56* came out and Shamim Ara was recognized as a new and upcoming star. From then on, she starred in many successful and super hit films, winning her fame and many awards.

Shamim Ara also holds the distinction of being the first successful female director of the Pakistani film industry. She is the recipient of many *Nigar* awards both for her acting as well as her directing skills.

In spite of being successful on the professional front, Shamim Ara's personal life was marred by heart ache. She got married three times, only to lose her husbands to death or divorce. Her fourth marriage to writer and producer Dabeer-ul-Hasan was finally successful and he wrote the screenplays for most of the films she directed.

In 2010, she went into a coma after undergoing brain surgery.

Swaran Lata

Swaran Lata was a Pakistani film actress who started her career in the film industry before partition in India and later moved to Pakistan. She was known as the "Tragedy Queen" because of her emotionally charged performances, the tragic roles she played and her impeccable and emotion-laden dialogue delivery.

Swaran Lata was born in December 1924 into a Syal Jatt Sikh family in Rawalpindi, British India. She did her Senior Cambridge from Delhi and then joined the Academy of Music and Arts, Lucknow. Her family moved to Bombay in the early 1940s from where she started her film career. She married Nazir Ahmed, a famous fellow actor, director and producer and converted to Islam, changing her name to Saeeda Bano. The husband and wife pair went on to create many successful films together.

Swaran Lata started her career as a stage actress. Her first film *"Awaaz"* was released in 1942. Swaran and Nazir migrated to Pakistan at the time of partition. They left everything they possessed in Bombay and shifted to Lahore where they had to start from scratch and in the process became one of the pioneers of Pakistan's film industry.

Swaran Lata was the heroine of Pakistan's first ever silver jubilee film 'Pherey'. For this particular project, she was coached in Punjabi language by Baba Alam Siahposh, a Punjabi poet, who was also one of the lyricists of the film's songs. She played the role of the heroine in *Laarey, Naukar, Heer* and as a character actress in *Sawaal*, all of which were her famous films. From 1960 onwards, she reduced her onscreen appearances and mainly shifted towards character roles.

Swaran Lata worked with great names like Prithviraj Kapoor, Motilal and Dilip Kumar in India and with Santosh Kumar, Darpan, Inayat Hussain Bhati and Habib in Pakistan. She passed away at the age of 83 in Lahore on February 8, 2008.

Tahira Mazhar Ali Khan

Tahira Mazhar Ali Khan is an activist who has struggled for human rights, particularly women's rights. Her father, Sir Sikander Hayat Khan, was the Prime Minister of United Punjab from 1937 to 1942 and her mother was the daughter of Nawab Muzafar Ali Khan, a prominent landlord of Punjab. Tahira Mazhar Ali studied at the Queen Mary School, Lahore and, from the beginning, was a confident and outspoken student.

In 1942, when she was just seventeen, she married Mazhar Ali Khan, a student leader and a communist. Marriage marked the beginning of her political activism. Impressed by the ideals of the Communist Party, she worked at the grassroots level for at least two years. During this time,

Baji Rasheeda, a prominent political activist became an inspiration for her. Tahira's husband later became a famous journalist and held various editorial posts at *Pakistan Times* and The *Dawn* before editing his own publication, *Viewpoint*, until he died. Tahira's political horizons broadened with her husband's active life as a journalist.

After her marriage, she worked for the Women's Defence League, an organization for women. After partition of the subcontinent, Tahira Mazhar Ali worked for displaced women, mobilized women workers, and cautioned them against the perils of capitalism. During Ayub Khan's regime, her organization invited women from Vietnam to visit Pakistan. In 1950, with support from the Communist Party, Tahira formed the Democratic Women's Association. She worked with very meagre resources fighting against the establishment for people's rights.

She lives in Lahore but due to ill health is no longer actively engaged in any social or political work.

Lady Viqarunnisa Noon

Lady Viqarunnisa Noon was a multifaceted woman who held many different positions. She was a committed social activist, the head of the Pakistan Red Cross (Red Crescent) Society and President of the Social Welfare Council of West Pakistan; she was a dedicated political activist who was part of the Pakistan Movement, Organizing rallies and processions for the Muslim League and a member of the Punjab Provincial Women's Subcommittee; she was Pakistan's Ambassador to Portugal from 1987-1989; for more than a decade, she was the head of the Pakistan Tourism Development Corporation, a tenure which is still remembered as a time of major achievements, improved facilities and an improved profile of Pakistan and, for a brief while, she also served as the Federal Minister for Tourism and Culture. She was one of the founding members of the All Pakistan Women's Association (APWA), and founder and chair of the governing body of the Viqarunnissa Girls Secondary Institute in Rawalpindi and the Viqarunnisa Noon School, Dhaka, both well renowned educational institutions, as well as being the founder of the Sir Feroz and Lady Viqarunnisa Noon Educational Foundation; and, she was a senior and executive member of organizations like the Family Planning Association of Pakistan and the National Crafts Council of Pakistan, among others.

Lady Vicky Noon, as she was fondly known, was born 'Victoria' in July 1920 in Austria. However, she moved to England for her education and grew up there. While in England, She came to know the then High Commissioner for the Government of India, Feroz Khan Noon, whom she married, converting to Islam and changing her name to Viqarunnisa.

In 1950, when Noon was

appointed the first Pakistani Governor of East Pakistan, Lady Viqarunnisa started her extensive social work, including the founding of the Viqarunnisa Girls School in Dhaka, which still prospers in what is now Bangladesh. She accompanied her husband when he was appointed Chief Minister of the Punjab in 1953, Foreign Minister in 1956 and then the seventh Prime Minister of Pakistan in 1957, until President *Iskander Mirza* declared martial law and abrogated the constitution in October 1958.

In 1959, she was awarded Pakistan's highest civilian award, the *Nishan-e-Imtiaz*.

In her later life, she spent a lot of time in her home in Abbottabad and in Islamabad, finding solace in creative expressions like painting and writing.

After recurring bouts of illness, Lady Noon died on 16th January, 2000.

Zari Sarfaraz

Zari Sarfaraz was a renowned political activist and committed social worker of the Pakistani province of Khyber Pukhtunkhwa, where she served in several capacities to work towards the improvement of society, especially of women. She was also an astute business woman, successfully running her family's sugar mills, in an area where women rarely stepped outside their homes.

Zari Sarfaraz, the daughter of *Mohammad Sarfaraz Khan*, a wealthy landlord of the area, was born on July 27, 1923 in Mardan, Khyber Pukhtunkhwa. Although Zari wanted to become a medical doctor but her father's early death forced her to take up the responsibility of managing the family property and businesses. She was briefly married to a relative, who died very early too, due to illness, and she never had any children of her own or remarried, preferring instead to dedicate herself to public service and a number of new business ventures.

From around 1943-44, Begum Zari Sarfaraz successfully expanded her family business, including the Premier Sugar Mills and Distillery Company Ltd, in Mardan, and also set up other entrepreneurial ventures in various places.

Zari also became deeply interested in the rapidly expanding Pakistan Movement. She became a leading young member of this movement and played an active role in furthering the Muslim League's cause. After the Independence of Pakistan in 1947, she remained an active political worker and leader of the Muslim League and in due course was elected as a member of the West Pakistan National Assembly in 1962.

As an active politician, during the Gen Zia-ul Haq era, she headed the 15-member Pakistan National Commission on the Status of

Women in 1985 and recommended drastic changes in the existing laws to end discrimination against women. During this time, she also served as the Federal Minister for Women Development. She also headed the *All Pakistan Women Association (APWA)*, and was a life member of the *Pakistan Red Crescent Society*.

Zari became the president of *TB Association and Frontier Association for Mentally Handicapped*. She also served as head of provincial Zakat council. She was also the chairperson of *Trust for Voluntary Organizations*. She travelled extensively leading a number of delegations and attended conferences in UK, USA, Africa, China and the Middle East.

Zari was the recipient of *Queen Elizabeth II Coronation Silver medal* in 1953, two times recipient of *Human Rights Society of Pakistan* (1998 and 1991) and *Pakistan Liberation Movement* (1995).

Begum Zari Sarfaraz died in Islamabad in April 2008.

Zehra Nigah

Zehra Nigah is one of the most renowned female Urdu poets from Pakistan. She is one of two female poets to gain recognition in the 1950s when there were no women poets and the *mushairas* were completely dominated by men. She is also a well respected scriptwriter and has written several serials for television. She is the recipient of many awards, including the Pride of Performance, for her literary endeavours.

Zehra was born in Hyderabad, India and migrated with her family to Pakistan after partition. She comes from a family deeply interested and involved in the creative arts. She was one of ten children, and her other siblings include many famous names like *Anwar Maqsood*, a satirist, writer and public speaker, *Fatima Surayya Bajia*, also a celebrated scriptwriter of some of the most successful plays in Pakistani television's history, *Zubaida Tariq*, cooking expert and *Mrs. Kazmi*, a famous dress designer.

Zehra Nigah's interest in poetry and writing began in childhood. By the time she was 14, she had learnt the poems of many famous poets by heart. When she was in school, she was asked to write and recite a poem in a *mushaira* organized by the All Pakistan Women Association. Her participation in that *mushaira* was the beginning of what would turn out to be a remarkable career.

Zehra Nigah writes mostly about being a woman and the trials and tribulations associated with being one. She writes about society, social issues, norms and relationships, viewed through the eyes of a woman but relevant and true for all humanity.

Zehra Nigah has three published volumes of poetry: *Shaam ka Pehla Taara*, *Waraq* and *Firaq*.

OFF THE RECORD

It took me two years to actually find the 'courage' to start this book. It took me another year to find the right team who would help in the nitty gritty details of translating the text, writing the profiles, editing and then re-editing the many drafts. It took me yet another 'many' months to find 'that personal' time which would make me 'free'.'Free to once again go back in time and reconnect with these wonderful women; free to recapture those moments spent in their company; free to give wings to my words which would fly away with my imagination.

The muse is an elusive being. It talks to you.It beckons you. It pulls at your heart strings. It keeps you awake at night. It bothers you when you are least receptive. It gnaws at your gut demanding expression. And then when you are finally ready, It floats away, a wispy thought and eludes your willing mind to put it into words.

People who know me well would describe me as a disciplined person over all. However being a wife, a mother and a grandmother not to mention a professional 'of sorts' puts many demands on my time. And then one is not growing any younger. Harnessing all of that together to put this book has been at times a tiring and at times a frustrating affair. Many a time I contemplated disappearing for an extended period of time to concentrate on my thoughts and words but could never actually found the courage to put all my other commitments on hold and selfishly 'take time out' for myself.

I am now saddened by the fact that I must finally let go of a dream which has been my companion and best friend for so many months.

At the same time I am proud to share this dream with my readers. I can only hope they will enjoy this experience as much as I did in bringing it to them.

For some this might appear a 'dated' document as many of these amazing women have since moved on to their eternal bodes leaving me (and you) with only their memories and their words to remember them by.

Moneeza Hashmi